The Creative University

Creative Education

Series Editors

Michael A. Peters (*University of Waikato, New Zealand and
Beijing Normal University, P.R. China*)
Tina Besley (*University of Waikato, New Zealand and
Beijing Normal University, P.R. China*)

Editorial Board

Daniel Araya (*University of Illinois, USA*)
Ronald Barnett (*London Institute of Education, UK*)
Jonathan Beller (*The Pratt Institute, USA*)
Simon Marginson (*University of Melbourne, Australia*)
Peter Murphy (*James Cook University, Australia*)
Brian Opie (*Victoria University of Wellington, New Zealand*)
Peter Roberts (*University of Canterbury, New Zealand*)
Susanne Maria Weber (*University of Marburg, Germany*)

VOLUME 7

The titles published in this series are listed at *brill.com/crea*

The Creative University

*Contemporary Responses to the Changing
Role of the University*

Edited by

Birthe Lund and Sonja Arndt

BRILL
SENSE

LEIDEN | BOSTON

All chapters in this book have undergone peer review.

The Library of Congress Cataloging-in-Publication Data is available online at http://catalog.loc.gov

ISSN 2542-9418
ISBN 978-90-04-38412-5 (paperback)
ISBN 978-90-04-38413-2 (hardback)
ISBN 978-90-04-38414-9 (e-book)

Copyright 2019 by Koninklijke Brill NV, Leiden, The Netherlands, except where stated otherwise.
Koninklijke Brill NV incorporates the imprints Brill, Brill Hes & De Graaf, Brill Nijhoff, Brill Rodopi, Brill Sense, Hotei Publishing, mentis Verlag, Verlag Ferdinand Schöningh and Wilhelm Fink Verlag.
All rights reserved. No part of this publication may be reproduced, translated, stored in a retrieval system, or transmitted in any form or by any means, electronic, mechanical, photocopying, recording or otherwise, without prior written permission from the publisher.
Authorization to photocopy items for internal or personal use is granted by Koninklijke Brill NV provided that the appropriate fees are paid directly to The Copyright Clearance Center, 222 Rosewood Drive, Suite 910, Danvers, MA 01923, USA. Fees are subject to change.

This book is printed on acid-free paper and produced in a sustainable manner.

CONTENTS

Foreword: Knowledge Cultures   vii
   Michael A. Peters

Notes on Contributors   xiii

1. What Is a Creative University?   1
   Birthe Lund and Sonja Arndt

2. The Importance of Imagination in Educational Creativity When Fostering Democracy and Participation in Social Change   11
   Birthe Lund

3. Artistic Makings as a Method of Inquiry in Higher Education   31
   Rikke Platz Cortsen and Anne Mette W. Nielsen

4. 'Back to Bildung': A Holistic Competence-Based Approach to Student Engagement in Innovation Learning Processes in Higher Education   51
   Tine Lynfort Jensen

5. Creative Knowledge Work and the Impact of Instruction   65
   Susanne Dau

6. Constructivist Approach in Business Education with the Use of Virtual Simulations   85
   Anna Wach

7. The Role of Education in Academic Ecosystems   103
   Joakim Juhl and Anders Buch

8. Exploring Universities as 'Organisations That May Learn'   121
   Bente Elkjaer and Niels Christian Mossfeldt Nickelsen

9. Creative and Inclusive Universities in the Globalising Learning Economy   139
   Bengt-Åke Lundvall

10. Peer Production and Collective Intelligence as the Basis for the Public Digital University   157
    Michael A. Peters and Petar Jandrić

11. Logical Foundation of Inductive Meaning Constructing in Constructivist Interactions   177
    Farshad Badie

FOREWORD

Knowledge Cultures

Knowledge Cultures is a multidisciplinary field that draws on the humanities and social sciences at the intersections of economics, philosophy, library science, international law, politics, cultural studies, literary studies, new technology studies, history, and education. The new field serves as a hothouse for research with a specific focus on how knowledge futures will help to define the shape of higher education in the twenty-first century. In particular, it deals with general theoretical problems concerning information and knowledge production and exchange, including the globalization of higher education and the knowledge economy. In this mix the interface between publishing and academia is critical impinging on the development of the intellectual commons with an accent on digital sustainability, commons-based production and exchange of information and culture. The development of the economy of learning and knowledge networks merge with philosophical issues concerning the concepts of freedom, access and justice in the organization of knowledge production.

The world of higher education has been transformed in the last decade and will continue to change apace in the next decade. The development of the knowledge and learning economies emphasise the changing significance of intellectual capital and tacit knowledge in the forms of human and social capital for economic growth and development. Theories of human capital and intellectual property cast in their neoliberal forms have dominated the era of the knowledge economy. But in the digital age democratic questions concerning knowledge rights and equity, including the distribution, geography and access to knowledge, have become extremely important. There have been a number of trends that together provide the context for the transformation of higher education:

- The development of the symbolic economy has highlighted the general importance of symbolic goods and services for economic and cultural development;
- The symbolic economy has resulted in new labour markets with the demand for analytic skills and new markets in tradable knowledges;
- Developments in ICT, especially in informatics and telecommunications, have contributed to a variety of globalisation forms involving the exchange and flows of knowledge and knowledge services. These developments have the power to reshape university curricula and to transform traditional degrees and modes of delivery;
- The digitisation, speed and compression of communication has reinforced the notion of culture as a symbolic system and led to the spread of global cultures

as knowledge networks that increasingly define trade in services and stand at the heart of the knowledge economy;
- Digitisation increasingly defines not only the service economy but also the "culture industries", including the creation and dissemination of cultural products such as written works, musical works, recorded performances, and software and information databases. This sector includes publishing and software industries, internet publishing and broadcasting industries, the telecommunications industries, internet service providers, data processing industries and the like.
- Digitisation today is a national policy for the preservation of national archives and collections in museums, libraries, national research institutes and increasingly also part of national and cultural representation. Higher education, thus, both produces and relies on these innovations and developments as a means for its new modes of delivery, and for the storage, communication, distribution and retrieval of information and knowledge.

Knowledge and education are fundamentally social activities developed through language and communication within and across cultures. The value of knowledge and education are rooted in social relations. Culture structures the way people think, act and feel as well as knowledge practices and activities. "Markets" and "economies" belong to the discourse of economics, which comprise representational and technological practices that constitute the ways in which economic action is both formatted and framed. Today, more than any time in the past, the cultural has become the economic and the economic has become the cultural. This is the basic insight of the knowledge economy that is based on the facility with signs and symbolic analysis and manipulation.

The cultural economy rests on the production and use of knowledge and innovation, and communication through electronic networks that have become the global medium of *social* exchange. In this new configuration the production of new meanings is central to the knowledge process and media or communication cultures once centred on literacy and printing, now are increasingly centred on the screen or image and the radical and dynamic concordance of image, text and sound. The "culturalisation" of the economy is clearly evident in a number of related developments:

- The creation, development, distribution and production of both hardware and software as part of the information infrastructure for other knowledge and cultural industries;
- The growth of a highly stylised consumer culture where ordinary products are increasing aestheticised;
- The development of media cultures imbued with meaning in relation to questions of lifestyle and the "fashioning" of personal identity;
- The convergence of telecommunications with enter- and edutainment media cultures based on radio, film, TV, Internet, mobile phones with their assorted mixed and blended media;

- The significance accorded to signifying and other cultural practices in the actual organisational life of firms as well as in the production, design and marketing of products.

Within this matrix of development certain policy issues impinge on higher education policy. Take, for example, the future of the intellectual commons. If we accept the model of a networked communication system as a layered complex comprising three levels—physical infrastructure, code, and content—then the future culture wars will be determined by the meta-values of freedom and control, at each level. The battle for the control of intellectual property is a policy issue both for the creation, generation and development of knowledge, and for its use, transmission, storage and retrieval. In this debate we need to know a great deal more about the production of academic knowledge and its uses.

This is inevitably an issue that returns to its fundamental historical, economic and cultural questions concerning a 'work' and its 'authorship'. These questions, in turn, cannot evade the history of intellectual property and its modes of regulation and regimes emerging though the concepts of copyright, patent, and trade secrets. Insofar as the formation of the intellectual is closely tied to the development of literature as a public institution and to a reading public, the future of the intellectual commons will be determined by the ways in which questions of authorship and the ownership of knowledge are determined by universities and other HE institutions. This has led scholars to talk of the "end of the book" and to speculate on new forms of readership, authorship and scholarship, as well as to comment on the transformation of traditional modes of teaching and learning though lectures, seminars, and tutorials.

Increasingly knowledge shapes and defines electronic markets and trade in services determining portal power, knowledge trading futures, and 'know-who' markets of experts and authorities. Knowledge communities are now strongly related to knowledge markets, networks and innovation. Knowledge futures in the world of business are seen to promote product innovation as the key driver for company competitiveness. The marketisation of knowledge futures has eroded the status of public universities as the primary knowledge institutions and fostered the growth of non-traditional competitive providers, specialising in single or related subjects delivered through online or distance education.

In the information economy the effect of location is diminished as virtual marketplaces and virtual organisations offer benefits of speed and agility, of round-the-clock operation and of global reach. Knowledge and information "leak" to where demand is highest and the barriers are lowest and, thus, laws and taxes are difficult to apply on solely a national basis. The new information and communications technologies have accentuated and augmented aspects of the traditional industrial economy, making even more efficient international transactions and promoting flows of capital, goods, labour and services at the speeds of sound and light. This has led to the unparalleled growth of e-commerce and e-business, that is, electronically mediated business transactions to create and transform relationships for value creation among organisations and between organisations and individuals. At the same time there has been a growing convergence of specific technologies into new integrated systems. The radical and globalised concordance of image, text and sound has created new IT, media, telecommunications and information/ knowledge infrastructures and a global media network reflecting the emergence a Euro-American dominated global consumer culture with the rise of multi-national edutainment conglomerates in music, movies, publishing and TV.

These developments have led some economists to emphasise the growing importance of an international knowledge system as a basis for a source of labour value and productivity, research and technological innovation. They stress the growth of intellectual, human and social capital, all forms of capitalisation of the self. Human capital or "competencies" is the key component of value in the knowledge-based economy and one of the principal aims of knowledge management is to "extract" it from people's heads and to lock it into systems or processes as soon as possible where it has a higher inherent value and cannot "walk out the door". In knowledge capitalism, knowledge creation, diffusion and innovation are all important which is to acknowledge the centrality of knowledge and information to the processes of the sign economy and the symbolic society.

In the new context of transformation for higher education we need to explore theoretical issues with a specific focus on how *knowledge futures* will help to define the shape of higher education in the twenty-first century. In particular, this means a general theoretical concern for problems concerning information and knowledge production and exchange within the processes of the globalisation of higher education. It also means an ongoing investigation of forms of the knowledge economy, the economics of knowledge and higher education with a special attention to the interface between publishing and academia and the effects of the development of the intellectual commons, commons-based production and exchange of information and culture.

Philosophical issues arise around concept of knowledge in relation to its digital forms and digital sustainability; freedom, justice, the organisation and ownership of knowledge production, including non-proprietary models of information production. It also deserves a focus the development of learning and knowledge networks as expressions of the new logics of cultural.

In this new cultural political economy of education and knowledge there are opportunities for the consumer and user co-production of digital goods and services; peer-production of information and culture in the networked environment; and, the use of non-proprietary production models for educational development and global redistribution. These developments spawn the emergence of student and digital cultures, including free and open science with an emphasis on open scientific publication models.

The paradigm of collective intelligence has encouraged changing concepts of collective authorship, readership and scholarship, and new forms of curricula and scholarship using the Internet. These are in the main positive learning effects in the epoch of digital reason. There are also negative effects of 'cybernetic capitalism' that stultify and obstruct learning but that's another story.

Michael A. Peters
Beijing Normal University
Beijing, P. R. China

NOTES ON CONTRIBUTORS

EDITORS

Sonja Arndt, Ph.D., Senior Lecturer in the Faculty of Education at the University of Waikato, New Zealand. She works in the Centre for Global Studies and the Early Years Research Centre at that University, where her research intersects initial teacher education and philosophy of/in education.

Birthe Lund, Ph.D., Associate Professor in the Department of Learning and Philosophy at Aalborg University, Denmark. Her research focuses on design and evaluation of creative and innovative learning processes in education, as well as on philosophy of education.

AUTHORS

Farshad Badie, Ph.D., is a researcher at the Center for Computer-mediated Epistemology at Aalborg University, Denmark. He holds a Ph.D. in Human-Centred Communication and Informations and an MSc in Software IT and Computer Science. His research interests lie in the fields of formal and philosophical logic, semantics, knowledge representation, and dialogue analysis.

Anders Buch, Ph.D., is Professor at Aalborg University Copenhagen, Department of Learning and Philosophy. With Theodore Schatzki he has recently edited the volume *Questions of Practice in Philosophy and Social Theory* (Routledge, 2018). He is editor-in-chief of *Nordic Journal of Working Life Studies*.

Rikke Platz Cortsen, Ph.D., is Danish lecturer at University of Texas, Austin where she teaches Danish language and culture. She researches space and place in comics in the Nordic countries. Her latest peer reviewed publication (done as comics) is "Aesthetics of Black Metal in Nordic Comics" in *Danish Musicology Online* vol. 8 2016–2017.

Susanne Dau, Ph.D., MLP, RN, Associate Professor (Docent) and Head of the Research Program "Professional Development & Educational Research," Department of R&D, University College of Northern Denmark (UCN). Susanne conducts educational research within digital and blended learning, knowledge development, creativity and professionalism, using narrative and mixed methods.

NOTES ON CONTRIBUTORS

Bente Elkjaer, Ph.D., holds a chair within learning theory with special focus upon learning in organizations and working life at the Danish School of Education, Aarhus University. She researches at the 'crossroads' between educational and organisational research, and the way enterprises and people 'produce', learn and share knowledge.

Petar Jandrić, Ph.D., Professor and Director of BSc (Informatics) programme at the University of Applied Sciences in Zagreb (Croatia) and visiting Associate Professor at the University of Zagreb (Croatia). His research interests are focused on the intersections between critical pedagogy and information and communication technologies.

Joakim Juhl, Ph.D., Assistant Professor, Department of Development and Planning, Aalborg University Copenhagen, Denmark. Coordinator for the Techno-Anthropology BA and MA programs. Juhl is a junior council member of the Science and Democracy Network and his research focuses on the normative foundations of technological innovation and its relation to social expectations of science.

Bengt-Åke Lundvall, Pol.Mag, is Professor Emeritus at Department of Business and Management, Aalborg University. His research is related to innovation systems and learning economies. He has published more than 200 publications (see www.vbn.aau.dk). His book *The Learning Economy and the Economics of Hope* (2016, Anthem) brings together major research contributions since 1985.

Tine Lynfort Jensen, cand.mag., Associate Professor at University of Southern Denmark, works with teaching and research within the fields of entrepreneurship education and innovative learning processes in higher education. She has a special interest in students' individual and team-based competences in relation to creative processes.

Niels Christian Mossfeldt Nickelsen, Ph.D., is a trained clinical psychologist and an associate professor in leadership and learning at the Danish School of Education, Aarhus University. He researches on the practical effects of innovation for professional discretion, relations and tasks. His most read book is *Innovationspsykologi* (ed. with Mads Bendixen)

Anne Mette W. Nielsen, Ph.D., Assistant Professor, Department of Learning and Philosophy, Aalborg University Copenhagen. Research interests include young people's participation and agency in education, community projects and cultural institutions. She's currently engaged in a project about children and young people on the edge of society and their participation in formal and informal arenas.

NOTES ON CONTRIBUTORS

Michael A. Peters, Ph.D., is Distinguished Professor at Beijing Normal University and Emeritus Professor, the University of Illinois (Urbana Champaign). He works in the philosophy of education and political economy of knowledge and edits the SSCI journal *Educational Philosophy and Theory*.

Anna Wach, Ph.D., Assistant Professor, Department of Education and Personnel Development. Poznań University of Economics and Business. Poland. Her research interest concerns teaching and learning in HE, and academic development. She is a leader of a few programs in this area.

BIRTHE LUND AND SONJA ARNDT

1. WHAT IS A CREATIVE UNIVERSITY?

INTRODUCTION

The chapters in this book reflect philosophical, cultural, social and pedagogical aspects of The Creative University. The book sets out a broad theoretical framework for a critical and pro-active reading of the educational development of 'the creative university'—as a metaphor for something existing, as something still to come, and as something that is arguably also at risk. The book includes dialogues between playful creative learning processes and contemporary concerns in society and the wider world, questioning the changing role of universities. It is a passionate engagement with the world-wide importance of the notion of a creative university.

The nature of 'producing' innovative and creative students is theorized, discussed and explained from various perspectives in throughout the book. The authors confront some of the difficulties faced by practitioners, the professors and lecturers within the university, by theorising and seeking to understand the connections and challenges within contemporary universities, and their implications as they strive to become creative universities. The chapters represent a range of responses to the question: What is a 'creative university'? This was the theme of The Creative University Conference at Aalborg University, Denmark, in August 2016, and the chapters in this book are a selection of the papers presented at the conference. The different chapters therefore reflect the fostering of creativity and knowledge cultures that can respond to this inherently complex problem. They illustrate various sources from which stimuli for change and innovation may arise, and the different forms they might take, in addressing pedagogical, technological, economical and organisational changes in universities.

The 'creative university' is first of all a response *to societal changes*, which call for new ways to conceptualise, address and enact education and research within the university, and as such, creative innovations at individual, collective, organisational, and institutional levels become critical.

A university is a place where education and research take place. The chapters in this book concretize and theorise what makes these two core activities creative, and what implicates them in the new field of knowledge cultures, as Michael Peters outlines in the foreword. Knowledge is regarded as human social and intellectual capital, to be developed within the university, in increasingly creative and innovative ways. Indeed, creativity and innovation are seen as something so integral to universities, that those universities which do not live up to the task of being creative and innovative risk failure, being labelled as unattractive and being rendered undesirable. Being labelled as creative is a positive, appealing branding in a competitive world in which 'knowledge production' is intensified. Processes of creativity, innovation and chance are central to universities, and a university's success is—apparently—based on the ability to nurture creativity and to manage change at all levels. In the commercial world creative ideas are expected to be transformed into new products, creative values are sought after, and, following this logic, universities of today are expected to prepare students to fill those demands of innovation and creativity.

In the development of knowledge economies, a discourse of creativity constitutes a change in educational and research-related understandings of the development of societies, competition, and social change. *Education* in the creative university is therefore seen as building knowledge cultures that include both the playfulness and the emotional and creative dimensions of teaching and learning. These creative dimensions, illustrated and theorised in the following chapters, highlight students' and teachers' micro-level experimentations with the construction of knowledge. The contributions show how building such knowledge cultures relies on learning environments and organisational structures that are fundamentally challenging, as well as supportive. The *concept* of the creative university is a response to the growing world-wide interest in teaching methods and pedagogies that develop students' innovative and creative thinking, where students as well as teachers are expected to break with habitual actions and thought.

When separating innovation from creativity, creative efforts are often seen as self-expressive and intrinsically motivated. They distinguish creativity from innovation by suggesting that the former is driven by intrinsic motives, whereas the innovation is driven by extrinsic incentives and by the need to surpass previous achievement levels or standards. This not only situates the creative university within dominant contemporary economic, outcomes-focused ideologies, but it indicates that emotions are linked to creativity and imagination. In that respect separating innovation from creativity emphasizes the crucial importance of emotions in the design of innovative learning processes—for students as well as teachers, lecturers and professors in the university. Making this explicit, the Creative University Conference drew on the special character of Aalborg University, and its defining strong focus on student-defined and constructed, problem-based learning and research. By crossing disciplinary and paradigmatic boundaries, the intention of the conference was to reveal new potential for fresh, innovative solutions to contemporary concerns within existing practices and knowledge cultures. A particular feature of this approach at Aalborg University is the engagement of students in the identification of pressing problems, and their development of creative and innovative responses to these problems through collaborative research and assessment. As Lund suggests in her chapter in this book the idea that this approach arose in Denmark, and that it has widely influenced educational thinking in the past 30 years, creates a fitting historical backdrop for extending these dialogues through the conference, and for collating them in this collection of chapters from the conference.

THE CONCEPT OF CREATIVITY

The conference focus draws our attention to the concept of creativity, as reflected in this book. Great thinkers like Einstein and Dewey have pondered what it means to be creative, and their ideas are still reflected in conceptualisations of creativity today. There are many answers to the question: what is creativity? Creativity can refer to a person, place, processes or products (see Lund, chapter 2 in this book). It can be found in cultures, in groups, and in small children, and there are ongoing debates on how to measure, utilize and improve creativity. Consequently, there is no single answer to the question we are dealing with in this book, as the concept of creativity itself is dynamic and it is approached from different perspectives.

An examination of the history of research on creativity suggests that many ideas and issues within the field of creativity have been discussed for hundreds of years, showing the interrelatedness of the research and contemporary conceptualisations of creativity (Runco & Albert, 2010). The earliest Western conception of creativity was the Biblical story of creation given in Genesis, from which followed the idea of the artisan doing God's work on earth. The most significant distinctions were made in the mid-1700s when separating the idea of 'creativity' from 'genius', 'originality', 'talent' and formal education, however still no concept of 'creativity' existed at this time. By the late 1700s imagination itself was accepted as governing artistic creativity. During the eighteenth century four accepted distinctions were made of the idea of creativity, which remain present today: (a) genius was divorced from the notion of the supernatural, (b) potential for creativity exists in all individuals, (c) talent and genius were to be distinguished from one another, and (d) their potential and exercise depend on the political atmosphere at the time (Runco & Albert, 2010).

Today, creativity is studied by educators, psychologists, sociologists and scholars in many diverse fields. As creativity refers in various ways to the potential danger that originality and individualism pose in the context of compliance, authority and the maintenance of social order, the 'creative university' may be perceived as a threat to the established and consensus-oriented university. This is particularly so when pedagogy and opportunities to develop and exhibit what might be seen as 'radical creativity', that is, the unexpected, becomes valued and challenges current control and measurement systems, as reflected in the chapters in this book. The vision of emotions and creativity as critical elements in teaching and learning positions the university as both formal and informal, flexible and responsive, and open to diverse, innovative, and exploratory constructions and approaches to multiple knowledges and knowledge cultures. A creative university then must balance both playfully wild, uncontrollable processes of idea generation, as well as existing rituals, traditions, histories and other already valued understandings of development, learning and knowledge. This vision for the creative university then involves teachers and learners in a reflexive social, organisational and cultural stock-take and opportunities for change, through emotional, innovative knowledge cultures. Each of the chapters in this book takes up this challenge in different ways, as we outline in the following section.

PRESENTATION OF THE CHAPTERS

Micro-Level/Pedagogical Level: Teaching and Learning in the Creative University

Birthe Lund points towards the neglected relationship between democracy, creativity and social change, inspired by John Dewey's work. She argues for the importance of pedagogy that fosters students' imagination of what they want their world to look like or be, whilst being 'educated' in the broader sense. This implies students' right to equality and democracy, founded on a pedagogy that recognises everyone's right to creativity and a voice, not just those who are special, talented or gifted. Lund argues for the importance of imagination in social change, by transforming and materialising ideas and actions. Her research points to the importance of culture and places them as central creative agents, as shown in her analysis of the creative alliances between students and the community in the protests against nuclear power plants in Denmark during the 1970s. Twenty years later, ongoing public resistance and the visible alternative—the world biggest windmill, in Tvind—paved the way for Denmark's huge windmill industry. In this sense active resistance, collaboration, knowledge sharing, and a common vision of sustainable energy, grew out of a shared creative resistance. Thus, they created what Dewy describes as "images-of-things-that-might-be".

Lund's innovation narrative illustrates how technological change is connected to a history of pedagogy in which children have increasingly been given a voice over time. She discusses why the ability to imagine and visualise that which does not exist becomes a powerful gift in students' process of self-cultivation, and in the aim for producing engaged, responsible and active new members of society. This, she concludes, must be reflected in universities of today, in order for them to be labelled as a creative university.

Rikke Platz Cortsen and Anne Mette W. Nielsen point towards the importance of engaging students as independent thinkers and actors in a continuous and creative inquiry process. They outline how students are encouraged to explore productive failing and new multimodal critical thinking in a theory course titled *Practice in Theory*. The two main objectives of the course, as they state, are, firstly, "to investigate and understand theories of practice", for example "philosophical concepts of practice and the role of practice in the construction of different theories and research methods". The second objective "was to expand the students' repertoire of inquiry methods and have them employ multimodal methods anchored in explorative and creative 'makings'". The course involved students' embodied interactions with digital technologies, frequent testing of code and other functionalities. 'Making' became central in this theoretical course as another way of discussing how embodied interactions with materials are integral in constructing and understanding theory.

This work of 'making' involved a process of decoding and recoding where the students used such activities as writing, cooking, drawing, movie making, baking, sculpting, and collaging to pick apart artworks and theoretical texts, reworking them to expose the 'put-together-ness' of the materials. It involved creative explorations in a continuous reworking of the conclusions and preconceived understandings. Inspired by Latour's researching of social interactions, this approach emphasises how the social organises, produces, stabilises and globalises practices. Introducing it into traditional academic institutions might cause resistance from students or be quite challenging for them, since it breaks with a number of the traditional roles and rules of teaching within the humanities and social sciences. It requires discussion and clarification of how individual inquiries might be valid; qualify, as 'well or badly composed' for example, in different group sessions. This poses an immediate problem in today's higher education environment: it is time-consuming and there is no clear measurement or 'correct' process or way forward. Instead, the students' open-ended making puts forward other kinds of alternatives than teaching 'to the test', or through familiar pedagogies.

Tine Lynfort-Jensen argues for bringing Bildung back on the agenda. She sees it as a vital aspect of higher education, and as important to supplement instrumental measures of education. Lynfort-Jensen argues that in the University, students are stimulated to engage in learning processes to develop in ways that are expected and beneficial for themselves and society. Since what is known as the 'ontological turn' in higher education, students are expected to develop themselves as human beings, and Lynfort-Jensen claims that Bildung can be revitalised through a more holistic approach to student engagement, competences, and learning, and to expand the discussion of the purpose of higher education. This chapter outlines how research shows that engagement increases when students interact with the surroundings and participate in experimental activities, in 'real-world' agendas, in co-assessment and in the wider community. In the chapter, 'Bildung' refers to "broad understandings of learning both in- and outside of schools", while 'education' is seen as situations where there are "concrete learning goals for a professional field". Education, however, appears to have replaced Bildung.

The chapter connects students with others in similar teams as a lever for encouraging innovation and learning. Lynfort-Jensen suggests that meeting people with diverse profiles and experiences through this process leads to an enhancement of Bildung in the educational system. It can be supported by allowing students to reflect upon identity in relation to practical work with other students from different disciplines.

Susanne Dau draws on different perspectives on the role of instruction in creativity, knowledge development, and learning. The question addressed in her chapter focuses on instruction in undergraduate teacher education and its influence on students' creativity and knowledge creation, whereby creative knowledge work is expected to contribute to student engagement and commitment. Dau's contribution to existing knowledge is founded on a metaphorical phenomenological-ecological approach to learning as 'wayfinding'. Dau uses Ingold's description of wayfinding, where "… people do not traverse the surface of a world whose layout is fixed in advance" and sees wayfinding as connected to narratives of prior journeys. When learning is understood as wayfinding, Dau claims, it addresses a range of social, and relational aspects of knowledge development. She outlines the role of a belief mode and a design mode to conceptualise and address knowledge development from a work-life perspective. Problematising these focus areas, she suggests improvements through working with the examples of problem-based learning, design-based learning, and project-based learning, in a focus on everyday realities rather than abstract questions. Dau posits knowledge creation as a learning process that takes place within different dimensions of knowledge and in the interactions between these dimensions. The concept of creativity in this chapter draws on earlier research revealing that environment, situation, experiences, motivation, instructions, and interpersonal relationships support knowledge creation, creative knowledge work and instruction. Finally, the narrative of creativity and learning reveals how student flexibility is essential for creative work, for instance, in their approach to assignments and their openness and curiosity towards learning processes.

Anna Wach describes how business education strives towards teaching that aims to develop a range of pro-active and creative attitudes and related skills, including analytic competences, teamwork, discussion and decision-making skills. She describes how teachers "mainly apply a traditional content-centred approach and focus on the predictable aspects of organisational life, ignoring the paradoxical and unpredictable characteristics of the contemporary business world". Business education is criticised for the lack of integration of issues and the lack of combining different subjects, such as finance, accounting, management or marketing. This implies a shift from a teacher/content-centred model to a student-centred model. Wach describes classes using simulation to develop cognitive, social and interpersonal competences as well as competences related to business orientations. The application of strategic management simulations is evident in two European Union programmes, whereby the aim of the simulation is to run a company and manage it to maximise its economic profit. The role of the teacher shifts to that of a designer of student activities, acting as a moderator/facilitator, instead of as an information source or provider. The student must then be an active builder of his or her own cognitive structures, involved in multilateral activities including problem solving and team-based learning. The existing body of literature and studies highlighted in the chapter show that students' approach to learning will largely depend on the way classes are taught by the teacher rather than on their own individual characteristics (including motivation).

WHAT IS A CREATIVE UNIVERSITY?

Joakim Juhl and Anders Buch add nuance to understandings of the dynamics of academic ecosystems and their (de)stabilising institutional mechanisms within the university. They define academic ecosystems as 'ecologies of practices', constituted by a multitude of for example, teaching, leadership, administrative, student, and research practices, that are situated and interwoven in complex ways. By zooming in on the concrete 'doings', 'sayings' and 'relatings' of actors in their socio-material contexts in university settings, Juhl and Buch present a clear view of the reproduction and transformation of scientific research and education. They outline the development of a Design & Innovation programme focused on analysing the problems to be solved—before deploying technical tools to design solutions. Instead of modelling its structure on academic disciplines, the authors outline how problems are introduced from within. This programme highlights problem-based learning (PBL) as an innovation of the Technical University of Denmark (DTU). The programme presents a resistance against the ways in which engineering previously had been thought and taught at DTU. Radical educational reforms turned Danish universities into economically autonomous institutions and exchanged universities' collegial self-governing systems.

Meso-Level: University as Societal/Organisational Institutions

Bente Elkjaer and Niels Christian Mossfeldt Nickelsen also address the shifting roles of universities. They highlight the impact of the Danish University Act of 2003, which converted universities into self-governing institutions administered by university boards, of which external stakeholders make up the majority. The changing role of universities implies a gradual transformation of employees, from academic to an employee in the knowledge industry, bringing with it a shift from relative autonomy to being subordinated to a greater degree to hierarchical structures. They emphasise how these changes imply a greater emphasis on external funding and on performance measurements.

Elkjaer and Nickelsen use an organisation studies lens to examine universities as learning organisations that consist of many staff members working together, engaged in their work, and open to opportunities to learn. They understand organisational learning as "the creation of an environment that is conducive to problem solving, and related to the work practices at hand". Universities are variously presented as "loosely coupled" and "organised anarchies" before moving on to a contemporary reading of texts where universities are seen as more tightly coupled organisations, similar to business enterprises, as the result of public sector reforms. The authors propose a conceptual development related to tasks, practices, and experiences, in order to understand the energies and passions that may drive organisational learning in universities. They introduce these notions to consider universities through a 'grass roots' approach, rather than maintaining a focus on management and control.

Bengt-Åke Lundvall poses the question: "How can universities respond to current challenges emanating from the growing role of knowledge and learning in global competition?" And he answers, reflecting Peters' foreword, that first, changes in the global knowledge landscape imply that universities in Western countries need to pay more attention to creativity. Secondly, greater attention must be paid to inclusion within universities, following the increasing polarisation of societies where economic inequality is combined with the opening up of cultural gaps between creative metropoles and regional peripheries. This reflects Lundvall's research on innovation systems and the learning economy combined with research on creativity. One important outcome of the globalisation process as highlighted in Lundvall's chapter is that the knowledge gap between OECD-countries and major Asian economies such as China and India has been reduced over the last couple of decades. Lundvall argues that the predominance of global ranking systems and the single-minded focus on bibliometric indicators as performance criteria undermine creativity. Following this argument, local university administrations have implemented new forms of management where the emphasis is upon the use of standardised indicators measuring the university's outputs. The dominant focus is on indicators that are comparable across the world, and one aim is to raise universities' position in global rankings. He claims further, that the format of the standard scientific article gives little room for radically new ideas and for developing new theory. In general, although the individual researcher is expected to add something new in each scientific paper, the general emphasis is on continuity rather than novelty. Lundvall refers to studies showing that extrinsic incentives have a positive impact upon quantitative variables, but that when it comes to quality, intrinsic motivation is the most important factor. The incentive system is crucial for the creative use of knowledge, as Lundvall claims, and creativity thrives when individuals and teams are driven by enthusiasm and passion. Examining how the combination of management control and extrinsic incentives undermines creativity, Lundvall uses bibliometric studies to show, for example, that the focus on 'high quality journals' in connection with ranking of institutions systematically disfavours interdisciplinary research.

Michael A. Peters and Petar Jandrić describe universities from a philosophical perspective as 'engines of innovation' for 'fast capitalism' dealing in 'fast knowledge', 'fast publishing' and 'fast teaching'. As an example, they cite Massive Open Online Courses (MOOCs), where 'knowledge' becomes confused with information, and is seen as having a rapidly decreasing half-life. Recent developments have brought about significant changes in the political economy of the university, and information and communication technologies have simultaneously brought about new affordances for, and new restrictions to, human creativity. They argue for a conception of the creative university that embraces user-centred and open-innovation public ecosystems based on the shared ethos underlying 'co-creation', 'co-production', and 'co-design' and that articulates the ideal of a philosophy for the public digital university. Without undermining the importance of psychology, they transfer questions pertaining to creativity from the realm of individualist approaches into the realm of the social sciences. The chapter defends "a paradigm of creativity as a sum of rich semiotic systems that form the basis of distributed knowledge and learning". It reflects a view of "creativity as enabled or permitted by the new digital infrastructures of human culture in the twenty-first century" – primarily focused on technical infrastructure, code, and content. Making new rules creates a new game, Peters and Jandrić argue, based on Wittgenstein's conception of language games.

Peters and Jandrić's chapter describes the changing roles of universities—from pursuing 'the quest for universal truth' to a focus on 'quality assurance' in the discourse of excellence, where neoliberal managerialism becomes the dominant model of knowledge performance. Structural transformation toward the knowledge economy is based on the production of knowledge, investment in human capital, and the diffusion of ICT requiring 'management'. Neoliberal knowledge management rests on the principles of homo economicus that are radically at odds with distributed knowledge systems.

Farshad Badie focuses on the process of meaning. He analyses meaning construction within constructivist interactions, using a semantic framework of logical and [formal-]semantic characterisations of 'concept', 'definition', and 'meaning'. Creative universities, he argues, must consider meaning as the active and dynamic process of knowledge construction. According to this research, he states, "a creative university can be regarded as a Constructivist Learning/Mentoring Community that corresponds with (i) constructivist learning/mentoring processes, (ii) constructivist interactions between mentors and learners (as well as learners and learners), and (iii) collaborative meaning construction that supports collaborative knowledge building".

Badie uses an activity-based approach to communication analysis that argues that information and understandings are shared through communication, and that this occurs "with varying degrees of consciousness and intentionality". Interactions between learners and mentors can be interpreted through their 'co-activations', that is, their shared actions and interactions. Badie uses a constructivist model of learning and knowledge as an explanatory, heuristic developmental framework to relate genetic epistemology to a developmental theory of knowledge. In the context of learner-mentor interactions, the constructivist model of learning can explain how the phenomenon of 'interaction' supports the generation of meaningful understanding based on his/her conception of the world.

CONCLUDING COMMENTS

The chapters in this book illustrate various iterations of the contemporary university as creative universities. Enmeshed in multiple transformations that challenge but also affirm traditional pedagogies, orientations, and expectations for the future, they collectively argue for innovations towards increased creativity. As Peters' foreword stresses, continual transformations in the "development of the economy of learning and knowledge networks merge with philosophical issues concerning the concepts of freedom, access and justice". The chapters follow explicate diverse examples of the growing new field of knowledge cultures, within universities and in society as a whole.

We would like to acknowledge all participants in the ongoing dialogues on the concept of creative universities, in particular those who contributed to the Creative University conference in Aalborg in 2016. Our thanks go to all chapter authors for reworking their presentations and for sharing them with us for publication in this book. We thank also Brill | Sense and Professors Michael Peters and Tina Besley as series editors, for publishing this collection. Further, we thank the Department of Learning and Philosophy, Aalborg University and the Obel Family Foundation for the financial support for editing and proofreading services, and we are enormously grateful for Ulla Burskov's invaluable support with editing, formatting and generally bringing this book together.

This book adds to previous publications in this series, and we hope it will further provoke and inspire ongoing engagement with the possibilities and knowledge cultures surrounding the concept and enactment of the Creative University.

REFERENCE

Runco, M. A., & Albert, R. S. (2010). Creative research: A historical view. In J. C. Kaufman & R. J. Sternberg (Eds.), *The Cambridge handbook of creativity*. New York, NY: Cambridge University Press.

Birthe Lund
Aalborg University
Aalborg, Denmark

Sonja Arndt
University of Waikato
Hamilton, New Zealand

BIRTHE LUND

2. THE IMPORTANCE OF IMAGINATION IN EDUCATIONAL CREATIVITY WHEN FOSTERING DEMOCRACY AND PARTICIPATION IN SOCIAL CHANGE

INTRODUCTION

This chapter investigates the connection between democracy and creativity and social change. The Swedish author of children's books, Astrid Lindgren, underpins the importance of imagination as part of social change: 'Everything great that ever happened in this world happened first in somebody's imagination' (Lindgren, 1987). Here she was echoing John Dewey, who portrays ideas as 'images-of-things-that-might-be' (Dewey, 1938/1976). But in order to transform and materialise an idea, human action is needed. It calls for reflection that draws on knowledge and experience in order to determine whether the 'might be' can be transformed into 'are'. This means that transformation processes include dialogue processes, interaction, and negotiation. To me, the essence of innovation is that, in contrast to creativity, the latter may appear through the idea or the vision itself.

This position also indicates that conceptualisation of innovation and creativity is a cultural conceptualisation. When creativity is personalised (e.g. as special talents or giftedness) it may influence students' personal interpretation of being creative, or not, and such self-cultivation may influence student's behaviour and agency in the long run.

In the Nordic countries it is the intention that all students experience equality through having their ideas and views taken into account; in addition to being educated with an aim of being able to take part in rational discussions, where major points of view are weighted according to evidence, rather than the position of the speaker as either student or teacher. This also implies welcoming students' ability to imagine what *they* want *their world* to look like (or to be) when being 'educated' in the broader meaning of the term. When I analysed the following actual and complex historical innovation and transformation process, the role of imagination as a 'connector' between pedagogy and innovation presented itself through studying the social and cultural dimensions of innovation and creativity—not as distinct and separate areas of studies, but in connection to each other.

The chapter consequently discusses why the ability to imagine and visualise the non-existing seems to be a powerful gift in students' self-cultivation process when aiming for engaged, responsible and active new members of society.

CONCEPTUALISING IMAGINATION

Although the educational philosopher John Dewey is first known for emphasising experience, defined as the result, the sign, and the reward of interaction between organism and environment; for Dewey imagination is, in itself, a vehicle of learning. Experience is a transformation of interaction into participation and communication, and the results might be art, as he describes in *Art as an Experience* (Dewey, 2005). Art is physically manifest in the 'expressive object' as the development of an 'experience'; the fundamental element is not the 'work of art'. Significant experiences and emotions are qualifications of a complex experience that moves and changes. He claims that all building up of experience take places place through the image (Dewey, 1976). He likens imagery 'to the motor power of an idea'. Dewey hereby portrays ideas as images-of-things-that-might-be, which requires action in order to determine whether the 'might be' can be transformed into 'are' (Chambliss, 1991). So, imagination and sense are included in reasoning, and imagination is the embodiment of ideas in an emotionally charged sense.

Dewey reconciles reason with passion. Compared to a deductive and rational model of calculation, it is distinctive for Dewey's notion of practical reasoning that emotions play a constitutive role in conducting deliberation, because the imaginative exploration is imbued with feelings and other qualities (Dorstewitz, 2008). It has a projective dimension, as it incorporates both the ability to synthesise certain possible and anticipated outcomes, as well as the ability to produce a complex interpretation of a looming situation. The imaginative as well as the intuitive aspects of thinking then point towards the role of feelings and emotions as a bodily experience too. Nevertheless, the concrete image has an effect on the course of action taken and, in turn, it may be transformed by that very action. According to Dewey, imagining and taking action are not different kinds of experiences, but phases in a continuing stream of experience and it is a necessity for images to be formed in a social context, as imagination is influenced by existing images such as cultural symbols and signs.

When Einstein praises the value of imagination over that of knowledge, he is referring to his (bodily) feelings of being on the right track. To him, imagination becomes a vehicle of learning, by which he brings new realities into existence, even though science describes reality which is not only not present to the senses, but not perceptually available at all. Scientific thinking moves beyond the present information to the senses by referring to non-existing objects:

> I believe intuition and inspiration […] At times I feel certain I am right while not knowing the reason. When the eclipse of 1919 confirmed my intuition, I was not in the least surprised. In fact, I would have been astonished had it turned out otherwise. Imagination is more important than knowledge. For knowledge is limited, whereas imagination embraces the entire world, stimulating progress, giving birth to evolution. It is, strictly speaking, a real factor in scientific research. (Einstein, 1931/2009, p. 97)

Formation of images, emotions, and feelings that arise through our imaginative connection and engagement with the contexts help us to understand and make sense of ourselves and the world. Along this line, Dewey considers imagination to be a power in acting, at work to *bridge* 'the new, or hitherto foreign' element in poetry, art, or science. He treats imagination as a stage of knowledge and the images as the motor power of an idea. The power of imagination is then to realise what is not present, rather than making up anything which is unreal. We are not to choose between imagination and knowledge; rather, imagination is an important part of the knowledge creation process, of thinking.

From a psychological perspective, the imagining of an alternative to the present situation is crucial to the generation of emotions, as imagining a future alternative to the present one can create fear, hope, or anger, and let us become aware of things that are not present. In this way, imagination includes the past, present and future, it reflects memories and conceptualises thoughts on an individual level (Ben-Ze'ev, 2000). Consequently, emotions are an integrated part of the way we experience and make sense of ourselves.

To sum up: emotions influence our imagination and imagination allows us to be aware of what is not present—and it is creative potential, as recognised by both Einstein and Dewey. Imagination refers to the faculty for or the action of forming new ideas, images, or concepts of external objects not present to the senses, as shown in art and science, and daily life. Imagination then refers to the ability to show and demonstrate creativity, which is sometimes manifested in innovations and creative thoughts and ideas. In Figure 1, I illustrate how knowledge creation includes imagination and creativity in both ongoing constructions and reconstructions as responses to the culture and social context.

This understanding indicates the socially embedded character of innovation and creativity, and the social and collective development of imagination as embedded in social structures and dynamics, point towards the cultural dimension of creativity development by symbols and images. From this conceptualisation follows that creativity development is not to be separated from knowledge creation in general, or from access to cultural symbols—education, which defines *educational creativity as a society embedded issue*, will be further developed in the following sections. The term educational creativity refers to and overlaps with the use of creativity for insight into problem-solving in other subject areas: creative ideas for teaching, teaching for children, and attempting to enhance their creativity (Smith & Smith, 2010). The first argues that creativity is an element of thinking, linked to problem-solving. The second element points to the educational system and the way we teach, and the last refers to general attempts to develop children's creativity. A century ago, when relating creativity to problem-solving and thinking (by including imagination), John Dewey integrated all these elements in his pedagogical and philosophical approach to education; forming a new pedagogy and innovating the dominating educational system, stating that (all) students are to be explorative, experimental, and reflective.

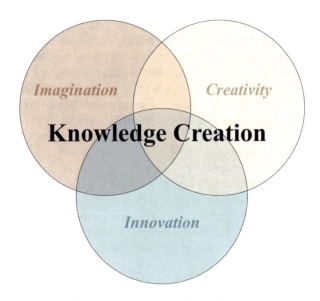

Figure 1. Knowledge creation embedded in culture and social context

CONCEPTUALISING CREATIVE THINKING AND DEMOCRACY WITHIN EDUCATION

Today, educational creativity is a global political issue. It is being framed as essential 21st century skill[1] in the United States of America; in some ways echoing Dewey's pedagogical ideas from the 19th century. Twenty-first century skills are framed by Partnership P21, based on collaborative partnerships among education, business, community, and governments leaders:

> Learning and innovation skills increasingly are being recognized as the skills that separate students who are prepared for increasingly complex life and work environments in the 21st century, and those who are not. A focus on creativity, critical thinking, communication and collaboration is essential to prepare students for the future. (P21, Framework for 21st Century Learning, n.d.)

The P21 statement above indicates the risk of being left behind if students are not taught to be creative and collaborative. Along this line, in Europe, the EU Youth Strategy aims to support the development of creativity among young people and facilitate and support young people's talents and entrepreneurial skills. The Exceptionally talented students must be given opportunities for further development. This challenge to equality intentions is manifested by the fact that in Denmark it is prohibited by law to separate students based on skills and different abilities until grade 9 or 10. If creativity is defined exclusively as talent and personal giftedness, the cultural, social, and embedded aspect of creativity is missing, and this may in the long run influence students' agency and ideas of what democracy means and implies.

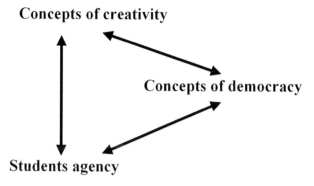

Figure 2. Agency, creativity and democracy

Figure 2 illustrates the interplay between concepts of creativity and concepts of democracy.

If students experience that some students are selected and given extra resources in order to develop their creativity based on grades, efforts towards enhancing creativity may challenge general equality efforts, such as the development of democratic values and norms in schools, explicitly expressed in the goals of the Danish national curriculum.

Education itself is conceptualised as *a human right* due to the historical Bildung tradition. The concept of Bildung is an educational category, dealing with normative aspects of teaching and learning. It encompasses the idea of education as a societal phenomenon which has human prosperity and development as its aims. This is reflected in the United Nation's goal to achieve free universal primary education for all, underpinned by the argument that education will enable a more fulfilling life: 'To embrace the broad range of life experiences and learning processes which enable children, individually and collectively, to develop their personalities, talents and abilities and to live a full and satisfying life within society'.[2]

Education is, furthermore, conceptualised as *capital*—it is regarded as a personal and/or national economic investment; reflecting students' productive capacity and competence evaluation. Development of creativity is valuable to societal growth as creative industries have a double impact on the economic system—they increase the gross of domestic product and create new jobs and value added. Creative industries may improve the evolution of economy, connected with social and institutional development (Martinaitytė & Kregždaitė, 2013). Education should be measured and compared from this perspective, with the level indicating the wealth of the country.[3] Because social changes are reflected in education, education seems to be a battlefield for different political and economic interpretations of its role, resulting in continuous negotiations of what it actually means to be educated.

Consequently, education balances between being *a human right* and *human capital*. This enables different valuations of the need for education, the role of creativity, and what is meant by the term 'education', related to being educated in a cultural and moral sense, which is often neglected within the innovations discourse of education (Lund, 2011, 2017).

A PEDAGOGICAL INNOVATION INITIATED BY LINDGREN'S PIPPI STORIES

Dewey's philosophy is in favour of a naturalistic approach that views knowledge as arising from an active adaptation of the human organism to its environment. In Dewey's philosophy and pragmatism, education is for life, it is about intellectual, moral, and emotional growth and the evolution of a democratic society. Today, education in science and technology are especially recognised as strong innovative forces, while the role of the arts and humanities tends to be neglected drivers; hence, I will point to development of new ideas within the field of pedagogy by part of departure in arts.

The Swedish author Astrid Lindgren created and expressed new images of children and children's position in society when she, in the 1940s, gave public voice to the perception of schooling from a child perspective. In the long run she paved the way for progressive pedagogical ideas in Sweden by reaching a broad audience. She reaches children through an aesthetic and emotional experience, as her books appeal to children's experiences and feelings of being subordinate to the dominance of adults. This understanding of childhood was new as well as very provocative, but over time it was accepted and approved, and gained political acceptance and support. As a result, Sweden became the first country in the world to legally prohibit physical punishment of children. In this way, Lindgren contributed to important *pedagogical* innovation and social change.

According to Rogers' innovation stage model, Diffusion of Innovations, this illustrates how art may contribute to innovation carried out through a process of social construction by an adoption of a new way of thinking. It is a theory that seeks to explain how, why, and at what rate new ideas and technology spread. Similarly, material inventions, as innovations, are embedded in culture and reflected by creations of new meanings on a collective level when forming a new attitude to a problem. In his book, *Diffusion of Innovations*, first published in 1962, Rogers argues that diffusion is the process by which an innovation is communicated over time among the participants in a social system. He documents the persuasion stage of an innovation—the decision process—often involves the ability to think hypothetically and counterfactually as well the ability to project into the future, as forward planning (Rogers, 1983, p. 174). This indicates to me the importance of imagination and the ability to be open, playful, and envision 'what might happen if we' in order to diffuse innovation.

The actual societal impact of an innovation may depend on who sees and formulates the need for concrete innovation, and how the expected consequences are framed through different discourses. In this way, innovation is embedded in communication and participation in social systems. When Astrid Lindgren created the imaginative figure Pippi, she also created a new (adventurous) social conceptualisation of what it might mean to be a girl.[4] Despite protests uttered by some, her work was admitted to the canon of children's literature in Sweden and Germany almost straight away. Later the 'diffusion' was enhanced by the filmed versions in the late 1960s and early 1970s, and hereby Lindgren's work gave children public access to new images of being a child, as well as new concepts of gender, democracy, and behaviour across the world. Besides questioning gender roles and equality, the figure Pippi questions what being educated means by playing an imaginative 'what if' game: what if children had more money, had avoided traditional upbringing, were living alone, and were stronger than most grown-up men? What would the world then look like? Pippi does not show any kind of inferiority or any sign of being inferior to any authorities (police, principals, etc). Despite being rich and the strongest girl in the world, she is non-violent and shares her wealth, based on the philosophy: 'When one is especially strong, one has a particular obligation to be kind to others'. Thus, the character Pippi constantly questions the given concepts of socialisation and what it means to be educated, as indicated in this dialogue:

> [Teacher:] "Think how embarrassing it will be for you to be so ignorant. Imagine when you grow up and somebody asks you what the capital of Portugal is and you can't answer!" "Oh, I can answer all right", said Pippi. "I'll answer like this: 'If you are so bound and determined to find out what the capital of Portugal is, then, for goodness's sakes, write directly to Portugal and ask". "For that matter, I've been in Lisbon with my papa", she added, still standing upside down, for she could talk that way too. (Lindgren, 1987, pp. 23–26)

She has the kind of imaginative creativity that allows her to devote a day to searching for a 'spink' together with Tommy and Annika, while searching for something which has no name yet and something they do not know. This shows important aspects of language and language games, of naming and expressing. As Michael Tholander concludes, based on his reading of this Pippi story: 'It [new words] allows you to transcend the limits that language appears to set before you, and to strive for something new, something adventurous, something joyful' (Tholander, 2016, p. 110).

Even today this adventurous figure will not adjust to any school systems. Viewed from the concept of PALS (Positive Behaviour in Leaning and Interaction) she might be diagnosed as disruptive, disturbing, unprepared for learning, etc. Seen from the point of view of a progressive creativity discourse which values ingenuity and fantasy, she might be labelled curious, caring, innovative, socially responsible, etc. In that sense, Astrid Lindgren's novels and their characters clearly display the challenge to our school systems, by posing the question: do our school systems create enough space for the disruptive and adventurous students?

Along this line, education must, to some extent, welcome the new and the unknown and learn to deal with the unpredictable, as well as the unpredictable students. In the Pippi stories, she is representing the *newcomer*—the one who is introducing new ideas and information (Gert Biesta's (2013) use of this term, inspired by the term

Natality by the philosopher Hannah Arendt). Each birth represents a new beginning and the introduction of novelty in the world, by acting:

> The new beginning inherent in birth can make itself felt in the world only because the newcomer possesses the capacity of beginning something anew, that is, of acting. (Arendt, 1958, p. 9)

Arendt claims individual's show 'who' they are and reveal their unique identities through action and speech. In the Pippi novels, the transcendence appears through the creation of a new language, the creation of new images of being a child, and of children's civil rights. In this sense, the progressive pedagogical ethos of the novels by Astrid Lindgren is almost a reflection of the essence of Dewey's insistence on pupils' rights within education. His ideas of being educated are later reflected in Pippi's ideas, as he values the importance of 'keeping one's soul', being allowed to be authentic, curious, and gain the ability to learn and value own meanings and experiences over barren discipline information (Dewey, 1938). Bildung, as well as being educated within the framework of progressive pedagogy, implies an embodied integration of character and mind, a fusion of meanings and values of facts, as well as supporting students' desires and imagination. But, in order to become intellectualised, such desires are transformed into a genuine interest in problems provoked by the observation of things. Dealing with real challenges and objects which one (students) really cares about and feels strongly for, ought then to be reflected in the creation process and awaken students' motivation per se (Dewey, 1933).[5]

Problem formulation and problem-solving are essential in his pedagogy, as problem-solving itself entails imagining other events similar to or different from the experienced. Imagination then develops during a process of creative thinking in which students are encouraged to ask stimulating and critical questions (just like Pippi).

INVENTION AND IMAGINATION IN THE 1970S

While the problem-solving elements of Dewey's pedagogy has aroused renewed interest in the 2000s (Renier, 2016), the democratic, critical, and social aspects of his theory are played down, contrasting with the problem-based learning appearing in the 1960s and 1970s. At that time the Scandinavian countries were particularly oriented towards the international reform pedagogic theory and its appreciation of the child's personal potential. New space was provided for pupils to develop creativity, as well as having a say within education. In 'the golden era of Nordic social democracy', social virtues, such as equal opportunities, co-operation, and solidarity were considered the main formation goals of compulsory schooling. This was reflected in comprehensive schools as both political objectives and as democratic socialisation of pupils (Telhaug, Medieås, & Aasen, 2006). During the construction of the Nordic welfare states at the time, massive investment in public education took place.

Besides general investments in further education/higher education, during the '70s nuclear power plants were introduced as a potential solution to the lack of energy from oil, due to the international oil crises in 1973 which affected the economy, resulting in a large recession. At the time, power supply was publicly owned and solely based on oil and coal power plants. Raw materials were needed, and education was regarded as both human capital and as a public good. The political response consisted of investment in 'more education' and the creation of conditions providing less dependency on oil. The dominating political discourse within the power supply area favoured public nuclear power plants.

In Denmark, the innovation narrative told about the Tvind windmill reflects an upcoming new *Weltgeist* in the 1970s. Established authorities were challenged by young people with new ideas about democracy and education, and by upcoming new and radical ideas and movements, such as women's liberation movements and anti-nuclear movements, all of which expanded during the 1970s. At the same time, there was growing environmental awareness towards ecology among young people. In this *Weltgeist*, the educational reforms of the 1970s had their starting point. Hegel's concept of *Weltgeist* reflects the belief that each time period and its unique spirit is a stage in the development of World Spirits itself and individuals are themselves expressions of their place in history and its limitations (Magee, 2010). Imagination flourished and was manifested by societal change and technological inventions that reach into the society of today.

New Pedagogy at University Level—Problem-Based Learning and Critical Pedagogy

Returning to the 1970s, we recognise this *Weltgeist* as reflected in critical pedagogy which was deliberately practised at the new universities in Aalborg and Roskilde as problem-based learning. This meant, student-defined problems were setting the agenda for students' research. The new university pedagogy made way for studies based on problem formulation and problem-solving through investigative initiatives driven by students and teachers in common. (In the early years, this policy and pedagogy resulted in huge public debates and resistance, especially towards Roskilde University, as it was considered too revolutionary, but today Aalborg University is known as a university whose graduates are excellent cross-disciplinary and collaborating employees). In the beginning, the university pedagogy was influenced by the key assumption that critical pedagogical practice has the potential to promote transformation of individuals and society (within the arts and social science studies). Ideologically, this pedagogy seeks to develop a critical awareness of problems, power structures, and inequalities. Within this framework, a potential creation and recreation of democracy is linked to students' engagement with communities and authentic learning (like building a windmill and being engaged in the solution of real societal problems).

Founded in 1974, Aalborg University constitutes a new educational response in a period of time when the city of Aalborg found itself in an almost existential crisis, heading towards a transformation process during which it developed from being an industrial town with shipyards and cement plants, towards becoming a city that is rooted in what we now consider to be 'the knowledge society'. The number of blue-collar jobs was rapidly declining, and huge public investments were no longer a generally welcomed public solution to the economic crises due to higher taxes. But, some collaborating 'innovative' citizens expected the university to transform the city and its reputation as a 'working-class' city. Later the number of students grew quickly, from 3,000 to 20,656 in 44 years, and created an enormous impact on this transformation process.

The Tvind Windmill Innovation Narrative and the Windmill Industry

The educational innovation within the worlds of universities (44 years ago) signifies how educational innovation and new ideas were contested in social and political processes; worked out by complex processes of social construction and reconstruction; and influenced by the actual culture, history, economy, values, and zeitgeist of the time. During the same time period, the idea of building the world's biggest windmill was fostered by mainly young people and students. It originated in the social movements and organisations of the 1960s and 1970s, when students, as well as some teachers from universities and high schools, actively participated and supported processes towards a more renewable energy supply. On May 29 1975, students at the Tvind Folk High School[6] took the first step towards the creation of the windmill, and in the same year the nuclear power plant in Barsebäck in Sweden opened, close to the city of Copenhagen.

The windmill soon became a symbol of the movements against nuclear power plants and in favour of renewable energy, as stated by one of the pioneers in the movement for renewable energy, J. Maegaard: 'The Tvind mill has become a legend'. Maegaard says, that

> it was a realization of an idea at the Tvind schools in Western Jutland, in the 1970s, when teachers and students designed and built their own power plant for their own schools—the world's largest wind power plant at the time. For their own money. They built it for the sake of natural energy, for the sake of a humane society—against monopolisation in the energy sector and against nuclear power. (Maegaard, 2009, author's translation)

The Tvind windmill became a technological sensation. In May 2005, Tvindkraft's 30th birthday was celebrated. It is still producing electricity today, while the Swedish Barsebäck nuclear power plant was decommissioned (Olsson, 2005), although there is now growing support to nuclear power plants in Sweden. Denmark later reduced its dependence on imported oil by developing the North Sea gas and oil fields, as well as requiring central electricity generating plants to switch from oil to coal.

THE IMPORTANCE OF IMAGINATION IN EDUCATIONAL CREATIVITY

Today the plants base their production primarily on sustainable energy by combining hydropower plants from Norway and Sweden with windmills in Denmark.

The Tvind windmill story of innovation illustrates a growing competition between two different technological responses to the oil crises at the time. In the construction of the forthcoming innovation narrative I am inspired by basic and very early innovation theories by Everett M. Rogers and creativity theories by Mel Rhodes (known as the Man Behind the Four P's of Creativity) in order to investigate the interconnection between creativity and innovation, as I take a special interest in the sociocultural dimension of innovation and creativity when studying the potential relation between space and place, the present and the future, while going back in time.

As creativity itself is a complex and multifaceted phenomenon, there is no general definition of the term. Creativity definitions tend to be placed in either the product, the process, or the person. Mel, Rhodes, a pioneer in the field of creativity studies, long ago pointed at 'Person, Process, Press and Products' (the four P's) as relevant aspects of creativity, but I find the *interplay* and connections between these relevant to explore. When taking an interest in the creative *Person*, which is often the case within education, one attempts to apply creativity to intelligence, talents, and habits. *Process* refers to motivation, learning, thinking, and communicating. As no one is living or operating in a vacuum, Rhodes expects all to experience a psychological *Press* from the environment, depending on the interaction between human beings and their reaction to the environment, as well as the press from the environment. Since great inventions very seldom are the work of any one mind, they often have social causes, such as changed needs and opportunities (Rhodes, 1961).

Ideas are embodied into tangible forms which Rhodes calls Products, and each of them represents a record of thinking at some point in time. In order to explain the relationship between the four P's, Rhodes came up with the suggestion to investigate 'the nature of the creative process from product to person and thence to process and to press' (Rhodes, 1961, p. 309). In the following, I am going to suggest a twist to his proposal, by including the four P's: Person, Process, Press and Products, in order to investigate the nature of the creative process on a bigger scale. I will analyse the Product: the idea of building the biggest and most powerful windmill in the world in two years at the Tvind Folk High School in Denmark; the People, meaning students and laymen interacting with some experts and citizens; the Press, meaning resistance of the time and space in history, and the Process, studied by analysing the influencing factors—the interconnection between the four P's.

THE INNOVATION CONTEXT

As ownership and access to resources tend to influence innovation processes we need to contextualise the innovation. Until recently, the energy sector in Denmark was vertically integrated and comprised about one hundred utilities (mainly co-operatives or municipally owned). The public opinion against nuclear power plant could not be ignored by public companies. The small utilities were grouped into two partnerships, Elsam and Elkraft, which controlled generation, import, and export of electricity, and planned generation and transmission expansions (Organisation for Economic Co-operation and Development [OECD], 2000). Historically, the industry has to a large extent been run on a non-profit basis. The powerful corporation, the Danish Collaborative Energy Company: Gyllingnæs/ELSAM, was actively supporting nuclear power plants in Denmark in 1973 and was considering the locality of Gyllingnæs in Jutland as the place to build the power plant. At the time, the energy policy discourse was primarily focused on financial issues but, due to public movements, opponents managed to change the agenda from technical issues to safety and environmental topics. Simultaneously, a general public protest against nuclear power plants began to grow internationally, and various emotional and art-based expressions influenced the discourse. The global movement was indicated by the badges saying: 'Nuclear Power? No Thanks' (the Danish artist Anne Lund created the badge (Figure 3) in 1976, and later it was translated into 45 languages). In a polite way it showed opposition to nuclear power, while at the same time its smiling sun in the middle of the badge pointed in the direction of sustainability.

Figure 3. Anti-nuclear badges

THE INNOVATION NARRATIVE UNFOLDING

During this period, the idea of building the biggest windmill in the world came up and involved a group of young students at a Danish Folk High School, together with a bunch of other primarily young people who decided to realise their shared vision by building the world's biggest windmill. Against all odds, they succeeded when several hundred very young people were gathered to physically build the mill. They erected the 100 metres high concrete windmill without any form of professional expertise in building windmills. Due to the collaborative efforts of lay men and engineers working voluntarily, they also developed the technical skills needed during the process. Before the internet, they looked for inspiration all over the world, as well as seeking inspiration from knowledgeable engineers and craftsmen, and they were successful.

Historically, the project draws on inspiration from the physicist Poul la Cour, who in 1891, as teacher of science at Askov Folk High School, was experimenting with wind power for the production of electrical power and was part of the co-operative movement at that time.[7] The young people from Tvind gained popular support from all over the country. At the time, various artists and artistic expressions, such as theatre and popular music, expressed concerns about nuclear power plants. One especially ironic song, welcoming a nuclear power plant, created a new discourse as it became clear that no one, in fact, wanted the plant in their back yard. Industries argued that compared to the efficiency of a nuclear power plant, windmills—with their low capacity—could not reasonably be the answer to the political and economic challenge the society was facing. Wind power was not regarded as a serious alternative, and the project did not get any economic support from the state. However, as the area was not regulated at the time, everyone was allowed to build a windmill close to their own residence in order to produce wind power for their own use, so the Tvind mill did not meet any restrictions.

Later, the technical innovations represented by the windmill were recognised by Vestas Ltd, when celebrating the 30-year anniversary of the mill,[8] A pioneer from Vestas windmills expressed his admiration:

> With your wind turbine you made it possible for me to keep believing that one day we too could produce a wind turbine with your capacity. You have also managed to keep the windmill maintained and even develop and install new technology—such as the new converter. More than forty years ago you, Tvind, had the courage to fire up the debate about energy—nuclear power versus other energy sources—including alternative energy such as wind power. (Midtby, 2015)

Engineering students from Aalborg University also paid particular interest in the possibilities of wind power and alternative energy, and many students later graduated with a green profile and paved the way for the university's current position within production and development of windmills.

The (controversial) political concept of this particular Folk High School Tvind may have obscured the importance of this technical innovation. The innovation narrative shows how perception of an innovation (nuclear power plants) led to its rejection in the persuasion stage of the innovations process, due to lack of public support. Protest movements influenced the decision state and were strong enough to enable the politic change several years later. The persuasion stage prepared for the public acceptance of another innovation (the windmills) by forming a directly observable physical appearance of a powerful windmill, with one very clear function: to produce electricity without dangerous waste products. This invention obviously made sense to the people involved in the processes as well as supporters, and it later inspired a reinvention of windmills and thereby restructured the entire energy structure, eventually turning it into a huge industry.

The building of the windmill tells the story of the innovative power of a public movement which encompasses culture and traditions from the past by bearing the pedagogy of the folk high schools as well as the co-operative movement in mind.

Given the widespread acceptance and execution of the concept, this narrative shows the power of simultaneous collaboration across different sectors and fields; turning a vision into a powerful observable image through the combination of practical and theoretical knowledge. Although at the time it looked like a fight between David and Goliath—a fantasy, one big windmill versus nuclear power plants—a powerful idea was fostered, and a new discourse was created. Inventors later recognised the challenge, reinvention took place, and development of new knowledge during the process led into the implementation of the idea now backed by public funding and venture capital. Today no one questions the value of the windmill industry, but its origins seem to have been forgotten, and thereby the progressive innovation drives in collective movements.

CREATIVITY DEVELOPMENT AND IMAGINATION IN EDUCATION

The innovation narrative of the Tvind windmill manifested the power of collective problem-defining and problem-solving processes within a pedagogical institution, although the project would not have been realised without support from the surrounding community. The project is evidence that technological innovations are grounded in impartial factors like imagination and emotions.

The emotional driving force behind the creation was 'fear' of nuclear power plants and their waste products, scepticism and 'anger' towards powerful experts, 'hope' by creating an alternative future, and 'trust' in the collaborative in order to overcome the lack of specific knowledge. In this climate, new important and alternative knowledge was created by seeking and introducing knowledge from various sources and, in the end, sharing the advanced technical knowledge for further generations to use, as technology in this project was deliberately not patented.

The innovation story demonstrates the dynamics between imagination, creativity, and innovation as parts of a complex knowledge creation process. This is illustrated by Figure 4. In the constant process of moving from insecurity towards certainty and back, knowledge is produced by creating, playing, and expressing new ideas and conceptualisations. The innovation itself is shown in actualising new ideas. By being open to ideas, and through dealing with uncertainty when playing with new ideas and expressions, the participants moved toward 'certainty' by creating and manifesting new technology; they were able to change the existing culture (and concepts) and, in the long run, the society around them.

Although arts and humanities are regarded as 'soft' knowledge areas, artistic knowledge implies the ability to cope with uncertainty when operating in an open field, while technical knowledge is polarised as 'hard' knowledge, dealing with subjects that can be quantified, captured, and codified. A (false) duality between the two areas may hide potentials and the need for correspondents in order to come up with new solutions, i.e., to societal challenges. Art and artist create and reflect new visions and ideas which may influence what the world will look like in the future, as art is able to communicate shared emotional responses to different subjects.

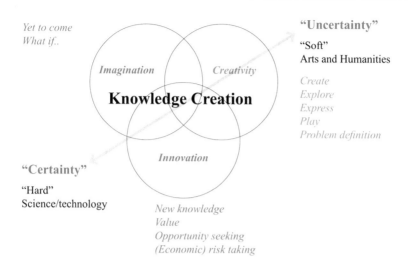

Figure 4. Knowledge creation in the space between uncertainty and certainty

This study of an innovation process further supports the system model by Csikszentmihalyi (1996) in which he includes the study of the social and historical milieu in which creativity and innovation unfold, while showing the importance of ideas and the support of these, as well as the crossover between different sectors and knowledge domains.

In this case, creativity development was part of a social response to critical situations, and the response was realised by involving cross-sectorial and *across*-knowledge domains. The innovation—the product—was realised by commonly developed imaginations in different materialisations. From a pedagogical perspective, it points towards the emotional aspects of innovations as students' passion seems to create the mental energy needed to continue and fulfil an idea. Subjective individual experience contributes to the mobilisation of *shared emotional* experiences, leading to new common social actions and societal change influencing the future direction of society. In this case, the students participated in a self-cultivation and educating process as agents, and the creation of meanings was related to their desires and imagination. Through this process they learned to think, to question, to feel, and to act when solving problems, in an interconnected learning process, as expressed by Dewey:

> Human beings are not normally divided in two parts, the one emotional, the other coldly intellectual—the one matter of facts, the other imaginative […] There is no integration of character and mind unless there is fusion of the intellectual and the emotional of meaning and value, of fact and imaginative running beyond facts into the realm of desired possibilities. (1933, p. 278)

This means that the emotional aspects of learning and thinking are to be welcomed in order to make the right decisions. Dewey perceived learning as social and dynamic and, most importantly, affected by the quality of interaction between person and environment, since knowledge and skills from one experience become an instrument of understanding in the coming situation. As the image has an effect on the course of action taken and in turn may be transformed by that very action, during this process change occurs in both the self and the environment when interacting.

To be innovative from this perspective, some routine habits are to be challenged, as they are narrowing the field of further experiences in contrast to that expansion of the students' meaning-horizon, which seems to be the essence in innovating thinking processes.

CONCLUSION

The innovation narrative implies that creativity and imagination today are valued as *a means* to economic growth. This awareness is shown through political and economic support for the fostering and creation of an 'entrepreneurial mindset' and talent development within education. Along this line, it is worth mentioning that no single person was ever acknowledged as *the* inventor of the Tvind Mill, opposed to the tradition of recognising great inventions by recognising *the* inventor. The windmill project implied the competency of forming and establishing cross-sectorial collaborative networks, where sustainable technological knowledge developed from dealing with insecurity and complex problem-solving; however, the production of the Tvind mill itself was not an isolated and goal-directed rational innovation process sparked by a recognised need and driven by the market and profits. As the analysis shows, the ground-breaking idea was not fostered out of the blue by special talents, but by mutual and cross-sectorial efforts. By participating in this building process from the beginning to the end, this group of young people experienced physically the potentials in contributing to the realisation of a common imagination and its resulting ideas. They learned by experimenting and trying out new things. In a pedagogical terminology, this constituted authentic learning situations in a very open educational environment. Due to the historical tradition of the Folk High Schools, in Tvind there are no exams and students are not receiving any grades. There is no fixed curriculum, and although students have to pay tuition fees, the Danish state supports this kind of school financially. This creates the time and space to think and to experiment, being inspired by actual cultural and societal challenges.

The innovation narrative further indicates the importance of social movement as an agent of change. In this case the anti-nuclear campaign paved the way for a technological alternative originated through a common bottom-up process, as an imaginative and emotional response to insecurity, initiated by questioning and challenging the established knowledge, politics and expertise within the field. This points towards an important aspect of knowledge creation being the human capability of imagining other events similar to or different from the one experienced. This creative attitude thrust together curiosity, formulation of new questions, and generation of possible expansions and testing of theories when acting. Important new knowledge seems to result from a sense of insecurity and intuition, as well as from questioning established truths and convenience;, thus the ability to move back and forth between 'uncertainty' and 'certainty' until a solution is created (Figure 4) is both fruitful and needed in order to innovate.

This narrative incorporates the role of the arts in innovation processes—as its ability to provoke and inspire by expressions of new visions manifested in shared cultural symbols (lyrics and stories). Some of these images possess worldwide appeal (like the Pippi stories and the sun badge), as artistic expressions are part of the way humans express and experience themselves emotionally when creating meaning in actions and beliefs. Through art and artistic expression, we make sense of ourselves individually and in common, which seems to support and enhance the power of collaboration. Csikszentmihalyi (1996) underpins that what we call creative is never the result of an individual acting alone, it is the product of three shaping forces—social institutions (fields), a stable cultural domain, and the individual, who brings about change in the domain that the field will regard as creative. For me, the innovation narrative points to the fact that creativity is essentially connected to the ability to imagine how things could be different, and connected to questioning: to the belief that the world can be changed. The innovation narrative further shows that in order to create real change, an image must be shared and supported, emotionally or/and economically across domains. But innovations also imply power issues manifested in laws and access to resources in time and space (e.g., if the Danish energy sector (and the power plants) at the time had not been publicly owned, it would have been far more complicated to politically influence the energy policy and create alternatives). The result might be a product (as the bottom-up windmill innovation shows) or a story (such as Astrid Lindgren's) that innovates the way we conceptualise education, gender, or pedagogy. This does not imply that all imaginative or creative ideas are considered progressive or deserve to be realised; education has an important role to play in order to support critical reflection and moral aspects in knowledge creation, in order to educate.

Schools, universities, and society in general ought to welcome and reinvent reform pedagogy, as learning to think and to question *might* lead to progress, depending on how the critique is expressed and how we deal with it within a democratic setting. Our common future may very well depend on our ability to collaborate globally and internationally in order to solve our greatest common challenges, such as inequality and climate change. Consequently, education must encourage *all* students to have a voice, to criticise, and to welcome ideas and imagination in order to acknowledge the strong connection between democratic formation in education and students' creative potentials within—as well as outside—universities.

NOTES

[1] Partnership P21's mission is to serve as a catalyst for 21st century learning by building collaborative partnerships among education, business, community, and government leaders. http://www.p21.org/members-states/how-to-get-involved

[2] Since 2000, the UN has been promoting the Millennium Development Goal to achieve free universal primary education for all, regardless of gender, by 2015.

[3] The Human Capital Index ranks 130 countries on how well they are developing and deploying their human capital potential. The Index assesses Learning and Employment outcomes on a scale from 0 (worst) to 100 (best) across five distinct age groups to capture the full demographic profile of a country.

[4] Which later became world famous in different variations. Only in 2008 in a new French version of Pippi was allowed to present herself in an uncensored version! (Munck, 2008).

[5] Which is a challenge as students, schools and education may have different understandings of what 'real challenges' means.

[6] The Danish folk high schools offer non-formal adult education. Most students are between 18 and 24 years old and the length of a typical stay is 6 months. The folk high schools are boarding schools without academic requirements for admittance and there are no exams. The concept is associated with N.F.S. Grundtvig (1783–1872), a Danish philosopher, poet, educational thinker and clergyman. The concept arose in the 19th century and is one of the cornerstones of the Danish educational system.

[7] La Cour's mill produced electricity for the folk high school and later also for people in the town Askov, and some experience from this project was transformed into the new project. (This windmill was operating until 1968.)

[8] Today, Vestas is one of the largest wind turbine companies in the world. It has an operating income on 906 million EUR (2015). Vestas windmills used to produce 22 kW or 30 kW, and just recently started to produce 55 kW. In comparison, the Tvind windmill's turbine had a 1725 kW generator capacity.

REFERENCES

Arent, H. (1958). *The human condition.* Chicago, IL: University of Chicago Press.
Ben-Ze'ev, A. (2000). *The subtlety of emotions.* Cambrige, MA, & London: MIT Press.
Biesta, G. J. J. (2014). *The beautiful risk of education.* London: Paradigm Publishers.
Chambliss, J. J. (1991). John Dewey's idea of imagination in philosophy and education. *Journal of Aesthetic Education, 25*(4), 43–49.
Csikszentmihalyi, M. (1996). *Creativity—flow and the psychology of discovery and invention.* New York, NY: Harper Perennial.
Dewey, J. (1933). *How we think.* Boston, MA: D.C. Heath.
Dewey, J. (1938). *Experience and education* New York, NY: Collier Books.
Dewey, J. (2005). *Art as experience.* New York, NY: Perigee Books. (Originally published in 1934)
Dewey, J. (1976). Creative democracy: The task before us. In J. Boydston (Ed.), *John Dewey: The later works, 1925–1953* (Vol. 14, pp. 224–230). Carbondale, IL: Southern Illinois University Press. (Original published in 1939)
Dirkx, J. M. (2001). The power of feelings: Emotion, imagination, and the construction of meaning in adult learning. *New Directions for Adult and Continuing Education, 89*, 63–72.
Dorstewitz, P. (2008). *Imagination in the deliberation process.* Technical Report 04/08 Centre for Philosophy of Natural and Social Science Contingency and Dissent in Science, The London School of Economics and Political Science, London.

Einstein, A. (2009). *Cosmic religion and other opinions and aphorism.* Mineola, NY: Dover Publications, Inc. (First published in 1931)
Kaufman, J. C., & Sternberg, R. J. (Eds.). (2010). *Cambridge handbook of creativity.* New York, NY: Cambridge University Press.
Kümmerling-Meibauer, B., & Surmatz, A. (Eds.). (2011). *Beyond Pippi Longstocking: Intermedial and international aspects of Astrid Lindgren's works.* New York, NY: Routledge.
Leddy, T. (2016). Dewey's Aesthetics. In E. N. Zalta (Ed.), *The Stanford encyclopedia of philosophy* (Winter 2016 Edition). Retrieved from https://plato.stanford.edu/archives/win2016/entries/dewey-aesthetics/
Lindgren, A. E. (1987). *Pippi Longstocking.* London: Puffin Books.
Lund, B. (2011). Hvordan udfordrer innovationspolitikker uddannelsessystemet og etablerede dannelsesidealer. In J. H. Midtsundstad & T. Werler (Eds.), *Didaktikk i Norden* (1st ed., pp. 81–99). Kristiansand: Portal Forlag.
Lund, B. (2017). Managing students' emotion in order to foster innovation: View on entrepreneurship education in school. In T. Chemi, S. Grams Davy, & B. Lund (Eds.), *Innovative pedagogy: Recognition of emotions and creativity in education* (1st ed., pp. 91–105). Rotterdam, The Netherlands: Sense Publishers.
Lybæk, R. B., & Møller, P. (1999). *Ny planlægningsstrategi for implementering af vindkraft i den offentlige planlægning: Ressourcebegrebet som grundlag for vindmølleplanlægning.* Roskilde: Roskilde Universitet. (Rapportserien, Institut for miljø, teknologi og samfund, Roskilde Universitetscenter; no. 75)
Martinaitytė, E., & Kregždaitė, R. (2013). Creative industry impact on economy growth. *Societal Studies, 5*(4), 1094–1108.
Maegaard, P. (2009). Tvindmøllen viste vej. *Nordisk Folkecenter for Vedvarende Energi.* Retrieved November 19, 2017, from http://www.folkecenter.dk/dk/rd/vindkraft/48017/tvindmollen
Midtby, J. (2015). *Speech given at the 40th anniversary of the Tvind Windmill.* Tvindkraft: Vestas Wind Systems Ltd. Retrieved November 19, 2017, from http://www.tvindkraft.dk/…/575-jens-midtiby-at-vestas-wind-systems-ltd
Munck, A. (2008, April 19). Franske oversættelser gjorde kål på Pippi [French translations destroyed Pippi]. *Politiken.* Retrieved February 6, 2018, from https://politiken.dk/kultur/boger/art4741658/Franske-overs%C3%A6ttelser-gjorde-k%C3%A5l-p%C3%A5-Pippi
OECD Reviews of Regulatory Reform: Regulatory Reform in Denmark. (2000). *Governance.* Paris: OECD Publishing.
Olsson, K. (2005, May 12). Barsebäck lukker og slukker for atomkraften [Barsebäck closes and turns off nuclear power]. *Politiken.* Retrieved February 6, 2018, from https://politiken.dk/indland/art5006432/Barseb%C3%A4ck-lukker-og-slukker-for-atomkraften
P21, Partnership for 21st Century Learning. (n.d.). *Framework for 21st century learning.* Retrieved April 29, 2018, from http://www.p21.org/about-us/p21-framework
Renier, S. (2016). The many lives of John Dewey's 'democracy and education'. *European Journal of Pragmatism and American Philosophy* [Online]. doi:10.4000/ejpap.448
Rhodes, M. (1961). An analysis of creativity. *The Phi Delta Kappan, 42*(7), 305–310. Retrieved from http://www.jstor.org/stable/20342603
Rogers, C. (2002). Defining reflection: Another look at John Dewey and reflective thinking. *Teachers College Record, 104*(4), 842–866. doi:10.1111/1467-9620.00181
Sawyer, R. K. (2010). Individual and group creativity. In J. C. Kaufman & R. J. Sternberg (Eds.), *The Cambridge handbook of creativity* (pp. 366–380). New York, NY: Cambridge University Press.
Smith, J. K., & Smith, L. (2010). Educational creativity. In J. C. Kaufman & R. J. Sternberg (Eds.), *The Cambridge handbook of creativity.* New York, NY: Cambridge University Press.
Talentudvikling evaluering og strategi af Arbejdsgruppen til talentudvikling i uddannelsessystemet. (2011). Retrieved Novermber 09, 2017, from https://uvm.dk/-/media/filer/uvm/udd/folke/pdf11/110414-talentrapport-hele.pdf

Telhaug, A. O., Mediås, O. A., & Aasen, P. (2006). The Nordic model in education: Education as part of the political system in the last 50 years. *Scandinavian Journal of Educational Research, 50*(3), 245–283.

Tholander, M. (2016). Pippi Longstocking as Friedrich Nietzsche's overhuman. *Confero, Essays on Education Philosophy and Politics, 4*(1), 97–135. doi:10.3384/confero.2001-4562.160111

Birthe Lund
Department of Learning and Philosophy
Aalborg University
Aalborg, Denmark

RIKKE PLATZ CORTSEN AND ANNE METTE W. NIELSEN

3. ARTISTIC MAKINGS AS A METHOD OF INQUIRY IN HIGHER EDUCATION

INTRODUCTION

Academic practices have been going through rapid changes in recent years in the way they operate, as well as their role in society (Hayles, 2012). University students are still expected to acquire new knowledge and think critically within their field of studies while facing new modes of thinking and a more unpredictable post-graduation future (Barnett, 2004). In our teaching we have addressed these changes through multiple intersecting pathways. The ambition is to engage the students as independent thinkers and actors in a continuous and creative inquiry process, where they are encouraged to explore productive failing and new multimodal modes of critical thinking. In this chapter we provide examples of how we framed the processes the students went through and analyse the key components that allowed them to access new areas of thought and acquire new (artistic) strategies to work with.

The way research and education relate in academia have gone through rapid changes in recent years, and the way these academic practices relate to society is changing accordingly (Hayles, 2012). Our chapter offers an exploration of new ways of engaging students as independent thinkers and actors through a discussion of the multimodal academic practices employed in a theory course, 'Practice in Theory', which we taught at the Department of Arts and Cultural Studies, University of Copenhagen in 2014. The course had two main objectives: The first objective was to investigate and understand theories of practice, for example philosophical concepts of practice and the role of practice in the construction of different theories and research methods. The second objective was to expand the students' repertoire of inquiry methods and have them employ multimodal methods anchored in explorative and creative 'makings'.

The course followed the threefold conceptual definition of 'making' proposed by media theorist and literary scholar Katherine Hayles in her book *How We Think*:

> The idea of practice-based research, long integrated into the sciences, is relatively new to the humanities. The work of making—*producing something that requires long hours, intense thought, and considerable technical skill*—has significant implications that go beyond the crafting of words. Involved are embodied interaction with digital technologies, frequent testing of code and

other functionalities that results in reworking and correcting, and dynamic, ongoing discussion with collaborators to get it right. (Hayles, 2012, p. 19, emphasis added)

In the quote, Hayles underlines how the ways in which we develop knowledge are embodied and interrelated with—and in fact indistinguishable from—the material processes constituting it. To understand academic work as a work of *making* makes visible how new multimodal and collaborative practices impact our work with text: how we read, write, and ultimately reflect upon the subjects at hand. A growing integration of digital technologies in the Humanities and qualitative Social Sciences involves, Hayles argues, collaboration around collecting, storing, and analysing material in relation to extensive databases, integration of conceptual developments with design, navigation, and graphics, and differentiation of front-ends including e-books, blogs, and research-related webpages hosted by individuals, collaborative research-projects, or whole universities. Drawing upon the work of media theorists Marshall McLuhan, Lev Manovich, Mark Hansen, and Jonathan Crary among others, Hayles thus unfolds the idea that 'we think through, with, and alongside media' (Hayles, 2012, p. 1) and convincingly demonstrates a shift in humanistic inquiry across the way we conceptualise projects, implement research programs, design curricula and educate students.

Hayles suggests that these new multimodal and collaborative practices not only integrate new formats of scholarly work, they also make the assumptions and organisational patterns of print visible as media-specific practices, thereby opening up the largely invisible presuppositions of the Age of Print accessible for rethinking and reconceptualisation. This sudden visibility, Hayles argues, integrates an *expanded* concept of text to her argument of how digital media has extensive theoretical, organisational, and pedagogical implications. This expanded understanding of text does not necessarily involve leaving skills, thoughts, and expressions of print-based practices behind, but opens up an understanding of reading processes in research and teaching as multiple and distinct. Hayles names these differing types of reading *close reading*, *hyper reading*, and *machine reading* (Hayles, 2012, pp. 55–87). Up until now close reading has been at the core of many humanities subjects, but the appearance of digital media has highlighted how scholars and students frequently hyper read (scanning for patterns, skimming a text for keywords and phrases, reading several texts simultaneously by flipping back and forth between them) and are aided in their pursuits by machine reading (archival searches, search engines, and other big data interpretation by digital programs). Hayles underlines that it is not a question of hyper and machine reading replacing close reading as the core practice shaping research and teaching, but rather that we understand how all three modes of reading impact how we work with text, i.e., how we read, how we write, and ultimately, our possibilities for conjuring up new ideas and reflecting upon the subjects at hand. Adding that code, graphics, animation, design, video, and sound are increasingly important guides in how research navigates in meaning shaping processes, Hayles integrates an expanded concept of text to her argument that digital media has extensive theoretical, organisational, and pedagogical implications.

With an emphasis on the importance of Hayles' nuanced view of reading as threefold, as well as the importance of the act of making in the creation of new thoughts and reflection, we decided to make multimodal production processes an integral part of our reflection and teaching. This put *making* at the centre of our theoretical course as yet another way of discussing how embodied interactions with materials are an integrated part of constructing and understanding theory.

MAKINGS AS WAYS OF 'KNOWING-IN-AND-WITH-UNCERTAINTY'

The employment of multimodal methods anchored in explorative and creative 'makings' meant that the students—apart from multiple ways of reading—used different artistic strategies to produce reflection *into* the artworks and theoretical texts discussed during the course. This work of 'making' involved a process of decoding and recoding where the students used writing, cooking, drawing, movie making, baking, sculpting, collaging, etc. as processes to pick apart the artworks and theoretical texts and rework them in a way that exposes the put-together-ness of this material.

We suggest that these kinds of 'makings', in close tandem with reflective inquiry, are essential for students to develop the means to think about and act upon the complex world they are part of (e.g., Barnett, 2004). Rather than focusing on specific knowledge and skills, this approach helps students develop sophisticated strategies to examine, take apart, and reconfigure theories, materials, and contexts. Educational thinker Ronald Barnett proposes this direct involvement of students in the academic production of knowledge itself as the main path of future learning (Barnett, 2004). By avoiding the academic 'cul-de-sac' of generic knowledge on the one hand and the purely problem-solving limitations of the so-called 'mode 2 knowledge' (Gibbons et al., 1994) on the other hand, Barnett (2004) turns the educational task towards what he calls a knowing-in-and-with-uncertainty:

> Under such conditions [learning for an unknown future], a double educational task arises: First, bringing students to a sense that all descriptions of the world are contestable and, then, second, to a position of being able to prosper in such a world in which our categories even for understanding the situations in which we are placed, including understanding ourselves, are themselves contested. (pp. 252–253)

In the quote Barnett argues that 'uncertainty' is no longer something to be done away with, nor a ground conquered through the educational process, but a *groundwork* to interact with in order to meet a future that is unknown. When everything is unclear, the very act of wondering—to step back, to look closer, and to express: *I really don't understand*—becomes desirable.

The way we chose to examine the double educational tasks of bringing students to contest concepts and theories, and at the same time be at ease when embedded in this on-going inquiry process, included an emphasis on the composite and complex nature of problems and, hence, the need to keep the process of inquiry open. In the course 'Practice in Theory' it meant a continuous rework of the conclusions and preconceived notions through creative explorations. In doing so, we not only want to underline the changing relation of academic practices to society, but also to address the challenges many universities face today in an exceedingly competitive and competency focused university environment. For us, the course offered an opportunity to counteract the push to streamline academic teaching through standardisation, budget cuts, and accountability (e.g. Tuchman, 2009). The students' open-ended makings positioned as an integrated part of their reflective inquiry (emphasising collaboration and differentiation) put forward alternative strategies to teaching for the test. Being comfortable with working in uncertainty and accepting that these creative makings could end up complicating their subject or falling apart made the students accept 'wrong' outcomes as productive rather than as failure. Furthermore, when working with makings, time can expand excessively—through hours and hours of rework and reconnection—but also condense it. This includes how long it takes to access the makings for an external viewer. The massive contrast of the morphable timescapes characterising these processes breaks down the way the ECTS-system divides studies and study-time into hourly-defined components and challenges the idea that a certain amount of learning can be done in a certain amount of time.

PRESENTATION OF THE COURSE

We begin the presentation of the course by introducing one of the main inspirations for the strategies employed in the course—anthropologist and philosopher Bruno Latour. First, we will specify our use of his concept of 'compositionism', and then present his use of artistic strategies. The chapter presents the elements of the course and examples of student 'makings' as well as an analysis of what can be said to characterise student-driven inquiries that use artistic strategies. We conclude in a discussion of the potentials of employing artistic strategies as a way of empowering students to engage with and face uncertainties.

We co-taught the MA course 'Practice in Theory' in the spring of 2014 at the Department of Arts and Cultural Studies, University of Copenhagen, Denmark. The MA students at Modern Culture courses hold BAs in a wide variety of subjects in the humanities, primarily from the aesthetic disciplines: literature, art history, music, dance, performance, and theatre. Hence, the student population is a cross-disciplinary group; the department's focus on the multiplicity of artistic forms allowed us to draw on works, artists, and research from a very diverse area of the cultural sphere, where each student had additional knowledge and input to contribute from their main field.

The ambiguity of the course title 'Practice in Theory' was intended, and it emphasised how the two concepts are interrelated and how they informed each other as the teaching progressed. It meant that we discussed practice as a philosophical concept, practice-led research, practice-based research, as well as different forms of artistic research and the difficulties involved in qualifying and evaluating the approaches within the organisational context of museums, universities, and other research and teaching institutions. Simultaneously, we used multimodal artistic strategies to explore, identify, and comprehend complex concepts and relations within the theories we studied, in order to advance the students' understanding of intricate problems. Through the shaping of materials, visualisations, and the construction of three-dimensional objects, the 'makings' permitted the students to spend considerable time analysing patterns and rethinking the mediations. The creative makings allowed the students to try to refine technical skills during the course, as well as when they made an e-book as a final product of the class. The latter provided the students with editorial skills, an understanding of working with images in digital formats, as well as structuring content and preparing it for publication.

Practice in Theory

Introduction to practice through various concepts	The relationship between practice and theory	Ways to navigate the research field theory/practice
1. Feb. 7th Intro: Mapping, curating, archive and experiment as possibility **2. Feb. 14th** John Dewey: Practice philosophy On praxis, practices and 'practical turn' **3. Feb 21st** Bruno Latour: "compositions" On inter-objectivity, black boxes and compositions	**4. Feb 28th** Art academy – the art institution On exchanges between theory and practice **5. March 7th** Visit at CIID (Copenhagen Institute of Interaction Design) On how theory is drawn into practice **6. March 14th** Summing up + Kathrine Hayles: Different readings	**7. March 21st** Research approaches (I) On artistic uses of natural science technologies: the lab as practice **8. March 28th** Research approaches (II) Robot technology as practice **9. April 4th** Research approaches (III) Comics Drawing Style, Constraint and Theory: Drawing as practice

10. Bookcamp

11. April 25th Own connections and exam preparation

Figure 1. Overview of the course 'practice in theory'

We met with the students once a week for three hours over a period of 14 weeks. The classes alternated between lectures, guest lectures, sharing of creative makings, dialogues, field trips, and, finally, a whole day where we, together with the students, produced an e-book with insights and makings from the course. In preparation for each class, the students read theoretical texts, engaged with various artworks, and produced multimodal, inquiry-driven makings into the assigned theories, concepts, and/or artworks. During class, we held lectures or had guest lecturers present their research, works, and theories to us. By the end of each class, we, along with the students, presented our makings in an 'exhibition', allowing in-depth discussions on the makings, and on the artworks and theories we had explored, often with questions and reflexions involving the guest lecturers present and drawing on their feedback.

INSPIRATION: BRUNO LATOUR AS A *COMPOSITIONIST* PRACTITIONER

A core element in the course was our use of artistic strategies to identify and comprehend complex concepts and relations. This approach was inspired by the work of Bruno Latour. Known primarily for his contributions to the early development of Actor Network Theory (Latour & Callon, 1981); his manifold, artistically inspired inquiries into the organisation of the social are often overlooked. This is regrettable since these multimodal explorations form the stepping stones for many of his major written works.[1]

Latour's use of artistic strategies includes mappings, re-enactments, and curatorial practices, all of which emphasise how he understands new theories and concepts as experimental ways of *presenting* or studying the world rather than revealing it. Hence, one of Latour's main points in *The Pasteurization of France* (1988) is that 'to discover is not to lift the veil. It is to construct, to relate, and then to "place under"' (Latour, 1988, p. 81). This radical understanding of academic scholarship as embedded in the construction of the social is later developed by Latour in the essay *An Attempt at a 'Compositionist Manifesto'* (2010). Here Latour suggests that critique as a privileged access to the world of reality has been a utopian construction relying 'on the certainty of the world *beyond* this world. By contrast, for compositionism, there is no world of beyond. It is all about *immanence*' (Latour, 2010, pp. 474–475). This replacement of critique with compositionism has three important implications for this chapter.

The first aspect is the impossibility of 'the discovery of a true world of realities lying behind a veil of appearances' and, instead, the necessity to assemble the world and compose it (Latour, 2010, p. 474). Latour here defines social order not as an already existing and certain given, but as a process that requires constant reworking or 'translation', involving the interaction of multiple actors. Researching these interactions emphasises how the social organises, produces, stabilises and globalises practices. The second aspect is how composition (from the Latin *componere*) 'underlines that things have to be put together' thereby underlining both heterogeneity (the diversity of composite materials) and elusiveness (compositions are fragile, revisable) (Latour, 2010, p. 473). Part of this second aspect is that compositions can always be decomposed, taken apart, and put together again (involving repair, care-taking, reassembling, and stitching together) in a new configuration or constellation. The third aspect refers to the artistic and musical dimensions of the concept introducing a focus on 'the crucial difference between what is *well* or *badly* constructed, *well* or *badly* composed', thus underlining aesthetic processes as reliant upon the possibility of redoing failed compositions: 'a composition can *fail*' (Latour, 2010, p. 474).

THREE EXAMPLES OF LATOUR'S USE OF ARTISTIC STRATEGIES AS *COMPOSITIONISM*

In our course we introduced compositionism as a way to give form and compose, but also as a way to deduce or underline relations or associations proposed in theories and concepts, hence perceiving them as scholarly 'makings', which is to say, something that also has been given shape or has been composed (Hayles, 2012). We presented the three artistic strategies inspired by examples from Latour's work: mapping, re-enactment, and curating. The three examples share certain qualities in that they all explicitly *compose* the object of study: they take apart, reconnect, and reconsider the compositions. As Latour notes, artists are always concerned with *how* to represent and *through which medium* to represent the powers that be and the connections between things, people and situations (Latour, 2005, p. 16). As such, the redoing of the work at hand is at the centre of all three strategies, but each of them employs a different approach to putting things together.

Mappings: Paris: Invisible City (2006, First Published in French in 1998)

The first example by Latour is his *Paris: Invisible City* (2006), a web-collaboration with the photographer Emilie Hermant. Through an interactive mixed media inquiry into the city of Paris, they create a layered portrait of the invisible networks that make Paris liveable: 'Our photographic exploration takes us first to places usually hidden from passers-by, in which the countless techniques making Parisians' lives possible are elaborated (water services, police force, ring road: various "oligopticons" from which the city is seen in its entirety)' (Latour, 2006, p. 1). The aim of the work is to enable the reader or viewer to take a new look at the city at the same time acknowledging that it is not possible at a single glance. In the quote above Latour introduces the concept of *oligopticon* (from the Greek *oligo* meaning 'little'); hereby underlining that any effective overview is defined *not* by seeing the whole (as in Bentham's idea of the 'panopticon') but instead by seeing *little* (and seeing it *well*).

This seeing *little and well* involves spatio-temporal orderings that extract, leave out, and establish boundaries. The spatio-temporal orderings are constituted, formed, or *composed* through a multiplicity of materials, relations, and scales we called *mappings*. Not a mapping which plots places within the usual cartographic co-ordinates of latitudes and longitudes, but the kind of mappings which make different types of connections (powers) visible. In the introduction of mapping provided to the students we focused on the parts, the linkings, and the visibilities that the oligopticon's 'seeing little, but seeing it well' allows. We introduced the approach of artist and cartographer Dennis Wood, as developed in his book *Everything Sings* (2010), where he focuses on how mapmaking changes what can be seen and what cannot be seen. Mapping helps build the world by showing certain connections, putting elements together in particular constellations. Maps can make things and connections visible or disappear. When Denis Wood maps the jack-o'-lanterns in his neighbourhood he is not just showing representations of pumpkins but highlighting socioeconomic differences and patterns that point to the way the community is put together, and in turn, what might take it apart.

Working with *Paris Invisible* and *Everything Sings* together, we introduced our students to creative mappings as a way to get to know, make visible, and produce the places, theories, artwork, and things we encountered in class: that is, how to see little, but see it well.

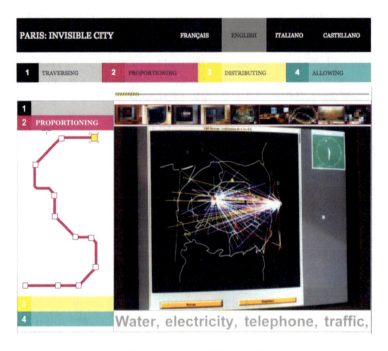

Figure 2. Latour 2006, plan 20

Re-enactments: The Tarde Durkheim Debate (2007)

The second example by Latour is his *The Tarde Durkheim Debate*—a performance concerning the nature of sociology and its relation to other sciences. It staged a debate between the two sociologists Gabriel Tarde and Emile Durkheim at the Ecole des Hautes Etudes Sociales in 1903. The performance is composed as a montage of quotes from the written works by Gabriel Tarde and Emile Durkheim, since nothing had been preserved from the original debate except for a brief summary. Even if Latour did in one sense completely reinvent this particular debate, he did, in another sense, just assemble paragraphs Tarde and Durkheim *had* in fact written, but put forward in a way that suggests Tarde as the 'winner' of the debate (thus replacing Durkheim as the father of sociology).

This way of retracing events, situations, theories, artworks, or other assemblages that allows the elements to be composed differently with different results we called *re-enactments*. In re-enacting the Tarde Durkheim debate, Latour alters the causality of events in the history of science (in the case of sociology) while at the same time showing the reversibility of it. Hence, re-enactments help answer questions of how assemblages are put together, what the connections (powers) that hold them together are, and how they might look different—not at random, but as consequences of a recomposition of particular elements. As with the first strategy, re-enactments focus on the remaking, the representing of processes where the thinker (Latour), the artist, or—in our case—the students go back over material that is then reconfigured. The point of the re-enactment is *not* to redo a thing, a situation, or a line of events precisely, but to allow for another understanding of the studied object through the recomposition of its parts. In class we presented this approach through artist Pia Arke's ethno-aesthetic explorations of the individuals appearing on old photographs from Greenlandian village Scoresbysund, her family's home-village (Arke, 2010). Arke had stumbled upon the photos in archives in Washington D.C. and brought copies back to Scoresbysund to identify (and name) the then anonymous 'village-members' and reprint them as part of her oeuvre. This re-enactment of the photos by explorers and employers of the colonial era were put into writings by the students during the first class as an act of translation. This provided them both with a sensibility towards media-specificities and let them explore re-enactments as a recomposition of material. The writings also allowed the students to experiment with ways of sharing their explorations and reflections with the rest of the class.

Curatings: Making Things Public (2005)

The third example by Latour is *Making Things Public*, an exhibition by Latour and artist, art theorist, and director of Zentrum für Kunst und Medientechnologie (ZKM) in Karlsruhe, Peter Weibel. Just like *Paris: Invisible City,* the exhibition at ZKM aimed to explore a hidden geography; but while the *mapping* of the multimedia project involves orderings that extract, leave out, and establish boundaries, Latour states that in the exhibition they 'simply want to pack loads of stuff into the empty arenas' (Latour, 2005, p 17). In this creation of a public space 'thick with things, crowded with objects' Latour draws on philosopher John Dewey's concept of the public as a non-institutional, not pre-existing space where agents (humans as well as non-humans) get together to solve those matters of concerns that institutions and organisations are not able to solve (Dewey, 1927). By bringing matters of concern together in the same space, the public can listen to other voices, share knowledge and—maybe—come to an agreement.

This way of gathering differing assemblages we called *curatings*. It is characterised by confronting the challenge of renewing politics not through solving or explaining problems, but through allowing disagreements and agreements as coexisting in an ongoing, multi-voiced recomposition of the matters of concern. To speak politically in Latour's sense thus describes 'a risky and tentative set of experiments in probing' (Latour, 2005, p. 14). Just like politics revolve around problems that people are implicated in, the exhibition involves the spectator in various and not always directly traceable ways.

> At times the relation will be traceable in a sort of one-to-one connection ('I did this, and here is what happened'), but at other instances the whole effect will be entirely lost ('I did nothing, and here is what happened'), while at some other times the effect will be direct but on some other visitors. (Latour, 2005, pp. 38–39)

Performing politics as relational and sometimes phantom-like emphasises curatings as a composition strategy focusing on the multiple ways objects (both things and people) can come together in agreement and disagreement to examine the matters of concern. We put forward this approach through what we called a 'curated assembly' with inspiration from author and museum director Peter Seeberg and his curatorial practices at the small regional museum of Viborg (Seeberg, 1975). In his juxtapositions of everyday objects, Seeberg unfolded complex stories of life accompanied by a text—often in the shape of dry registrations or (seemingly, but not quite) ready-mades (e.g. his overviews of genealogies). By letting the students experiment with curatings as ways to have objects and voices come together they explored makings, not as defined and already settled assemblages, but as probings into how matters of concern can be examined.

EMPLOYING ARTISTIC STRATEGIES AS MULTIMODAL INQUIRY METHODS IN OUR TEACHING

In class we introduced these three artistic strategies, mappings, re-enactments, and curatings, as multimodal inquiry strategies to identify and comprehend complex concepts and relations within theory and artworks. In the introduction we used both the above-mentioned works of Bruno Latour, and the works of a variety of artist-theorists, between them Wood, Arke, and Seeberg, to broaden the perception of the students.

At a first glance, it might not be immediately clear how the makings that were made by the students in class (e.g. crochet pieces, baking, building a sculpture, drawing, or making a flavoured jelly block) can further their independent thinking, support critical reflection, and enhance their ability to engage in complicated inquiries. However, this variety of creative methods and explorations are characterised by sharing the approach of compositionism: analysing works and advancing the understanding of intricate problems by putting together and taking apart materials and allowing the possibility of failed assemblages (which is such a crucial aspect of compositionism) in order to understand a given problem, artwork, situation, or theory. For a more in-depth description and discussion of what characterises the way we employed mappings, re-enactments, and curatings as multimodal methods in class, we offer two concrete examples presented by the students as responses to assignments in class.

Figure 3. Cardboard project made by student as part of class exercise

The Cardboard Project

> A piece of cardboard lies on the floor, a strong smell of glue surrounds it. I sit next to it and try to keep three beads together while the glue between them dries. The drying provides me with a break to think, which I hadn't planned on. But it allows me enough time to restructure the plan for the cardboard project. (Quote from the e-book produced at the end of the course, see Figure 1)

The first example of a student 'making', the cardboard project is a study of three robotic artworks: Ken Goldberg's *The Telegarden* (1995–2006), Ken Feingold's *Where I can see my house from here so we are* (1993–1995), and Stelarc's *Fractal Flesh* (1995-). In addition to reading a number of academic articles about the works, this student created the cardboard project to explore how these artworks stage net-based interactivity. It was made for a session where the robot art researchers Gunhild Borggreen and Elisabeth Jochum visited our class to present and discuss their research into robotics, performance, and art.

In the above description of putting beads, cardboard, glue, and a number of other components together, the student underlines her inquiry as a practice where different elements are connected. By making a composite sculpture, she is able to take the

41

different artworks apart, make selected components visible across the three works, and thereby understand their mechanisms and relations. It is a process that decodes and recodes the object. Crucial in the quote is how the very act of making provides her with both time, material and technical skills to step back, go through her analysis again and realise that the components had to be connected differently. The elements had to be recomposed.

What the student introduces here is an understanding of *mapping* as an active and changing coproducer of the world (Kitchin, Perkins, & Dodge, 2009, p. 21). The student is not trying to represent the artworks or reveal a certain truth behind them but rather to examine how they are put together by paying attention to the elements and connections that comprise them.

This kind of *productive* mapping highlights, as Latour puts it, how 'all these unusual visits' make it possible 'to take a new look at a more theoretical question' (e.g. Latour & Hermant, 2006, Level 4). In line with the strategies employed in *Paris: Invisible City* this mapping aims to represent the theories and artworks as assemblages, i.e. a multitude of spatial-temporal orderings, and explore, not what they mean, but rather what elements in these assemblages have not had sufficient attention paid to them, and what becomes visible when we emphasise *this* aspect? By highlighting certain elements, connections, and aspects through the cardboard project ('seeing little, but seeing it well') the student discovers that the act of composing is a continued process of reworking (regrouping, revisiting, failing and recomposing) that makes the interactions of a constellation visible and, thus, accessible to other map-readers (e.g. the class).

Knitting the Concept

Another student used crochet to retrace how theory and practice were interrelated in a theory of practice-based research, by participatory arts professor Brad Haseman (2006). The student used coloured yarn to present the various elements of the theory and their interconnections. She used the visual materialisation to decode and represent how various strands of theory and practice might interweave, take detours, and make unexpected turns. The example is particularly interesting because it involves two makings, since the student realised—during the process of crocheting—how the theories would appear differently if some of the elements had been connected differently, thus having to recrochet the conceptual combinations in a new composition. This making was produced for a class with comics artist/researcher Simon Grennan. He discussed the importance of sketches and controls in the work, with comics drawing as artistic research, much like the crochet project has both a sketch (or a crochet pattern) as well as a theory behind it that was redistributed and recomposed through the process of crocheting, and recrocheting.

In her examination of a theory, this student went through a sophisticated series of events closely re-enacting Haseman's description of the relation between theory and practice. She used this crocheting re-enactment to realise and share the elusiveness

ARTISTIC MAKINGS AS A METHOD OF INQUIRY IN HIGHER EDUCATION

Figure 4. Crochet pieces done by student as part of class exercise

of how an assemblage was put together. She went through another re-enactment, which recomposed the elements in a way that made the important parts of this particular theory visible—hence allowing for another understanding (appearance) of the theory.

'THICK WITH THINGS, CROWDED WITH OBJECTS'

While the cardboard project and the crochet pieces are examples of individual student makings, we also made sure that the students shared and discussed their explorative works and findings throughout the course. These instances of collaborative thinking we defined as *curatings*; in which the students could present their makings, i.e. which matters of concerns they had examined, the challenges and obstacles they had stumbled upon, the way they had made certain elements visible, and what their compositions had made them wonder about. The first type of curated 'assembly' was held by the end of each class, where we (students as well as teachers) presented our makings. We laid out the work on the tables or hung them on the walls in the classroom. If external lecturers were visiting, they would attend and we would use this exhibition-like area for discussing interpretations and doubts, as well as questions prompted by other students' work, perspectives from the lecture, or links to previous classes and makings. From the beginning the multimodal approach of the makings allowed students from very different backgrounds to engage in whatever performative, narrative, visual modes they preferred. It meant that the students were able to introduce and share the specific knowledge they had acquired during their various BAs or elsewhere. This kind of heterogenous public made room for agreements and disagreements of readings and interpretations that became very valuable for the way the students saw themselves as co-creators of the course and the knowledge produced in it. The second type of curated 'assembly' was part of the mid-term evaluation (*Summing up* Figure 1), where we, together with the students, created a blackboard overview of the first five classes. Each class was summarised on sticky notes by a group of students using their notes from class, the readings and artworks involved, and their own makings as references. During the presentation of each class, the other students and ourselves, as teachers, brought in new perspectives or drew linkages to other classes. The summing up paved the way for a presentation of the rest of the course, allowing us to introduce connections between the first part of the course, and the major theories involved, to the latter part's concrete examples of practice-based research (Figure 1). The third type of curated 'assembly' was the collaboration on an e-book at the end of the course. The students chose one of their makings from throughout the course, and the day started with an exhibition where the students introduced the work they had chosen to students from another class. This creation of a broader 'assembly' meant that our students had to make the linkages (the agreements and disagreements) between their explorative inquiries accessible to students who had not been part of the course. The next step was to create a small text to accompany each work, decide upon the order of works, peer review and edit each other's contributions, choose or make illustrations (scans or photographs) of their makings, and write an overall introductory text to the e-book. Apart from sharing their work and reflections among themselves and with a wider public, the e-book served as a point of reference for the individual oral exam they had to take in order to pass the course.

WHAT CHARACTERISES STUDENT-DRIVEN INQUIRIES USING ARTISTIC STRATEGIES?

The examples discussed above show a number of key components characterising the teaching modes we have been engaged in. During the course we noticed how artistic strategies further four specific key components through which the students were able to push themselves both further in their own thinking and in critically challenging established theories and concepts.

The first key component we noticed we call *material reflection*. The concrete engagement with the materiality of making cardboard projects, crochet pieces, videos, or drawings allowed the students to reflect on what they were doing and how they were composing their inquiry into the theory, problem, or artwork. The act of shaping the material forced the students to spend time with the material and go back over it, reread the theoretical text, or take a closer look at the artwork, repeat their process, and step back to see if the composition was 'well or badly composed'. When the student with the cardboard project waited for the glue to dry she had time to reflect upon what she was doing and use her own composition to make certain aspects of the works she was analysing more visible (and hence more accessible) to herself and, later on, to the rest of the class. Being involved with the material nature of wooden pearls, cardboard, and glue made her able to do a retake of what she was doing and reconsider, revise, and recompose her initial mapping. Sometimes, the materials resisted and 'talked back', forcing the student to pause and reconsider, unravel and recode the yarn as in the case of the crochet piece.

Students often struggle to spend time enough with assignments,—they do not always archive the desired process of stepping back, looking closer and wonder. The process of composing the makings and the way the materials resisted garnered insights and knowledge of how to explore complex matters of concern.

Furthermore, the experiments and productions allowed for the students to share misreadings or failures and discuss 'the crucial difference between what is *well* or *badly* constructed' in class, while introducing their work to the rest. The curatings also allowed the students' reflections to be shared in a much more convenient and accessible way than if we had exchanged written essays. This way of presenting invited us all into a situation where the works could be discussed and even redefined in a shared space. The concrete interaction with physical materials highlighted two aspects of the theoretical discussions: the importance of material reflection in the process, as well as in the sharing of knowledge.

The second key component we call *extended and different modes of attention*. Following Katherine Hayles, we worked with ideas about different modes of attention involved in research and learning (Hayles, 2012). As unfolded in the introduction, Hayles points to how technology has afforded modes of attention that differ from the classical print-based virtue of close and deep reading, where attention is paid to detail. By shaping their multimodal makings, the students experienced several types of attention where they had to close read texts, closely study artworks, and closely observe others' works but also where they took in the whole, skimmed the artworks, and got a sense of overall patterns in large and complex works. Working with the artistic strategies allowed them to scale a problem and discuss it with different approaches. The multiple ways of composing the works that happened both individually and collectively (during the curatings and the work with the e-book) all contributed to new ways of decoding and recoding, which promoted different modes of attention. Shaping materials and sharing this process in plenum helped expand the students' abilities to think thoroughly about very complicated challenges concerning mediations. This furthermore challenged the students' previous experience with the humanities as an unquestioned bastion of print-based knowledge.

One of the ways in which this paradigm of print is challenged is connected to sight as the dominant aesthetic way of structuring along the way print tends to organise arguments in certain ways. The concept of compositionism makes visible the plurality of aesthetic codifiers involved in scholarly inquiries and emphasises how the engagement with and exploration of indeterminate situations can integrate different aesthetic approaches as a core aspect of both research and teaching.

The third key component is *productive failing* as a major force in *knowing-with-and-in-uncertainty*. As we have already made clear, the materiality of the makings often emphasised a temporality that supported reflection. A big part of this was the room it afforded for failure. Productive failing has been increasingly erased from university teaching and the students are encouraged to get it right the first time (Biggs, 2003). Nevertheless, there are very important aspects of failing that make the student better versed in the material at hand because they have taken apart and put together the elements several times. This, in itself, makes the students more skilled and helps them build repetition as a way of bettering their work. The technical skills involved in the makings are refined through reworking and strengthens the students understanding of how materiality influences our way of thinking, while at the same time adding to their individual skillset. When things go 'wrong', it is possible to spot the potential for other connections and ways of reworking the material. The surprising twists and turns prompted by a material making process can make new avenues of inquiry visible or make preconceived notions more tangible.

We find that not knowing, not understanding, and, most significantly, *being comfortable in and with uncertainty* to be incredibly important abilities when engaging with complex problems and unstable challenges. Thus, the confidence that comes with being able to navigate uncertainty is one of the most notable qualities we found as a result of the course. Through failing productively on their own and sharing it collectively in class, the students experienced, in an embodied way, how their inquiries could be of interest and lead to further discoveries, even if they at first sight looked wrong or misguided. Rather than stating: 'that is wrong', we try to say: 'That did not show what we wanted, why is that?' Drawing a concept in a wrong way makes us realise what the concept is comprised of and allows us to re-evaluate our understanding of it. Makings make our own mistakes visible and therefore much easier to correct, rearrange, and understand.

The fourth and final key component we identified is *collaborative thinking*. Most of the makings done by the students were individual, but, as mentioned earlier, the sculptures, drawings, short writings, and collages allowed for easy access to discussions of the works. The regular exhibitions at the end of each class created little publics and, hence, supported the experience of inquiry as an overall collaborative and heterogenous effort of agreements and disagreements. Thus, the course was inspired by Latour's translation of Dewey's concept of little publics as spaces and arenas that enable us to get involved in complex matters of concern. A number of the concerns we engage in with students at MA level are issues that cannot be solved or agreed upon from the blackboard but require an emphasis on wondering and not knowing. We could also call it *not-grasping-alone*, emphasising agency as relational and hereby teaching students to take the problems and matters of concern into the common. In that sense, this kind of teaching, artistic strategies, and composition also become crucial conditions for education as the democratic experience so thoroughly discussed by Dewey (1934).

CONCLUSION

We suggest that mappings, re-enactments, curatings, and other artistic strategies can be productively introduced in a variety of courses as ways of enhancing students' engagement in material reflection, extended modes of attention, productive failure, and collaborative thinking. These aspects can be understood through Dewey's main argument in *Knowing and the Known* (1960) where he underlines the importance of furthering a kind of inquiry-driven teaching that states the exploration of a problem also involves the very composition of it. Interacting with written text and artworks, as well as reflecting upon them through multimodal formats, are valuable paths for rethinking future scholarly teaching. However, the approach requires consistent use of different strategies and should not be treated as just another 'fun gimmick' or 'engaging take' on teaching. First, the introduction of this approach in traditional academic institutions might cause resistance from students or be quite challenging for them, since it breaks with a number of the roles and rules of teaching within traditional humanities and social sciences. Second, qualifying the individual inquiries requires discussion and clarification (what is 'well or badly composed') in different group sessions (here defined as curatings). This poses an immediate problem in today's higher education environment; the time-consuming nature and lack of clear measurement or 'correct' path.

However, this does not prevent artistic strategies from being taken from studies of aesthetics and modern culture and into other disciplines. Here they can provide a critical reflection model not oriented towards judging or revealing a truth, but towards what art theorist Irit Rogoff defines as 'a cultural inhabitation that performatively acknowledges what it is risking without yet fully being able to articulate it' (Rogoff, 2003). We found that artistic strategies enable us to work with student imagination and creativity, supporting two interconnected shifts in higher education's critical thinking and pedagogies: Both examples of student makings call attention to the experience of being able to keep the process of inquiry open and take a step back, reflecting upon and readjusting their initial analysis—a moment so critical to scholarly inquiries and so hard to reach during class. The examples also emphasise learning as a way of interacting with the world, here formulated by Biggs: 'As we learn, our conceptions of phenomena change, and we see the world differently' (Biggs, 2003, p. 13).

Compositionism as involving creative makings and artistic strategies then becomes one of the possible answers of how to make students familiar with navigating unpredictable post-graduation future(s) and uncertain world(s).

ACKNOWLEDGEMENTS

We wish to thank first and foremost the students at the course 'Practice in Theory'. Without their commitment, creativity, and curiosity, we would not have anything to discuss here and we would not have had this opportunity to open up the relationship between artistic strategies, teaching, and inquiry. We also want to thank the guest lecturers Gunhild Borggreen, Elizabeth Jochum, Pernille Leth-Espensen, and Simon Grennan who interacted with our students and helped us all go further in our thinking and doing.

NOTE

[1] E.g. the multimedia online project *Paris: Invisible City* (1998/2006) laying the ground for the later work *Reassembling the Social* (2005), where Latour unfolds his theory of assemblage.

REFERENCES

Arke, P. (2010). *Ethno-Aesthetics/Etnoæstetik*. Copenhagen: Pia Arke Selskabet & Kuratorisk Aktion.
Arke, P. (2010). *Stories from scoresbysund. Photographs, colonisation and mapping*. Copenhagen: Pia Arke Selskabet & Kuratorisk Aktion.
Barnett, R. (2004). Learning for an unknown future. *Higher Education Research & Development, 23*, 247–260. doi:10.1080/0729436042000235382
Biggs, J. (2003). *Teaching for quality learning at university: What the student does* (2nd ed.). Buckingham: Open University Press.
Dewey, J. (1927). *The public and its problems*. Athens, OH: Ohio University Press.
Dewey, J. (1934). *Art as experience*. New York, NY: Minton, Balch & Company.
Dewey, J., & Bentley, A. F. (1960 [1949]). *Knowing and the known*. Westport, CT: Greenwood Press.
Gibbons, M., Limoges, C., Nowotny, H., Schwartzman, S., Seot, P., & Trow, M. (1994). *The new production of knowledge: The dynamics of science and research in contemporary societies*. London: Sage Publications.
Haseman, B. (2006). A manifesto for performative research. *Media International Australia Incorporating Culture and Policy, Theme Issue "Practice-led Research", 118*, 98–106.
Hayles, N. K. (2012). *How we think*. Chicago, IL: University of Chicago Press.
Kitchin, R., Perkins, C., & Dodge, M. (2009). Thinking about maps. In R. Kitchin, C. Perkins, & M. Dodge (Eds.), *Rethinking maps: New Frontiers in cartographic theory* (pp. 1–25). New York, NY: Routledge.
Latour, B. (1988). *The pasteurization of France*. Boston, MA: Harvard University Press.
Latour, B. (2007). *The Tarde Durkheim debate, reenactment of 1903 debate*. Retrieved from http://www.bruno-latour.fr/node/354
Latour, B. (2010). Steps toward the writing of a compositionist manifesto. *New Literary History, 41*, 471–490.
Latour, B. (2012, February 17). *From critique to composition*. Talk at Dublin City University, Dublin, Ireland. Retrieved from http://wanderlustmind.com/2012/05/17/bruno-latour-reenacting-science-from-critique-to-composition-ecological-crises-digital-humanities-and-new-political-assemblies/
Latour, B., & Callon, M. (1981). Unscrewing the big Leviathan: How actors macro-structure reality and how sociologists help them to do so. In K. Cetina-Knorr & A. V. (Eds.), *Advances in social theory and methodology—Toward an integration of micro- and macro-sociologies* (pp. 277–303). London: Routledge & Kegan Paul.
Latour, B., & Weibel, P. (2005). *Making things public—Atmospheres of democracy*. Karlsruhe: ZKM.
Rogoff, I. (2003). *From criticism to critique to criticality*. Retrieved from http://eipcp.net/transversal/0806/rogoff1/en
Seeberg, P. (1975). *Brikker af en verden*. Viborg: Forlaget Komplot.
Tuchman, G. (2009). *Wannabe U: Inside the corporate university*. Chicago, IL: University of Chicago Press.
Wood, D. (2010). *Everything sings: Maps for a narrative atlas*. Los Angeles, CA: Siglio.

Websites

Feingold, K. (1993–1995). *Where I can see my house from here so we are.*
Goldberg, K. (1995–2006). *The Telegarden.*
Stelarc (1995). *Fractal flesh.*

Rikke Platz Cortsen
University of Texas
Austin, TX, USA

Anne Mette W. Nielsen
Centre of Youth Research
Campus Copenhagen
Aalborg University
Aalborg, Denmark

TINE LYNFORT JENSEN

4. 'BACK TO BILDUNG'

A Holistic Competence-Based Approach to Student Engagement in Innovation Learning Processes in Higher Education

INTRODUCTION

This chapter presents a competence based approach to enhance student engagement in innovation courses in higher education by focusing on holistic competences in learning and Bildung processes.

Some argue that the era of the 'Creative University' has begun and that co-creation and collaboration between different actors and institutions are needed to address the global environment, in which the students are the future inhabitants (Besley & Peters, 2013). Barnett conceptualises how both teachers and students can develop pedagogical and learning creativity capacities in the Creative University (Barnett, 2011).

With the increased focus on creativity, innovation and entrepreneurship, the 'Entrepreneurial University' challenges the traditional Research University and points to the need for pedagogies and educational politics that support student engagement in the creation of new methods, ventures and initiatives (Gibb, 2012; Etzkowitz, 2013).

Another related term, the 'Ecological University', emphasises connections between university, students and the surrounding society with the purpose to develop mutual solutions and create well-being for people and society (Wang, 2014). The ecological understanding of learning has, as its centre, interconnectedness through a multidisciplinary approach to knowledge and collaboration. Knowing, acting, and being are keywords in the Ecological University (Barnett, 2011a).

The educational policy system is being criticised for the emphasis put on more instrumental measures of education, forgetting the intrinsic values of Bildung (Hansen, 2008; Varkøy, 2010; Reichenbach, 2014).

At the same time, some aspects of Bildung seem to be associated with the upcoming forms of University, where students are stimulated to engage in their own learning processes to create the required development for themselves and society. In what is known as the 'ontological turn' in higher education, students develop themselves as human beings as part of getting an education (Fellenz, 2016).

The aim of this chapter is to argue that Bildung can be revitalised through a more holistic approach to student engagement, competences, and learning that supplements the discussion of the purpose of higher education. In the subsequent sections, theoretical concepts of learning, education and Bildung, student engagement, holistic competences, and effectuation are described in relation to higher education, followed by a methodological account for the data used in the chapter. Next, the results are discussed through the theoretical concepts. The chapter finishes with a conclusion and suggestions for further research.

INTERTWINED UNDERSTANDINGS OF LEARNING, EDUCATION, AND BILDUNG

Reviewing different perspectives of learning, education, and Bildung in literature leaves the reader with a mixed impression. While some argue that the concepts are dissimilar, others understand learning and education in such a broad sense that appears to be close to the Bildung concept. Here, the main focus will be theory that corresponds with Bildung to shape a point of departure for the holistic perspective.

Dewey's approach to experimental learning has inspired many variants of active learning, describing education and learning as effective when it 'happens within the actual life-experience of the learner' (Liszka, 2013, p. 782). Dewey argues for a holistic approach to learning, attempting to resolve many seemingly opposing perspectives and, instead, looking at the ways pupils and students draw on prior and current experiences at the same time (Dewey, 1916/1958; Hung, 2014; Gordon, 2016).

Lave and Wenger (1991) operate with a practice-oriented approach based on an interactional understanding of learning and identity building, with recognition of the individual cognitive, reflective, and embodied experiences. Learning and personal development are seen as processes of change in everyday practices in many aspects of a person's life.

Jarvis (2006) understands learning from an existential perspective. The dialectics between the individual and society are expressed in the term: 'being-in-the-world-with others'. In his model, learners go through several loops of situations, actions, experiences, and reflections, and are thereby continuously changing and becoming more experienced.

Yosef-Hassidim (2016) is inspired by Heidegger, describing education as essentially a transcendence to a world, a shift in one's life, an ontological difference. Education should create awareness of who we are as students and teachers—and thereby education and learning become existential goals.

A common key factor in these selected theories is the emphasis put on a the 'becoming perspective'. This understanding operates with an ontological approach to being a student. It is an identity formation in both time and space, and thereby a process of becoming. The becoming perspective underscores participation in everyday activities with others and the awareness of the many factors in a person's life that support learning, not isolated to a teaching situation in itself.

Bildung as a complex, historical term has been defined by many and used with both positive and negative associations (Reichenbach, 2003; Wimmer, 2003;

Hansen, 2008). Humboldt is often cited as a founding figure with the understanding of Bildung as a humanistic ideal of self-cultivation and self-transformation, although classical thinkers such as Kant and Hegel before him operated with variations of Bildung as a matter of personal growth through education, enlightenment, and self-realisation (Jessop, 2012; Fellenz, 2016).

In the work of Dewey, Bildung is defined as a person's (educational) development and an end-in-itself (Jessop, 2012; Reichenbach, 2014). Biesta (2007) defines Bildung as a self-educative process whereby an individual takes responsibility for personal and cultural maturation. Fellenz (2016) defines Bildung as:

> The processes of self-formation or of educating oneself [...] it is both autonomous self-formation and reflective and responsible action in (and interaction with) society. (p. 273)

Fellenz emphasises development of the self as being a holistic process, which consists of more than acquisition of knowledge and skills. Education is a process of becoming, a transformation over time (Fellenz, 2016). Reichenbach (2014) defines it as:

> The inner development of the individual, a process of fulfillment through education and knowledge [...] an amalgam of wisdom and self-realization. (p. 65)

Some researchers suggest that the concept has gained renewed attention because Bildung is *more* than education. Bildung refers to a broad understanding of learning in- and outside of school (Englund, 2002). Education refers to concrete learning goals for a professional field (Wimmer, 2003; Stojanov, 2012); at the same time, education appears to have replaced Bildung (Varkøy, 2010; Sanders, 2011).

There is a contemporary discussion in the field as to whether the concept of Bildung has any relevance in the postmodern world of instrumentalist and pragmatic approaches to education. Wimmer (2003) describes the current social transformations as a lever for a renewed debate about the future of Bildung. The connections and disconnections between the concept and economic values are evaluated in order to recognise both (Wimmer, 2003). Reichenbach proposes an understanding of Bildung as a *horizon* rather than a *toolbox*, leaving space for the dimensions of self-transformation as ends-in-itself in an educational path (Reichenbach, 2014). Varkøy (2010) criticises the instrumental pedagogical thinking of today as means-end driven and offers the metaphor of a journey as an alternative to illustrate the relationship between learning and education at the personal level; referring to Gadamer's concept of Bildung as a life-long process with no particular end. Hansen (2008, p. 96), in his review of books on Educational Philosophy, identifies a dissociation of Bildung in literature about the 'pragmatic turn' in the educational system, but at the same time there seems to exist a 'rewriting of Bildung in postmodernity'. Stojanov (2012) describes the 'world-encountering' aspect of Bildung as a way of getting beyond the particular towards imaginable alternative scenarios and therefore relevant in the postmodern age. In addition, the concept holds potential for identity development. Interestingly, Thompson (2005) distinguishes Bildung from education as a non-transparent process of identity transformation in the relationship with our-selves and the world opposed to a more conscious concept of education.

The literature suggests that Bildung can be put back on the educational agenda due to an upcoming inclination in the fields of learning and education towards self-determination, reflexivity, autonomy, engagement in the world, and personal development. Some argue that it cannot be reduced to mere education as it comprises more than learning skills with the singular goal of becoming a professional, while others, such as Heidegger, Dewey, Jarvis, and Lave and Wenger understand learning and education in such a broad sense that the concepts almost fuse. Bildung and the broad or holistic variants of learning and education include a personal, existential, and perpetual process of inner identity growth with an intrinsic value in itself for individuals and, therefore, society. This broad understanding calls for attention to theories about student engagement.

STUDENT ENGAGEMENT IN RELATION TO LEARNING AND EDUCATION

As with the other concepts in this chapter, engagement in general, hereunder student engagement, are treated from various perspectives and disciplines. In Dewey's work, there are many references to interest and engagement in relation to learning. He emphasises that learning and education is:

> About those situations in which one really shares or participates in a common activity, in which one really has an interest in its accomplishment just as others have. (reformulated in Biesta, 2010, p. 714)

In this respect, engagement is about participation through interest. Dewey writes about the learner: 'it is an intimate participant in the activities of the world to which it belongs' (Dewey, 1916/1958, p. 393). His concept of interest is related to personal engagement in learning processes. Students should take interest in learning from other people and the surroundings. He refers to a stream of literature on how to cultivate student interest (Jonas, 2011). Dewey defines interest as the identification of a subject with the object (an idea, a theory, a cause, etc). So, personal identification is necessary to create interest. Interaction with the object is part of this process. In his later writing, Dewey argues that interest is connected to development and possible experiences more than an expression of the accumulated knowledge in a given learner:

> Interests function as 'signposts' towards potential learning possibilities. [...] If we can discover a child's urgent needs and powers, and if we can supply an environment of materials, appliances, and resources—physical, social, and intellectual—to direct their adequate operation, we shall not have to think about interest. It will take care of itself. (Dewey, 1916/1958, p. 126)

Dewey's strong emphasis on experiences as a key factor in learning has inspired many present theorists. Illeriis argues that in order for somebody to use experiences in learning processes, the person needs to be personally engaged in the situation (Illeriis, 2016).

Hung (2014) points to Dewey's conception of existential engagement with place both in a bodily and affective way. Here, attention is focused on place as both the actual learning context and 'places' in the surroundings that the learner interacts with. An existential, self-renewing process at the personal level takes place through this interaction, including both body and soul and represents the engagement of a learner.

Student engagement framed as 'making community happen', combined with engagement beyond the classroom both on and off campus and activities to become a member of the university community, seems to make students more engaged in their educational journeys. The authors emphasise a 'becoming' perspective in relation to involvement in learning through participation with others (McGowan & Partridge, 2014). Student self-understanding is correlated to engagement and is supported through experimental approaches and guided critical reflection (Zajonc, 2013). Data-based research on student engagement indicates that engagement increases when students interact with the surroundings and participate in experimental activities; a large mixed methods study shows that 'real-world' agendas, active participation, co-assessment forms, and involvement of a wider community increase students' engagement (Evans et al., 2015).

The connection between personal engagement and personal points of departure for creativity and innovation is documented in the fields of innovation and entrepreneurship education (Sarasvathy, 2001; Jensen, 2014; Blenker et al., 2014). The subfield of innovation teaching focuses on student engagement due to the importance of getting students to activate themselves in the creating processes. Here, empirical studies show that students developing ideas based on personal interest and knowledge increases their propensity to start a new venture by 22% (Moberg & Vestergaard, 2013). A qualitative study on social entrepreneurship education indicates that successful entrepreneurial students base their social initiatives on personal engagement and experiences and tend to use social initiatives or ideas as 'case material' in various courses and assignments throughout their studies (Jensen, 2014).

Consequently, in the selected literature, student engagement is often linked indirectly or directly to interaction with the surrounding world, supported by various kinds of experimental, bodily, or personal participation. There is an aspect of identity building associated with the concept of student engagement, which expands the question of engagement from merely taking active part in concrete learning processes to a broader understanding of engagement as a 'becoming activity' within students—a form of Bildung process. If this is the case, it becomes relevant and interesting to take into consideration learning activities that could help students to work with identity building. In the next section, concepts of competences are considered, in order to describe possible scenarios for increasing students' awareness of the identity building blocks they enter the university and different courses with.

COMPETENCES

Competence, competency, and competences as concepts have different definitions and understandings in the research literature:

- Competence is a combination of a person's knowledge, experiences and abilities (Sundberg, 2001),
- Definitions of competence depend on people, goals and contexts (Stoof et al., 2002),
- The phases identification, assessment and recognition are important elements in a clarification process of competences and competence is the personal and independent use of knowledge and skills (Buhl et al., 2008),
- Competences are the conscious ability to use knowledge and skills in a given context (Danish Qualification Framework, 2008),
- Competencies become relevant due to student employability (Jones & Warnock, 2014),
- Personal-interpersonal competence as emotional knowledge capacity and social behavioural options (Seal et al., 2015),
- Competence is the ability to use knowledge in combination with personal prerequisites in a given, often unpredictable, situation (Illeriis, 2016).

Definitions specifically related to student learning and teaching have been developed in recent years (Field, 2006; Oganisjana & Koke, 2012; Jones & Warnock, 2014; Stecher & Hamilton, 2014; Seal et al., 2015).

Thröler (2011) discusses the concepts of competence, Bildung, and knowledge in relation to education politics and concludes that there is a tendency to merge competence and Bildung. This conceptual marriage has been criticised by the research community, arguing that competence is the (instrumentalist) ability to use knowledge and skills in any given context in, whereas Bildung is an inner personal development process. The above definitions reflect this standpoint as the majority include the emphasis put on usability and application rather than a person's intrinsic journey as a value in itself. Extrinsic goals for students and higher education institutions *are* legitimate in relation to funding and the opportunity to get a job after graduation, but, from a pedagogical perspective, it is interesting to look into the more holistic approaches to competences that can correspond with the Bildung element to explore how we can *also* reframe student learning and education as a person's own journey with value in itself alongside with instrumental purposes.

HOLISTIC APPROACHES TO COMPETENCES AND LEARNING

Holistic approaches to competences are elaborated in several fields (Sundberg, 2001; Beckett, 2008; Jensen, 2014). Vygotsky argues that the integration of everyday concepts and scientific concepts are necessary to obtain competence in both areas as they supplement each other (Vygotsky, 1987; Fleer & Ridgway, 2007) Children are seen as active agents in their own learning processes, and their everyday experiences and working theories serve as the potential to bridge between the daily life and the scientific world (Hedges, 2012).

Dewey shares the assumption with Vygotsky that learning is always contextual. He argues that the greatest danger of the modern educational system is the separation of life and school (Dewey, 1916/1958; Beck et al., 2014). According to Dewey, the most important task of the educational system is to develop people who are competent to act on the basis of reflections, experiences and knowledge and thereby participate in society. Dewey describes how teachers should start any subject in class by including the pupils' experiences and knowledge into the given subject, in order to facilitate a process where the pupils connect to it on a more personal level and to encourage interaction with the surroundings (Dewey, 1916/1958; Jonas, 2011). The concept of continuity plays a central role in his learning theory, as continuity allows for new experiences to build on earlier experiences (Illeriis, 2016).

Rømer (2015) illustrates how an Aristotelian dialectic combination of action and thought is a more fruitful approach to learning, and thereby criticises Dewey for placing too much importance on action. This is supplemented by Marshall and Thorburn (2014) in their article on a holistic approach to personal and social growth through the use of Aristoteles' concept of practical wisdom in education. They point to more experimental pedagogical methods to support the element of practical wisdom as personal and social growth.

Merleau-Ponty's embodied learning approach has also inspired the holistic approach. An individual is treated as:

> A whole being, permitting the person to experience him or herself as a holistic and synthesized acting, feeling, thinking being-in-the-world. (as cited in Stolz, 2015, p. 474)

Learning is not separate from our lived experiences and, therefore, it implies the 'wholeness' of the learner and not just reading or thinking about something to come to really know it. There has been a strong tendency in pedagogy to favor abstract and conceptual thinking, and there is a need to re-educate students to reconnect to their bodies in learning processes. This is supported by so-called Anti-Cognitivism, an understanding of cognitive processes as situated and embodied and labels it as a more holistic approach to learning (Simpson & Beckett, 2013).

Another recent trend in holistic thinking is the theory of learning ecologies, which parallels the Ecological University. Jackson, Barnett, and others argue that the boundaries between university and society should be dissolved in order to allow teachers and students practice 'ecocentric thinking' and thereby become actors in the world, and not isolated in classrooms. The ecological approach offers boundless space and fluid time. The ideal is symbiosis through co-operation. Curricula can also create connections between disciplines, courses, and learning settings, which support a breakdown between the silos of university and everyday life (Jackson, 2013; Wang, 2014).

The literature offers a number of holistic perspectives that point to an expansion of the instrumental perception of competence by including Bildung elements. From these inspirational sources, I am operating with an understanding of competences that encompasses identity building, happening in both time and space, and aimed at both Bildung and more instrumental purposes. The time dimension focuses students' attention on past knowledge and experiences in order to activate these in a present or future learning context. The space dimension is important to be able to include knowledge and experiences that are generated in several contexts from the students' daily lives besides their studies. In addition to this, the extension of space also allows for the students to draw upon knowledge and experience derived from interactions with other people or other people's knowledge and experiences. Human subjects as learners are, by mind and body, enrolled in society and their own personal history that includes past, present, and future experiences. As such, students are always 'dressed up' with knowledge and experience that they can learn to bring into play in various contexts for various reasons. Through teaching, students can be given tools that provide them with a more solid foundation for engaging in their own Bildung processes.

From the field of entrepreneurship, the theory of effectual logic can support the concrete holistic work with competences and Bildung.

EFFECTUATION THEORY

The effectuation theory has been developed within the entrepreneurship field with inspiration from theories of bounded rationality and non-causal behaviour. Empirical data about successful entrepreneurs show that they create new ideas and ventures from means and available resources within themselves and their personal and professional network. This working method is described through several principles, starting with the 'bird-in-hand' principle. Here, the entrepreneur develops ideas from three aspects: 'Who am I? What do I know? Who do I know?' (Sarasvathy, 2001; Read et al., 2011).

This working method has been applied in higher education to teach students how to become aware of their implicit and explicit resources and to activate them through effectual exercises (Jensen, 2014). As such, the effectuation theory implies a holistic view upon learning and development. The approach has many similarities with the learning ecology approach. Additionally, there appears to be a direct line to Dewey's thoughts on pedagogy in school, where the teacher should engage young people in concrete learning processes by showing them how they can use the experiences and knowledge that they already have and by interacting with the immediate surroundings.

The effectual bird-in-hand principle has inspired the holistic approach to competence development as a concrete working method for students in a research project described in the following sections.

PROJECT METHODOLOGY

Through educational action research, data were collected in a mixed methods research project at five innovation classes consisting of 130 students in 35 teams in 2014 at the University of Southern Denmark (Mandrup & Jensen, 2017). The mixed method design consisted of qualitative participant observation throughout the semester, two quantitative surveys in the beginning and end of the semester, qualitative interviews with the 35 student teams halfway through the semester, the students' formal end evaluation, and 47 randomly selected individual competence cards made by the students at the beginning and end of the course. The triangulation of these specific data expresses various illustrations of students activating holistic competences and personal engagement in their efforts to develop innovative ideas. For the purpose of this chapter, I will primarily focus on the competence cards as a representation of the students' self-reported, explicit work with their competences.

Competence Cards as a Tool to Engage Students in Holistic Learning and Bildung Processes

At the beginning of the course, each student created a personal competence card by doing a number of exercises addressing the three effectual questions: 'Who am I? What do I know? Who do I know?' from both an educational and a daily life perspective. The idea is to help the students integrate experiences and contacts from their daily life into the innovative working process, as well as encouraging them to draw on previous educational knowledge to develop ideas. In this educational learning context, the goal is not to teach the students to create new ventures directly, but to present them with a more holistic approach to learning and creativity that breaks down the barriers between other courses and their everyday experiences, with the purpose of developing new creations based on their competences. After the course ended, the students updated their cards with their perceived new competences and contacts. The competence cards thereby represent concrete examples of the holistic view of learning, engagement, and competences that are described through the above theories. In addition to this, the teachers used the individual competence cards as a tool to match 3–4 students in teams at the beginning of the course. The purpose of this is to combine different student profiles in complementary teams as a lever for innovation and learning by meeting people with other profiles and experiences through teamwork.

The Discipline Context

The discipline context of the gathered data is the humanities at The University of Southern Denmark. Students undertaking the Bachelor degree in International Business Communication are introduced to a mandatory innovation course at the 4th semester. The course is elective for other students from the humanities and the courses often include students from various disciplines at the humanities. Around 30–35 students attend each course. The students pass the course through active participation, consisting of the following requirements:

- Present a minimum of 80% of the time,
- Create personal competence card at the beginning and end,
- Active engagement in a team and the idea process throughout the course,
- A business plan or a project plan written together by the team,
- Presentation of team ideas at the end of the course.

RESULTS AND IMPLICATIONS

The results will be described in relation to each element in the first and the second version of the 47 competence cards. First, the educational and experiential aspects of 'Who am I?', then the educational and experiential aspects of 'What do I know?', and finally the two aspects of 'Who do I know?'.

The first dimension that the students address is the educational aspect of 'Who am I?'. Few students can describe their educational identity or profile in the first version of the competence cards. The teachers therefore discuss this issue with each student, but not everybody succeeds with the exercise. In the second version, after having gone through the innovative learning process, every student is able to put words on this. In the supplementary data from the final evaluation and the interviews, the students explained that the concrete work with their educational 'building blocks' in relation to their ideas and working together with people with other profiles than themselves had made it easier for them to recognise their own educational identity and to explicate this in the second version of the competence card. This indicates that enhancement of Bildung in the educational system can be supported by allowing students to reflect upon identity in relation to practical work with students from different disciplines and external persons.

In relation to the experiential aspect of 'Who am I?', the students were asked to reflect upon experiences and conditions from their daily life that have affected them and shaped their personal identity. Interestingly, some students quickly discovered patterns in their first version of the competence cards between these experiences and their specific choice of education. Others could identify linkages between their roles and experiences in their family background and the roles that they were likely to take in group work at the university. This tendency becomes even clearer in the second versions. As such, the data show that students can construct cohesive stories that include both their daily and their university life in a way that increases meaning to them, just by giving them time to correlate elements of their life.

Under the educational element of 'What do I know?', the students initially showed difficulties in remembering previous courses that could provide them with knowledge in their then-present innovation course. The teachers helped them list courses and write competence word for each course, and by working with the ideas in the innovation course, the students learned to activate knowledge from previous courses. This indicates that students need help to create linkages between courses and that awareness of relevant knowledge from previous courses often comes with action. It also refers to the extended time dimension of the holistic perspective on competences: there is a potential for the educational system to begin to perceive the educational path of every student as a chain of compatible courses rather than as independent knowledge units.

Almost every student was able to write 'What do I know' experiences in both the first and second version from their daily life outside the university context that they could activate in the innovation course. In the second version, many students qualified these experiences by explaining how they have used these experiences in the learning process. Most of them have also included new knowledge gained from the process into both the educational and experiential aspects of their competence cards. This suggests that students and their ideas benefit from attention to practical experiences and knowledge that competence exercises and practical processes provide.

Of the students, 24 out of 47 marked the teachers and other persons connected to the course as their new network in the second version of the cards. As such, the educational element of 'Who do I know' indicates a changed perception of relationship with teachers and other actors from the university sphere. This might indicate a stronger sense of belonging to the educational system.

With respect to the experience element of 'Who do I know?', the cards in the second version show that 80% of the students engaged in co-operation with external partners in the process. This shows a high degree of interaction with the surroundings, as suggested in the holistic perspectives on learning, engagement, and competences. The extended space dimension of the holistic approach engages the students in new contacts in and outside the university context, and leaves opportunities for expanding teaching in higher education.

In the final evaluation most of the students marked the competence cards as valuable to them and explained that they learned more about themselves as persons and professionals. Of the students, 30% gained knowledge regarding the further direction of their studies and future working life. As such, competence cards appear to function as inspiration to a more conscious Bildung process as well as an instrumental method of raising awareness of the study and work potentials that lie ahead.

CONCLUSION

This chapter focuses on a holistic approach to competences, learning, and student engagement through theoretical concepts and research data in order to put Bildung back on the agenda in higher education, without having to reject the more instrumental elements of usefulness for students and society.

The study shows that students, when space and time is created for reflection and holistic thinking, care about *both* the intrinsic and extrinsic values of education. Following this logic, there is no contradiction between Bildung activities and purposeful work with competences to prepare for the more instrumental elements of future study and working life.

The discipline context in the research project is innovation in the humanities. Recognising that both innovation and the humanities are well-suited contexts for working with student competences, as they represent the more ambiguous areas of higher education, I would still argue that the use of holistic competence cards could prove valuable as a general engagement tool for students and teachers in many other disciplinary contexts.

In relation to educational theory, the attempt to merge Bildung and goal-oriented dimensions of competences and learning through holistic perspectives calls for a deeper discussion of the Bildung concept in relation to present challenges in the educational system. How can we understand and define the intrinsic values of studying while at the same time acknowledging that students actually study for *something*? This chapter seeks to answer that question by dissolving the ostensible opposition between the two dimensions of learning and to bring Bildung back on the agenda as a vital aspect of higher education as a supplement to its instrumental purposes.

REFERENCES

Barnett, R. (2011a). *Being a university*. Abingdon: Routledge.
Barnett, R. (2011b). The coming of the ecological university. *Oxford Review of Education, 37*, 439–455.
Beck, S., Kaspersen, P., & Paulsen, M. (2014). *Klassisk og moderne læringsteori*. Copenhagen: Hans Reitzels Forlag.
Beckett, D. (2008). Holistic competence: Putting judgement first. *Asia Pacific Education Review, 9*, 21–30.
Besley, T., & Peters, M. (2013). *Re-imagining the creative university for the 21st century*. Rotterdam, The Netherlands: Sense Publishers.
Biesta, G. (2007). The education-socialisation conundrum or "who is afraid of education?". *Utbilding & Demokrati 2007, 16*, 25–36.
Biesta, G. (2010). This is my truth, tell me yours: Deconstructive pragmatism as a philosophy for education. *Educational Philosophy and Theory, 42*(7), 710–727.
Blenker, P., Elmholdt, S., Frederiksen, S., Korsgaard, S., & Wagner, K. (2014). Methods in entrepreneurship education research: A review and integrative framework. *Education & Training, 56*, 697–715.
Buhl, R., Højdal, L., & Enggaard, E. (2008). *Realkompetencevurdering—og anerkendelse*. Copenhagen: Videncenter for Uddannelses- og Erhvervsvejledning.
Dewey, J. (1916/1958). *Democracy and education*. New York, NY: Macmillan.
Englund, T. (2002). Higher education, democracy and citizenship—The democratic potential of the university? *Studies in Philosophy and Education, 21*, 281–287.
Etzkowitz, H. (2013). Anatomy of the entrepreneurial university. *Social Science Information, 52*, 486–511.
Evans, C., Muijs, D., & Tomlinson, M. (2015). *Engaged student learning: High-impact strategies to enhance student achievement*. York: Higher Education Academy.
Fellenz, M. (2016). Forming the professional self: Bildung and the ontological perspective on professional education and development. *Educational Philosophy and Theory, 48*, 267–283.
Field, H. (2006). Competency Based Teacher Education (CBTE): A review of the literature. *British Journal of In-Service Education, 6*, 39–42.
Fleer, M., & Ridgway, A. (2007). Mapping the relations between everyday concepts and scientific concepts within playful learning environments. *Learning and Socio-cultural Theory: Exploring Modern Vygotskian Perspectives International Workshop 2007, 1*(1), 24–45.

Gibb, A. (2002). In pursuit of a new enterprise and entrepreneurship paradigm for learning. *International Journal of Management Review, 4*, 233–269.
Gordon, M. (2016). Why should scholars keep coming back to John Dewey? *Educational Philosophy and Theory, 48*, 1077–1091.
Hansen, K.-H. (2008). Rewriting bildung for postmodernity; books on educational philosophy, classroom practice, and reflective teaching. *Curriculum Inquiry, 38*, 92–115.
Hedges, H. (2012). Vygotsky's phases of everyday concept development and the notion of children's "working theories". *Learning, Culture and Social Interaction, 1*, 143–152.
Hung, R. (2014). Learning as existential engagement with/in place: Departing from Vanderberg and the reams. *Educational Philosophy and Theory, 46*, 1130–1142.
Illeriis, K. (2016). *Læring*. Copenhagen: Samfundslitteratur.
Jackson, N. J. (2013, September). Learning ecologies. In N. J. Jackson & G. B. Cooper (Eds.), *Lifewide Magazine*. Retrieved from http://www.lifewideebook.co.uk
Jarvis, P. (2006). *The theory and practice of teaching*. New York, NY: Routledge.
Jensen, T. L. (2014). A holistic person perspective in measuring entrepreneurship education impact—Social entrepreneurship education at the humanities. *The International Journal of Management Education, 44*, 1–12.
Jessop, S. (2012). Education for citizenship and 'ethical life': An exploration of the Hegelian concepts of bildung and sittlichkeit. *Journal of Philosophy of Education, 46*, 287–302.
Jonas, M. (2011). Dewey's conception of interest and its significance for teacher education. *Educational Philosophy and Theory, 43*, 112–129.
Jones, H., & Warnock, L. (2014). *Towards a competency framework for student work-based learning*. York: The Higher Education Academy.
Lave, J., & Wenger, E. (1991). *Situated learning: Legitimate peripheral participation*. New York, NY: Cambridge University Press.
Liszka, J. (2013). Charles Peirce's rhetoric and the pedagogy of active learning. *Educational Philosophy and Theory, 45*, 781–788.
Mandrup, M., & Jensen, T. L. (2017). Educational action research and triple helix principles in entrepreneurship education: Introducing the EARTH design to explore individual activities in triple helix collaboration. *Triple Helix Journal, 4*(1). Retrieved from https://triplehelixjournal.springeropen.com/articles/10.1186/s40604-017-0048-y
Marshall, A., & Thorburn, M. (2014). Cultivating practical wisdom as education. *Educational Philosophy and Theory, 46*, 1541–1553.
McGowan, W., & Partridge, L. (2014). Student engagement and making community happen. *Educational Philosophy and Theory, 46*, 237–254.
Ministry of Higher Education and Science. (2008). *Danish qualifications framework for higher education*. Copenhagen: Ministry of Higher Education and Science.
Moberg, K., & Vestergaard, L. (2013). *Effektmåling af entreprenørskabsundervisning I Danmark—2013*. Odense: Fonden for Entreprenørskab, Young Enterprise.
Oganisjana, K., & Koke, T. (2012). Does competence-oriented higher education lead to students' competiveness? *Inzinerine Ekonomika-Engineering Economics, 23*, 77–82.
Peters, M. (2014). Competing conceptions of the creative university. *Educational Philosophy and Theory, 46*, 713–717.
Read, S., Sarasvathyr, S., Dew, N., Wilthank, R., & Ohlsson, A. (2011). *Effectual entrepreneurship*. New York, NY: Routledge.
Reichenbach, R. (2003). Beyond sovereignty: The twofold subversion of bildung. *Educational Philosophy and Theory, 35*, 201–209.
Reichenbach, R. (2014). Humanistic bildung: Regulative idea or empty concept? *Asia Pacific Educational Review, 15*, 65–70.
Rømer, T. (2015). Thought and action in education. *Educational Philosophy and Theory, 47*, 260–275.
Sarasvathy, S. (2001). Causation and effectuation: Toward a theoretical shift from economic inevitability to entrepreneurial contingency. *Academy of Management Review, 26*, 243–263.
Seal, C., Miguel, K., Alzamil, A., Naumann, S., Royce-Davis, J., & Drost, D. (2015). Personal-interpersonal competence assessment: A self-report instrument for student development. *Research in*

Higher Education Journal, 27, 3–10.
Simpson, D., & Beckett, D. (2014). Expertise, pedagogy and practice. *Educational Philosophy and Theory, 46*, 563–568.
Stecher, B., & Hamilton, L. (2014). *Measuering hard-to-measure student competencies*. Santa Monica, CA: RAND Corporation.
Stojanov, K. (2012). *The concepts of bildung and its moral*. Wiesbaden: Springer Fachmedien.
Stolz, S. (2015). Embodied learning. *Educational Philosophy and Theory, 47*, 474–487.
Stoof, A., Martens, R., Merrienboer, J., & Bastiaens, T. (2002). The boundary approach of competence: A constructivist aid for understanding and using the concept of competence. *Human Resource Development Review, 1*, 345–365.
Sundberg, L. (2001). A holistic approach to competence development. *Systems Research and Bahavioral Science, 18*, 103–114.
Thompson, C. (2005). The non-transparency of the self and the ethical value of bildung. *Journal of Philosophy of Education, 39*, 519–533.
Thröler, D. (2011). Concepts, culture and comparisons: PISA and the double German discontentment. In M. Pereyra, H.-G. Kotthoff, & R. Cowen (Eds.), *PISA under examination: Changing knowledge, changing tests, and changing schools* (pp. 245–257). Rotterdam, The Netherlands: Sense Publishers.
Varkøy, Ø. (2010). The concept of bildung. *Philosophy of Music Education Review, 18*, 85–96.
Vygotsky, L. S. (1987). Thinking and speech. In R. W. Rieber & A. S. Carton (Eds.), *The collected works of L. S. Vygotsky: Problems of general psychology* (Vol. 1, pp. 39–285). New York, NY: Plenum Press.
Wang, C. (2014). Curricula without boundaries: Developing an ecological connection for higher education curricula. *Educational Philosophy and Theory, 46*, 1402–1411.
Wimmer, M. (2003). Ruins of bildung in a knowledge society: Commenting on the debate about the future of bildung. *Educational Philosophy and Theory, 35*, 167–187.
Yosef-Hassidim, D. (2016). Awareness of wholes: The ontological difference as an educative source. *Educational Philosophy and Theory, 48*, 785–797.
Zajonc, A. (2013). Contemplative pedagogy: A quiet revolution in higher education. *New Directions for Teaching and Learning, 134*, 83–94.

Tine Lynfort Jensen
Institute for Language & Communication
University of Southern Denmark
Odense, Denmark

SUSANNE DAU

5. CREATIVE KNOWLEDGE WORK AND THE IMPACT OF INSTRUCTION

INTRODUCTION

Creativity and creative knowledge work are considered to be amongst the most important skills in the 21st century. Creativity has been advocated as a core element of human and economic capital. Hence, various education systems strive to foster creative students. Complex workplaces that are constantly evolving need creative employees to perform knowledge work.

Drawing on different perspectives on the role of instruction in creativity, knowledge development and learning, this chapter reveals how instructions can foster creativity. This chapter's contribution to existing knowledge is founded on a metaphorical phenomenological-ecological approach to learning as wayfinding. Learning, when understood as wayfinding, addresses the environmental, social, and relational elements in knowledge creation. The question addressed is how instructions in undergraduate teacher education influence students' creativity and knowledge creation.

The empirical findings presented draw on data from a longitudinal case study of one class of student teachers within a blended learning environment at University College North, Denmark. Empirical data were retrieved from four observation studies and eight focus group interviews during the period 2012–2015. The focus of the interviews and observations was students' knowledge creation in a blended learning environment.

Overall, the findings of the empirical study reveal how the students experienced learning as wayfinding. Furthermore, it was found that the teacher's instructions highly influenced the students' creative knowledge creation. One significant implication of this study was that instructions must facilitate students' self-directed engagement, social relationships, and autonomy if creative thinking and knowledge creation are to take place. The findings from the empirical study form the basis for the discussion of creative knowledge work and the impact of instruction.

KNOWLEDGE WORK

Knowledge work has been addressed as being essential for companies' competitive advantage (Blackler, 1995). Knowledge workers should bring new knowledge and development to the private and public sectors. Knowledge workers are recognised as self-managing, self-directed, and autonomous, but they may also be resistant to structural approaches concerning administrative and traditional operational work (Davenport, Jarvenpaa, & Beers, 1996). The basis for these knowledge skills is fostered by the education systems and the collaboration, instruction, and work carried out in studies preceding working life. It is argued that collaboration and collaborative environments provide the foundation for effective knowledge work (Sveiby & Simons, 2002; Hardy, Phillips, & Lawrence, 2003). This argument is also found in Nonaka and Takeuchi (1995) and their descriptions of how knowledge work is a matter of social knowledge creation and transfer of existing knowledge among people. They address the importance of revealing tacit knowledge, combining it with others' knowledge and integrating it in practice.

Bereiter and Scardamalia (2003) assert that to meet the demands of the 21st century, education needs to include the design mode. They employ a constructivist approach to knowledge work and define knowledge building as "creative work with ideas that really matter to the people doing the work" (Bereiter & Scardamalia, 2003). Thus, creative knowledge work is supposed to contribute to student engagement and commitment. Bereiter and Scardamalia (2003) conceptualise the role of a belief mode and a design mode in educational practice, addressing the knowledge work in education systems from a work-life perspective. In the belief mode, the concern is about what to believe; unlike the design mode, the belief mode is concerned with usefulness, improvements, and development of ideas and products. Bereiter and Scardamalia problematise the unilateral focus on the belief mode in many education systems. Instead, they suggest a design mode and, accordingly, idea improvement e.g., by working with problem-based learning, design-based learning, and project-based learning. The idea is to focus on idea improvement by addressing real-life problems, instead of simply asking the students questions. The purpose is for society to gain knowledge value or produce new and improved products. Hence, instruction modes are a central matter in fostering future knowledge workers.

CREATIVITY AND KNOWLEDGE CREATION

Creativity and knowledge creation are interrelated concepts addressed by various authors. Runco and Jaeger (2012) have argued that the problem of defining creativity lies in the fact that it is a new concept with no precise definition. However, they stressed that creativity is defined by the criteria of originality and effectiveness. Moreover, Bruner (1962) found that creativity required the element of surprise. Coupled with a human perspective, Guilford (1950) stated that individual creativity is about originality and novelty: raising new ideas through unusual behaviours, which is to some extent in accordance with Bereiter and Scardamalia's (2003) suggestion of a design mode.

Barron (1955) more specifically focused on the impact of creativity and originality, as he described it as a process of uncommonness and adaptation to reality. However, two years earlier, Stein (1953) had already revealed further levels to the phenomenon of creativity. Stein acknowledged that creative insight could emerge from existing knowledge. Moreover, Stein found that the environment has an impact on creativity. In addition, a person's sensitivity, problem-solving abilities, and intellectual or emotional flexibility may also have an impact. Stein's thoughts are similar to the concept of knowledge creation described by Von Krogh et al. (2000). However, they describe knowledge creation in the context of organisational learning, and not only as an individual matter, as follows: 'Knowledge creation at the individual level involves the ability to deal with new situations, events, information and contexts' (Von Krogh et al., 2000, p. 19).

According to Nonaka and Takeuchi (1995), knowledge creation involves a dynamic interplay between tacit and explicit knowledge, including four modes of knowledge conversation (socialisation, externalisation, combination, and internalisation). Knowledge creation is supported by autonomy, commitment, and inbuilt sociality (Von Krogh et al., 2000, p. 179). Knowledge creation is thus a learning process that takes place within different dimensions of knowledge and in the interactions between these dimensions (Dau, 2015).

The social dimension of creativity was recently addressed by Martin (2016), who found that motivation, engagement, instruction, and interpersonal relationships have significant implications for nurturing and sustaining student creativity, both in school and beyond. He describes how students' inclination, interest, energy, and determination to learn, work effectively, and achieve their academic potential are motivational triggers for creativity. Creative motivation is regarded as students' drive to use their imagination, existing knowledge, and original ideas to create something new or innovative (Martin, 2016). Martin revealed that students' engagement in the creative process is fostered by their connections to others, e.g., teachers guiding and supporting the students' creative processes.

The concept of creativity as it is used in this chapter draws on Von Krogh et al. (2000), Martin (2016), and Stein's (1953) findings, revealing that environment, situation, experiences, motivation, instructions, and interpersonal relationships support knowledge creation. Moreover, creativity is regarded as a concept that links the past and the future to the present, as creativity is not independent to prior experiences, and at the same time points towards the future.

This chapter's contribution to existing knowledge is founded in a metaphorical phenomenological-ecological approach to learning understood as wayfinding. This understanding is inspired by Ahmed's (2006) phenomenological theory of orientation and Ingold's (2000) ecological concept of wayfinding. According to Ingold (2000), all wayfinding is mapping, and 'in wayfinding people do not traverse the surface of a world whose layout is fixed in advance' (p. 155). Moreover, wayfinding is related to narratives of journeys previously made (Ingold, 2000, p. 155). Learning, when understood as wayfinding, addresses the environmental, social, and relational elements in knowledge creation.

This understanding of learning is applied to empirical data retrieved from a case study of blended learning which is described in the second of the following sections, and underpins the following research question: how do instructions in teacher and radiography undergraduate courses, influence student creativity and knowledge creation?

LEARNING AS WAYFINDING

Learning as wayfinding represents the epistemological foundation for understanding students' knowledge development in a blended learning environment. Blended learning concerns instructional planning rather than the process of learning (Oliver & Trigwell, 2005). It consists of a mixture of face-to-face and virtual instruction and collaboration, with the purpose of creating flexible delivery modes. However, learning as wayfinding is suggested as a way of addressing the students' learning in these flexible environments (Dau, 2015). As previously mentioned, learning as wayfinding draws on findings from a longitudinal research study (Dau, 2015), Ahmed's (2006) phenomenological theory of orientation and Ingold's (2000) anthropological descriptions of wayfinding. Ingold underlines that:

> in wayfinding, people do not traverse the surface of the world whose layout is fixed in advance—as represented on the cartographic map. Rather, they 'feel their way' through a world that is itself in motion, continually coming into being through the combined action of human and non-human agencies. (p. 55)

Ingold's definition of wayfinding implies that learning as wayfinding is a process that is contingent on people's creativity, as the ability to deal with new entities is considered a process of wayfinding. Ingold (2000) differentiates between wayfinding, mapmaking and navigation (p. 251). He juxtaposes wayfinding and mapping as ongoing cartographic processes which also concern mental representation. However, navigation is compared to map-using, following paths already made or represented. Map-making is the inscription practice afforded by prior mapping and map-making. Map-making is related to the human capacity to make a map. It is not about drawing a cartographic map on a piece of paper, but about processes of remembering, sensing, structuring, consolidating, and comparing. The questions *'where am I?'* and *'which way should I go?'* (Ingold, 2000, p. 237) are found in narratives of prior movements. How people find their way is thus characterised by complex structures that include complex processes (Ingold, 2000, p. 220).

Learning understood as wayfinding (Dau, 2015) is aligned with this description and thus comparable to a design mode, problem-solving, and creativity. However, it is described in relation to the affordance of situations and surroundings. Learning concerns the individual's thinking, emotions, embodied movements, and habits. Learning as wayfinding addresses individuals' interactions in social, physical and virtual settings and their use of artefacts. Learning though wayfinding is a process that includes spatial, moving, collaborative, structural, and social dimensions, as well as emotional and identity dimensions, where reflectivity, resources, frames, and references influence the learning process. Learning as wayfinding is characterised as processes that take place through mental, physical, social, and virtual orientations to gain knowledge, competences and skills. From an epistemological point of view, learning as wayfinding is based on a phenomenological-ecological approach to learning (Dau, 2015, p. 184). Hence, the conceptualisation of learning as wayfinding and its different dimensions bear similarities to theories of knowledge work and knowledge creation, such as Stein's (1953) understanding of creative insight as knowledge emerging from existing knowledge coupled with new elements, where thinking and habits seem to play a role; the emphasis placed by Von Krogh et al. (2000) on sociality as a basis for knowledge creation; and Martin's (2016) emphasis on sociality, situations, and experiences in knowledge creation. Learning as wayfinding is therefore emphasised as being the aim of engagement in creative processes and knowledge work, as well as the driver behind the creative processes. In the next sections, the narrative case study and its methods will be described to present the empirical basis of descriptions and discussions of creative knowledge work and the impact of instructions presented in this chapter.

THE NARRATIVE CASE STUDY

The empirical data of the narrative case study were retrieved from a larger study investigating undergraduate students' orientations within different learning environments, including the classroom, internships, home, and virtual environment (Dau, 2015). The aim was to obtain data for a longitudinal case study. In the initial case study, data were collected from two classes from University College North (UCN) in Denmark. The case study included student teachers and radiography students participating in blended learning courses. Data from the former have been analysed, as teacher education is paradigmatic for the question raised. The empirical data retrieved from the initial study aimed at investigating the students' orientation within different learning spaces, including the classrooms, the place of internship, the home, and the virtual environments (Dau, 2015). Participants were primarily selected using the 'snowballing' method (Goodman, 1961).

Data from the teacher education courses consisted of eight focus group interviews among students, lecturers, and internship supervisors. During the data collection period of 2012–2015, focus group interviews were carried out among the participants three times and observation studies were performed four times. The object of the interviews and observations was students' knowledge orientation and knowledge creation when participating in the blended learning course.

Ethical considerations were made prior to data collection. A confidential agreement was signed by the participants prior to the interviews and anonymisation of personally identifiable data was subsequently secured. Moreover, the participants'' integrity and their ability to withdraw at any time were also safeguarded.

A schematic overview of the empirical data and methods is provided in Tables 1 and 2.

Data analysis draws on narrative case study theory where the narrative forms the basis of the findings. A narrative form was chosen as it is one of few methods

Table 1. Schematic overview of the retrieved empirical data

Focus group and no.	Date	Numbers of informants	Duration	Transcripts single space – Font Times New Roman 12/ Calibri 11
Teacher students interview 1, 2 & 3	27.11.2012 02.09.13 23.04.2014	8 (1 male, 7 females) 4 (all females) 5 (all females)	1 1/4h 1 1/2h 1h	45 pages 31 pages 6 pages (selected quotes)
Teacher lecturers' interview 1, 2 & 3	04.12.2012, 07.10.2013 24.04.2014	4 (1 male, 4 females) 2 (1 male, 1 female) 2 (1 male, 1 female)	1 1/4h 1h 1/2h	35 pages 22 pages 4 pages (selected quotes)
Internship supervisors municipal school interview 1 & 2	04.03.2013 26.11.2013	2 (2 males) 2 (1 male & 1 female)	1h 3/4h	21 pages 20 pages

Table 2. Schematic overview of the methods

Date and time	26.10.2012 8.00-12.00	16.01.2013 8.00 - 15.30	12.04.2013 8.00-10.30	07.10.2013 10.30-11.30
Place	UCN classroom	Municipal school	UCN classroom	UCN classroom
Participants	32 teacher students and 4 teacher lecturers	1-3 students and 1-2 internship supervisors and 1 lecturer	32 teacher students and 4 teacher lecturers	32 teacher students and 4 teacher lecturers
Researcher's position	Non-participating observant	Non-participating observant	Non-participating observant	Participating observant - facilitator of evaluation
Documentation	Field notes on paper	Field notes on paper	Field notes on paper	Field notes on paper

of analysis that can reveal the complexity in which creativity emerges. Thus, we applied the critical-phenomenological-hermeneutical approach founded in Ricoeur's philosophy and described in the books of *Time and Narrative* vol. I, II and III (Ricoeur, 1984a, 1984b), and Ogilvy, Nonaka, and Konno's (2014) work. More information about the narrative approach used can be found in Dau (2014, 2015). The findings are presented in the next section as narrative themes indicated in the subheadings, followed by short narratives in quotations from the case study.

CASE STORY FINDINGS

The findings from the case study are presented as antenarratives (minor narratives revealing elements of the main plot). Three narratives are presented. The themes of the narrative plots are: (1) creativity and learning, (2) creativity and instruction, and (3) creativity and sociality. The findings are in the end of the section, presented in a conceptual model that frames the instructional elements that foster the process of knowledge creation and knowledge work.

The Narrative of Creativity and Learning

Creativity and learning are closely connected. Creativity facilitates students' learning processes and is acknowledged as a competence by lecturers. A lecturer in teacher education described it as a combination of self-efficacy, creativity, and fun in approaching assignments:

> But I think, they have self-efficacy. They are creative. They are fun, that needs to be acknowledged, and they approach the assignment in a relatively straightforward way, and I think you can get much out of it. (Focus group no. 3 with lecturers)

Creativity is related to the flexible environment made available by blended learning courses, which also create different learning pathways. A student teacher described the possibilities of blended environments as follows:

> You don't all have to be at the same place. Now we have been on Prezi where you can make a lot of things together without sitting together. The fact that you can make a lot of creative things and work together on assignments is mega exciting, I think. I think it is totally cool, but if you think it is just a mail to which you must reply, then you don't see the possibilities […] But if you see the possibilities, then I think that it is exactly as Henry (fictive name, male peer) also said, that it is very free, and you can 'walk many ways' where you can say […] In our Danish lessons (it is the opposite), you get an assignment on paper which we must answer. On the other hand, here, we get an overarching theme and we can decide for ourselves how we want to solve it. I think that is very positive. (Focus group no. 1 with students)

In the antenarrative above, it is obvious that the blended learning environment allows students to traverse the surface of an educational world whose layout is not fixed in advance, making room for their autonomy and engagement. The blended learning environment creates a space for knowledge work and knowledge development that may open for more creative processes than ordinary lessons. Moreover, the social space is afforded by the virtual environment's flexibility and the possibility of connecting, which is partly independent of time and space. Virtual space and the autonomy it enables creates intellectual and emotional flexibility, as well as the motivation to solve problems.

The creative, flexible approach to teaching and learning may conceal the outcome being practised, but even though the approach is not associated with prior school experiences and assessments, the learning outcomes are, nonetheless, significant. A student teacher described it as follows:

> For instance, as Dennis [fictive name] said, some of them were surprised because they realised how much they learned during the past year. We talked about it. 'Did we actually learn something this year?' Because we have just got a lot of ideas about how to teach, but we have learned a lot […] We have been in the world of ideas. It has all just become obvious, and we had thought that we have been lacking a professional base, such as when you say: 'Now you have learned this' or […] but we have, nevertheless, received professional content and at the same time … [the creative element]. We have been […] So, we have been duped one way or another. We just wanted an ordinary teacher education, but we got many more opportunities, and for that we are happy. (Focus group no. 2 with students)

The creative process is afforded by its novelty and adaptation to reality as illustrated in the antenarrative above. Novelty is a matter of breaking down the common understanding of teaching and learning and adding a new perspective and approach to the processes involved. The blended learning environment and the world of ideas make an effective surprise that triggers engagement in the learning process, and the students' prior experiences of learning are challenged and reflected upon.

The lecturers acknowledged the students' engagement and were also aware of the possibilities made available by the flexible, experimental approach fostered by the blended learning environment. A lecturer at UCN said:

> I think that they [the students] have been very open to new projects—a curiosity and determination to try something new and see what happens and be creative. I think it is a general competence that we can be proud of. The advantage here [of blended learning courses] has been that you could try something new. It has been legitimised by the conceptualisation of flexible education, and they have been the types of students who would like to try something out if they could be creative and use IT. (Focus group no. 3 with lecturers)

Like Martin's (2016) findings, the antenarratives from the lecturers illustrate how creativity is fostered by the students' inclination, interests, energy and motivation to learn. However, the newly added blended learning environment is the setting that creates the freedom to experiment and try something new in teacher training.

The Narrative of Creativity and Instruction

The pedagogical approach and instructions on how to use different online tools facilitate creativity when the tools are transferable and relevant to work-life practice. A student teacher said:

> We have been presented with different online tools that we can use, for instance, SkoleTube which has different programs like Go-animate and Prezi. I think that it is super cool that you can use it in the instruction [of pupils], and it works very well. Because you could clearly observe when we presented it for the senior pupils […] You have some pupils who are curious and pay attention to how it works. However, if I had stood at the blackboard and blah blah blah … So, it is nice that you have some tools that might foster their engagement. (Focus group no. 2 with students)

Another student teacher seemed to agree:

> It is nice as the others have mentioned that you get other ways of teaching, and you start being more self-directed in your thinking. How can I get IT into the instruction (at municipal school) and make it fun, so it isn't the same as before? (Focus group no. 2 with students)

The professional outcomes and the impact on the students' own teaching practice in municipal schools thus seem to play a significant role in the creative teaching practised. Originality and effectiveness, combined with the students' own use of IT and creative tools, create motivation and engagement, not only among the students, but also in their professional work in the internship.

The creative tools framing the students' needs do not have to be about the use of online media. Any instruction that is directed to practice and might engage the students is valued. A student teacher described it as follows:

> It is much more related to practice, not just to write something down … also in our own teaching. There is group work … You must make something that is different and new, something that you can use in a municipal school, and it doesn't have to concern media use. It can also be a poetry slam, how to make poems … just make something different happen. We are an experimental class and we are allowed to do a lot of things. It is cool that it is not the instruction we are used to and know. (Focus group no. 2 with students)

The experimental base offered by a flexible and varied approach appears to afford new approaches to the student teachers' own teaching in municipal schools. As such, creative knowledge work involves the ability to deal with new situations, events, information and contexts. Moreover, the motivation for their engagement is very clear, as efforts have direct implications for practice and professionals' work. Hence, transference is valuable for creative knowledge work to succeed.

In a similar way, the internship plays a crucial role in students' competence development and acts as a real-life experimental base for using newly gained skills or instructional methods. A student teacher described it in this way:

> Yes, I think … in the internship, we were wildly creative. I don't know if it always was by using IT, but it was just creativity that we had learned to make use of. I think it engages pupils if you want to illustrate something in a fun way.

> You can also see that they (pupils) paid more attention to the issue and thought that it was exciting and fun to do. In the internship, a boy said to me that he thought it was cool, because 'we didn't have to learn anything' […] then I said; 'I know that you made three poems in the last hour'. 'Oh my God', he was totally surprised, you know, but if you can hide the learning process by making it fun, making a movie or doing something different, then it is just […] We also had a class which involved making a book trailer, and a group—they were so committed to the assignment. They took a whole afternoon of their leisure time and filmed, and they sat for three other afternoons and edited it […] Yes, they were very engaged and made a good assignment, where afterwards when you consider the instructions that you gave, you think it is cool that some of your pupils also found it cool. (Focus group no. 2 with students)

Employing the new method in schools makes the learning process both goal-directed and engaging. It is not about creating knowledge just for fun, but also to achieve competences and learning. The quote above illustrates how the students dared to experiment and use newly acquired skills in real-life practice and how they experienced success when their pupils showed the same drive and engagement as they had themselves experienced as students. The hidden learning reveals how knowledge development is tacit in the beginning. However, when it is shared and expressed verbally, it is externalised by dialogue; for instance, in the case of the students sharing the observed learning outcome with the pupils. When newly gained, expressed knowledge is combined with prior knowledge and the theme of the course, and it can be internalised and stored in the memory and the body; thus, the knowledge again becomes partly tacit. Thereby, the knowledge creation process is made possible by sociality, knowledge sharing, and knowledge combination in a process between tacit and explicit knowledge, as Nonaka and Konno (1998) have also underlined.

The lecturers were also aware of the value of practice, and how instructions are central when it comes to raising creative skills and thinking among students. They talked about fostering a culture of curiosity:

> But I also think that many of them [students] begin to have some tools to manage it [the instruction in class] in different ways. It is important that you get a culture that is curious and experimental towards other approaches. That you can do something. Yes, I think it is typical for these students that they don't think 'what does she, Tania [fictive name for the lecturer], want us to do?', but instead, think 'could we do it like this?' They bring with them a curiosity that is worth a lot. (Focus group no. 1 with lecturers)

Acknowledgment of the students' self-directedness and engagement was also evident in the following comment by a lecturer:

> But I think that they are autonomous. They are creative. I think they are fun, and what you shouldn't overrule is that they approach the assignments in a

relative leaned-back way, and I think you can come far by doing so. (Focus group no. 3 with lecturers)

The lecturers' endeavours are acknowledged and appreciated by the students who experience very creative courses. Moreover, dedicated and enthusiastic lecturers are highly valued by the students:

> Thus, the teachers who are super engaged [...] It is always the best teachers that are passionate about what they teach, and it is also this kind of passion that we must show. Therefore, I think you must have a very inspiring approach. I also think that teacher education is good at finding creative ways by which we can learn and pass it on [to pupils]. So, I think it is great fun. Also, yesterday, we had a poetry slam. We had to think creatively immediately because we weren't provided with concrete instructions. Again, it is cool because we are not afraid of making mistakes. It makes a difference, yes [...] There was a loose frame, and this made it totally cool. It gives a crazy creativity to people when you have this autonomy. It is important to learn it [creativity] from the beginning. Yes, but as we have talked before about the creative element and other ways of learning [that can develop the profession] so that you can engage all pupils [...] And it is not only those who can manage to sit quietly on their chair and write notes that get involved, but also those who are less calm and might prefer to learn using their bodies. There are many ways of learning; some of it is has to do with learning how we can make people learn. How we can teach people who have difficulties following ordinary blackboard teaching [...] Yes, I think creativity is very important ... [and] variation, like when you are offered assignments and you get to try it on your own. We think it is fun. Perhaps there are also some pupils that think it is fun. I think I have experienced that. Instead of making them write an assignment—we also think it is deadly boring. So, I think that we get a lot of great tools we can apply in school, but we must also have a professional background and aims. I think there is a great mix here [at University College of Northern Denmark]. We know what the pupils are going through, because we have tried it, we have experienced it. I think the lecturers have a super creative approach. It really gripped me ... because I have had the opportunity to unfold creatively instead of sitting down all day. So, I think that we learn a lot from the different forms of instruction. (Focus group no. 1 with students)

The teacher's motivation and engagement, as well as instruction and interpersonal relationships, have significant implications for nurturing and sustaining student creativity in school. The teacher's passion directly impacts on the students' engagement and desire to solve the task given and to internalise the knowledge gained. The relationship and interplay between the students and the teacher create a sociality that is fundamental to knowledge creation.

Creativity is scaffolded by the relatively free structure, the autonomy given, the variation in instructions, and the allowing of experimentation. The focus on professional practice and the relevance of the methods in school settings are significant. Transferring creative learning experiences from one setting to another is crucial for the adoption of creative learning among the student teachers. The example of trying things out illustrates how the creative learning process is not only about cognitive and emotional competences, but also about the embodied nesting of skills and attitudes. The knowledge flow and adoption of acquired knowledge in practice is one of the main elements in the knowledge sharing process. It is achieved through mirroring the role models' tacit knowledge in practice and by the explication and dialogues among the students and the professional teachers. However, once again, openness towards new ideas is necessary in schools. A school internship supervisor described this openness:

> Well, I think we are very open minded towards new input at this school. We look forward to new input. I think it is also what you get as an internship supervisor when you choose to have students in the internship. The reason is that you get to see a lot of cool stuff such as new books, new instructional material and new thoughts […] Moreover, you get these discussions with students, right? (Focus group no.1 with internship supervisors)

As mentioned earlier, the lecturers are also aware of the transfer and thus of the knowledge development in the profession made available by the students in their periods of internship:

> Now, it can be a lever. It is also … It is hard to get the professional teachers in school to do it [use flexible solutions and IT]. There are some nerds in the schools who have knowledge in the area—whom you always can call. In this way [using the students' competencies], education provides a model which the students can bring into school. (Focus group no.1 with lecturers)

The transformation and development of practice are carried out partly through the students' participation in the internship. Among internship supervisors, creative insight is understood as emerging from existing knowledge while being coupled with new elements, as Stein (1953) has suggested.

The Narrative of Creativity and Sociality

Sociality, it seems, is the glue that binds knowledge creation to creativity. Sociality is one of the main elements in the learning process that scaffolds students' and lecturers' engagement and commitment. It matters to the students' experience of connectivity, identity formation and affiliation to the profession. Social relations to peers, lecturers and professionals are essential for inclusion in the community of practice. The students described how social relations were important to them and their learning process:

> Yes, we keep together. We do not always agree, but if we have an assignment then we talk about it. We confront one another's opinion. The better you are

socially, the more you dare to make ... or be unsure of the correctness of the answer. Because I have previously experienced [in high school] that if you were not sure which answer to give, you didn't raise your hand, where now I find that our class is very open-minded, and nobody thinks oh! It is much more direct and straightforward. It means a lot that social cohesion is here where great professional learning can take place. It is, nevertheless, also important to bring it into the classroom. Social aspects are important, and it must work. Yes, and everybody must be included. I want a class where I can meet and get some social connections, too; relationships, but to do that [online] it demands another relation. It can be great [online], but I think it is based on the experiences you have had together. I don't think you get new friends online and then oh. Friendship is founded here. We know people here and can follow what they are doing afterwards. (Focus group no. 1 with students)

Sociality creates a platform where students dare to make mistakes, experiment, and be creative. Their peers and mutual support create a space where knowledge development and learning are facilitated. Thus, the social environment is supportive and gives students access to knowledge sharing and new ideas. Online sociality is limited with respect to establishing relations, but it may be valuable afterwards when the formal learning process ends. Moreover, sociality in physical spaces has a strong effect on the students' commitment. A student expressed this as follows:

When you are together in a group, it might be that you would like to do something else, but you can sense: okay, now, this is what we are doing and what we must do. On the other hand, if I was at home and would fancy a cup of coffee, then there is nobody who ... there I dispose of my own time, whereas if you are in a group, you work more intensively while you are out here [at University College], because there are not as many temptations. It is, I think, that you postpone meeting your needs which you would not do at home. It is also observable in class that you postpone your needs. (Focus group no. 2 with students)

Commitment forms the basis of relations and trust that is essential to carrying out creative in-depth knowledge work. Peers are central to the students' identity and they described the importance of the connections, explaining that it is because of their age and because they need social ties that they physically meet instead of studying at a distance:

It has something to do with our age. Many of us are newcomers to Aalborg, so you search for new friends and social relations. We have the time to meet ... because our age is 19 to 21. You need to connect, also to the lecturers. So, you prefer to come here [at University College] and gain that proximity. You don't get the same if you are at home. (Focus group no. 3 with students)

Student identity formation thus plays a crucial role in the choices made by the students and their wayfinding and must be seen in the view of the students' past, present, and future, as illustrated by their reflections on why they need relationships and why they want a social environment. Thus, they map a surface of the world whose layout is not fixed in advance as they try to find their way in the blended learning environment. Their journeys are related to the narratives presented, which are also affected by their previously made journeys; for instance, those in high school. Sociality and interpersonal relationships nurture and sustain students engagement, triggering their imagination, ideas, and creative knowledge work. Hence, the social connections offer student confidence and knowledge sharing that might be useful in the internship; they not only achieve academic skills, but also the possibility of knowledge development in the profession. Physical, face-to-face sociality appears to form the basis for further connections and collaborations online. Therefore, the environment and timing play a crucial role in the students' relationships and consequently their creative knowledge work. This is consistent with Nonaka's (1998) description of sociality and interactions as being prior to knowledge online.

Relationships are not only fostered among the students, but also by their relations to the lecturers, as revealed in the previous section. Physical sociality and relationships are accordingly also a priority among the lecturers:

> There must be a lot of sociality in education, and it becomes more difficult if the instruction is solely internet based. Currently, it is not, but I have thought a lot about it, the mix. Blended learning ... then I have had some lessons that are solely online, right? And I have found that is it not clever because I came to teach in a space where the prerequisites were unrevealed. So, I must instead take a more varied approach to blended learning where the students and I have time together, trying to collaborate in a way where there is a sense of openness towards testing out new possibilities. Yes, because it is a process of socialisation here in the first semester. (Focus group no.1 with lecturers)

The relevance of sociality is also coupled with professional work and the students' future work-life. A lecturer emphasised apprenticeship as a way of illustrating knowledge creation and open-mindedness towards new ideas:

> Relationship competency is very important, right? But it is also because we are a communicative profession. We are a profession of relations. So that is why we apply the concept of apprenticeship during the study and focus on being open minded to all new ... and thus the width in the professions. Yes, it is about being curious towards all new things, also when it comes to group work, and they must accommodate some peers who are different and might have another discipline. Because they must have tolerance [in school] that extends beyond the normal. Yes, a spaciousness. So, we won't allow that they leave some out from group formation, because they must include all just like in the profession. (Focus group no. 2 with lecturers)

Sociality continues to be highlighted in the study. A lecturer says:

> I simply think that you can't underestimate it [sociality]. It is universal for humans. You value being together in the same room and observing how people are and act. Then it all become easier in real-life spaces because you have social needs. (Focus group no. 3 with lecturers)

Sociality becomes both a prerequisite and an existential foundation for the knowledge development being carried out. It creates a structure and a basis for the student's wayfinding and a space for identity formation that aims at supporting the professional work. Sociality appears to be the foundation for student creativity which is fostered by the role modelling carried out by the lecturers and in the activation of relationships. Internship supervisors also agree on the relevance of sociality:

> We talk a lot about relationships. Also, the profession as a teacher. That's also what I tell them (the students): 'What we look at is if you are looking. Do you have eye contact? Can you foster relationships and professionalism?' Yes, we talk a lot about relations and the like. In their first year, it is about their connection to children, building relationships, because if you haven't got a relationship with the children, they become indifferent. (Focus group no. 1 with internship supervisors)

Despite the complexity of real-life social practices, the students are good at creating relationships with the children at the school especially at the end of their internship period. The internship supervisors expressed it as follows:

> I think they [the students] have worked hard to create relationships with the pupils. They have clearly better experiences after they have been here for a while, because they have established relations to the pupils they know. There is no doubt that it is a borderless work in many ways because the relationships that we have spoken about are so important and something that affect us. So, you build a professionalism that makes it possible. I used to say, 'it is a miracle that teaching happens'. Relationships become important, because if there are good relations, teaching will succeed. So, it is all the feelings that are in motion and the presence and the relationships in the room that are essential. (Focus group no. 2 with internship supervisors)

The glue that fosters and keeps knowledge creation going thus includes relationships, interactions, eye contact, social environment, and attention towards the individual in the social setting. However, according to the internship supervisors, it takes some time to become familiar with the pupils and understand their preferences and prerequisites. Thus, the students 'find their way while walking the road'. The students internalise their experiences and new knowledge while processing their knowledge development; for instance, while they gain familiarity with the children and establish relationships. Sociality becomes both a condition and a driver for creative knowledge development and pupils' learning. The student teachers' learning in the school profession thus takes place through wayfinding. Moreover, their sensitivity, problem-solving abilities and intellectual or emotional flexibility seem to matter in the creation of relationships. The students' tacit and explicit interactions with peers, lecturers, internship supervisors, and children in the school are essential to enabling a creative approach to learning and knowledge development in different learning environments.

A Conceptual Model of Knowledge Creation in Education Courses' Instructional Practice

Based on the empirical findings, a conceptual model has been derived that illustrates the different elements in educational practice and in working with knowledge creation, where student learning is characterised as a process of wayfinding.

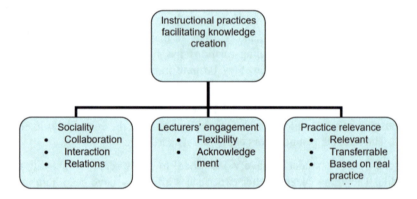

Figure 1. A conceptual model of elements in instructional practice facilitating knowledge creation

Figure 1 illustrates the elements in instruction that foster the process of knowledge creation and knowledge work in an educational blended learning context. The findings confirm the importance of sociality. Sociality is the foundation for creative work and an important element of the collaborative journeys and interactions. The relationships between peers, students, and lecturers provide the basis for collaborative knowledge work and student engagement in the learning process. Another important element is the lecturers' engagement. The empirical findings reveal how the lecturers' flexibility and instructional practices affect the students' engagement and participation in the knowledge work. Moreover, the lecturers' acknowledgement of students and their contributions to the knowledge work creates a platform on which knowledge work is carried out. Finally, the focal point of knowledge creation is practical relevance. It is crucial that knowledge work addresses real-life problems, i.e., knowledge work should address relevant problem-solving where knowledge has a direct impact on problems that have been observed and addressed in practice, helping students gain transferable knowledge and skills for future knowledge development in practice.

CREATIVE KNOWLEDGE WORK AND THE IMPACT OF INSTRUCTION

The findings from the case study reveal elements significant for the success of creative knowledge work and instruction. The narrative of creativity and learning reveals how student flexibility is essential for creative work; for instance, in their approach to assignments and their openness and curiosity towards the processes. Flexibility is also emphasised as being an important emotional or intellectual competence (Stein, 1953) that is fostered by the environment. The blended learning environment adds a playful and flexible environment, and under the right conditions this environment supports student competences and wayfinding and knowledge creation. Moreover, the importance of the world of ideas is revealed as being a central element in the creative process in accordance with Guilford's (1950) focus on raising new ideas and Bereiter and Scardamalia's (2003) view of a design mode.

The findings from the narratives confirm the relevance of self-directedness among students, which is also mentioned by Davenport et al. (1996). Self-directedness is a skill that the students can use in their future instructional practice as teachers.

In general, transference and practical relevance seem to matter in creative knowledge work; for instance, when students are inspired by passionate, engaged lecturers, they adapt their approaches and implement them in their own instructional practices with pupils. Practical relevance is also highlighted in the theoretical perspectives including Barron's (1955) emphasis on adaptation to reality and, indirectly, the conceptual model of knowledge creation, which is founded on a context of practice and work, in Von Krogh et al. (2000). Also, Runco and Jaeger's (2012) descriptions of originality and effectivity seem to match the idea of practical relevance.

All in all, the teaching that students are exposed to is crucial to how they become engaged and creative. Instructional practice is coupled with the lecturers' motivation, engagement, and passion, adding value and trust to student experimentation and creative play.

The engagement of lecturers is discussed in Martin's (2016) descriptions of drive and energy as the basis for creativity, and the idea of a design mode in educational practice as described by Bereiter and Scardamalia (2003) that implicitly includes teachers' engagement in moving educational practice away from a belief mode. The relatively free structure and the variety of methods offered by the blended learning environment and a design mode increase curiosity and open-minded attitudes, facilitating students' creative wayfinding.

Creative knowledge work is founded in sociality. Sociality creates a basis for collaboration, commitment, creative experimentation, and design processes, as acknowledged by Stein (1953), and Nonaka and Takeuchi's (1995) description of the interplay of tacit and explicit knowledge as well as Martin's (2016) emphasis on the social dimension. Relationships contribute a safety net where errors and failed attempts do not become a burden, but rather a basis for understanding and new knowledge. Hence, social relations and collaboration add a supportive social environment to student wayfinding.

DISCUSSION OF THE EMPIRICAL FINDINGS AND CONCLUDING REMARKS

The study's empirical basis is limited to two bachelor's degree education courses. More cross-sectoral and quantitative studies are required to test the reliability and validity of the findings in other educational environments. However, the findings do illustrate a connection between instruction and creative knowledge work that is missing from other studies. This connection highlights the importance of practice as a key element in the creative process and thus its direct relevance.

The case study's overall findings revealed how the students experienced learning as wayfinding. The findings of the case study illustrate how freedom and autonomy, as well as less regulated instructions, can afford knowledge creation and learning fostered by sociality, lecturers' engagement, and practical relevance. The experimental basis of blended learning appears to have generated more creative thinking than well-planned instructions with less structured, but goal-oriented instructions by furthering creativity in the students' study activities and knowledge creation. One significant implication of this study is that educational reflections must include the facilitation of students' self-directed engagement, social relationships and autonomy if creative thinking and knowledge creation are to reveal their potential for the benefit of the end users. Moreover, a key influence of learning by wayfinding is that it triggers students' curiosity and engagement and facilitates their self-directed, peer-supported, and instructionally-supported engagement and commitment, creating value for the professions' contemporary development. The study's findings regarding creativity confirm Bereiter and Scardamalia's (2014) findings which refute the existing underlying assumption that there is a lack of creativity in education because of contradictions and curricular constraints. However, there must be reservations for the study's results, as these have not included other forms of education than the courses in blended learning. Further studies of instruction's impact on creativity are thus recommended. For instance, studies in primary and secondary schools and in vocational education would be valuable.

CONCLUSION

The question of how instruction can foster creativity has been investigated using empirical data from a longitudinal case study of instruction in blended learning courses. Based on the case study, three narratives reveal the importance of instruction in student wayfinding and creative knowledge work. The first narrative has mapped the interplay between creativity and learning. It illustrates how the blended learning environment raises possibilities for experimentation, creative processes and knowledge development through different modes of instruction. The flexible learning environment creates a space that fosters motivation to solve problems and try something new.

The second narrative has reveals the interdependence between creativity and instruction. The importance of educational tools and knowledge transfer to work-life is emphasised. The use of creative tools in instruction appear to play a crucial role for student engagement and creativity. The lecturer's engagement and creative approach inspires the students to act accordingly. Creativity is afforded by a relative loose structure, the autonomy given, the legitimacy of experimentation, and the variation in the instructional delivery modes.

The final narrative solidifies the importance of sociality as a fundamental basis for knowledge creation and creativity in instructional practice. Sociality plays a significant role in students having the courage to fail and test new ways in teaching. Sociality thus becomes a prerequisite for student wayfinding and creative approach. The sociality that fosters creativity is both related to peers' social relations and commitments, and the relationship to lecturers and practitioners. Lecturer creativity has a spill-over effect when the students have a close relationship with them. The lecturers' and internship advisors' awareness of the social relationships is essential for fostering creativity and knowledge development in the educational practice. Hence the sociality and, accordingly, relationships, interactions, and collaboration are the drivers behind creativity.

In general, creativity and knowledge creation are found to have a central place in education, enabling students' skills through collaboration in the process of knowledge development and knowledge building, and providing the foundation for participating in the future knowledge society.

REFERENCES

Ahmed, S. (2006). *Queer phenomenology, orientations, objects, others*. Durham, NC: Duke University Press.

Barron, F. (1955). The disposition towards originality. *Journal of Abnormal and Social Psychology, 51*, 478–485.

Bereiter, C., & Scardamalia, M. (2003). Learning to work creatively with knowledge. In E. D. Corte, L. Verschaffel, N. Entwistle, & J. V. Merriënboer (Eds.), *Powerful learning environments: Unravelling basic components and dimensions* (pp. 73–78). Oxford: Elsevier Science.

Bereiter, C., & Scardamalia, M. (2014). Knowledge building and knowledge creation: One concept, two hills to climb. In S. C. Tan, H. J. So, & I. Yeo (Eds.), *Knowledge creation in education* (pp. 35–52). Singapore: Springer.

Blackler, F. (1995). Knowledge, knowledge work and organizations: An overview and interpretation. *Organization studies, 16*(6), 1021–1046.

Bruner, J. S. (1962). The conditions of creativity. In H. Gruber, G. Terrell, & M. Wertheimer (Eds.), *Contemporary approaches to creative thinking, 1958*. New York, NY: Atherton Press.

Dau, S. (2013). *The art of making interpretative research through the use of the threefolded mimesis*. In International Human Science Research Conference, Aalborg, Denmark.

Dau, S. (2015). *Studerendes orientering i fleksible professionsuddannelsers læringsrum: Et narrativt casestudie af vidensudviklingens veje og afveje*. Aalborg: Aalborg University press.

Davenport, T. H., Jarvenpaa, S. L., & Beers, M. C. (1996). Improving knowledge work processes. *Sloan Management Review, 37*(4), 53.

Goodman, L. A. (1961). Snowball sampling. *Annals of Mathematical Statistics, 32*(1), 148–170. doi:10.1214/aoms/1177705148

Guilford, J. P. (1950). Creativity. *American Psychologist, 5*, 444–454.
Hardy, C., Phillips, N., & Lawrence, T. B. (2003). Resources, knowledge and influence: The organizational effects of interorganizational collaboration. *Journal of Management Studies, 40*(2), 321–347.
Ingold, T. (2000). *The perception of the environment: Essays on livelihood dwelling and skill.* New York, NY: Routledge.
Martin, A. J. (2016). *Motivating, engaging, and instructing students for creativity*. Retrieved May 12, 2016, from http://www.lifelongachievement.com/image/data/Motivation%20and%20Creativity.pdf
Nonaka, I., & Konno, N. (1998). The concept of 'Ba': Building a foundation for knowledge creation. *California Management Review, 40*(3), 40–54.
Nonaka, I., & Takeuchi, H. (1995). *The knowledge-creating company: How Japanese companies create the dynamics of innovation?* New York, NY: Oxford University Press.
Ogilvy, J., Nonaka, I., & Konno, N. (2014). Toward narrative strategy. *World Futures, 70*(1), 5–18.
Oliver, M., & Trigwell, K. (2005). Can 'blended learning' be redeemed? *E-learning and Digital Media, 2*(1), 17–26.
Runco, M. A., & Jaeger, G. J. (2012). The standard definition of creativity. *Creativity Research Journal, 24*(1), 92–96.
Ricoeur, P. (1984a). *Time and narrative: Volume 1* (K. McLaughlin & D. Pellauer, Trans.). Chicago, IL: University of Chicago Press.
Ricoeur, P. (1984b). *Time and narrative: Volume 2* (K. McLaughlin & D. Pellauer, Trans.). Chicago, IL: University of Chicago Press.
Stein, M. I. (1953). Creativity and culture. *The Journal of Psychology, 36*(2), 311–322.
Sveiby, K. E., & Simons, R. (2002). Collaborative climate and effectiveness of knowledge work–an empirical study. *Journal of Knowledge Management, 6*(5), 420–433.
Von Krogh, G., Ichijo, K., & Nonaka, I. (2000). *Enabling knowledge creation: How to unlock the mystery of tacit knowledge and release the power of innovation.* Oxford: Oxford University Press.

Susanne Dau
Department of Research & Development
University College of Northern Denmark (UCN)
Aalborg, Denmark

ANNA WACH

6. CONSTRUCTIVIST APPROACH IN BUSINESS EDUCATION WITH THE USE OF VIRTUAL SIMULATIONS

INTRODUCTION

As business education should promote proactive and creative attitudes, as well as develop analytic competences and teamwork, discussion, and decision-making skills—which is particularly reflected in labour market expectations—it is worth reflecting on whether currently used approaches to teaching and educational strategies implemented by business schools meet the demands of students and employers. Although the need to shift the focus from the teacher/content-centred model to the student-centred model has been stressed in the literature on academic teaching for at least a few decades, the teaching reality of many universities is far from what theoretical formulae recommend.

Classes taught with the application of simulations are not an entirely new approach. Simulations are often used to practise specific skills in artificially designed conditions, which help to shape particular behaviour mechanisms. They are applied in the directive, expository model of teaching, where the sequence of actions is determined by a certain algorithm. However, when the goal of educational efforts is not only to provide declarative and procedural knowledge, but also to develop cognitive, social, and interpersonal competences as well as those related to business orientation, the role of simulations changes. According to the constructivist paradigm (Piaget, Vygotsky, Bruner), learning is based on learners' multilateral activity (the student-centred approach), during which they have an opportunity to expand and reconstruct individual structures of knowledge through solving a properly devised cognitive problem. Thus, it is particularly important to create learning by doing, hands-on, and situated learning cases, fostering creativity, which in turn will increase the impact of business education (Masek & Yamin, 2010).

The main aim of the chapter is to present what constructivist learning in business education with the application of strategic management simulations is. In the first part, I intend to discuss the characteristics and conditions of learning in the constructivist paradigm and the framework for designing classes according to this approach. Then, I will focus on the possibilities of supporting students' learning in business education, paying particular attention to simulation as a teaching strategy, and considering Amabile's (1983) framework of creativity. In the next section, I am going to describe strategic management games which are a product of two European

Union programmes. Based on the Kolb learning cycle, I will focus on designing and teaching classes with the use of virtual simulations. Finally, the results of the research on the constructivist virtual simulation-based learning will be presented.

THE SHIFT FROM TEACHING TO LEARNING

Today we observe a specific paradigmatic turn in academic teaching, expressed in the formula 'the shift from teaching to learning'. This approach emphasises changing the focus from the transmission of educational content to students and their activity and the role of the teacher as a facilitator. Barr and Tagg (1995), Ramsden (1992), Biggs and Tang (2007), Entwistle and Ramsden (1983), Fink (2008) and Prosser and Trigwell (2014) in particular suggest that the directive, expository teaching process should be replaced by a process with students and their multilateral activity in its centre. Thus, they propose a shift from theory and educational concepts based on the behavioural paradigm to the constructivist one, which seems to be the most popular and best known among cognitive and social theories (Fry et al., 2009). This constructivist approach is based on the works of scholars such as Piaget, Vygotski and Bruner (Fosnot & Pery, 2005), who created the key assumptions of educational constructivism; at the same time formulating its cognitive and social aspects.

According to educational constructivism, learning should consist of the learner creating notions and embedding them in the existing structures of knowledge. This takes place as a result of his/her involvement and multilateral activity, in referring to his/her prior knowledge and experience, and the possibility of negotiating meanings in social interaction (Fosnot, 2005). In accordance with the premises of constructivism, learning occurs when (Jonassen et al., 1999 as cited by Pritchard, 2009, pp. 32–33):

- the construction of knowledge rather than the reproduction of knowledge is paramount,
- new information is built into and added onto an individual's current structure of knowledge, understanding and skills,
- learners construct their own knowledge in an active way (active learning strategies),
- learners use their previous knowledge in building new knowledge,
- involves the use of variety resources,
- authentic tasks in a meaningful context are encouraged,
- reflection on prior knowledge is encouraged,
- collaborative work is encouraged,
- autonomy is encouraged.

Constructivism, as a theory of learning and cognition, explains how people learn, while at the same time becoming the framework for designing a teaching process, as it emphasises what students need to do to construct their knowledge, which, as a result, indicates what learning activities teachers should plan for them in order to achieve the learning outcomes (Biggs & Tang, 2007). It shows how the process of communication between the teacher and students should take place, what roles they have in this process, and what teaching strategies, educational media, forms of arranging educational space, and student evaluation techniques support the student-centred approach (Table 1). Similar lists were prepared by Barr and Tagg (1995), Kąkolewicz (2011), Sajdak (2013) and Wach-Kąkolewicz (2016).

Table 1. Class designing items according to student-centred approach

Communication process
Multidirectional communication Student-student, student-group, student-teacher, group-teacher relations, etc. Social interaction, discussions, negotiations
Goals and outcomes of teaching (learning support)
Help students to construct permanent knowledge (meaningful for the learner) Encourage students to establish the scope of goals on their own Shape cognitive curiosity and intellectual competences, such as: analytical skills, searching relations, synthesising, critical thinking, reflectiveness Resulting knowledge is permanent, holistic, declarative and procedural
The teacher's role and skills
Designer of students' activities (including cognitive ones) Moderator/facilitator instead of information source provider Content knowledge and advanced teaching skills
The learner's role and motivation
An active builder of his or her own cognitive structures Involvement and multilateral activity in problem-solving Intrinsic motivation, aroused cognitive curiosity
Teaching strategies and forms
Active teaching strategies (discussion, case study, brainstorming, Oxford debate, project, simulation) Team-work based learning
Educational media and IT
Hand on media, case study sheets, handouts and IT increasing student involvement
Space designing
Classrooms are laid out for group work, space arranged in any ways according to the class goals Classes inside and outside the university building
Students' assessment and class evaluation
The process of gaining knowledge and students' involvement and progress are assessed Assessment for learning Feedback Formative and summative assessment

The existing body of literature and studies (Marton, 1975; Biggs, 1987; Ramsden, 1988; Trigwell et al., 1997; Trigwell & Prosser, 2004; Trigwell et al., 2005; Prosser & Trigwell, 2014) show that students' approach to learning will largely depend on the way classes are taught by the teacher rather than on their individual characteristics (including motivation). The student-centred model supports and reinforces a deep approach to study; it may also change a surface approach to a more active one. Students who adopt a deep approach focus on studying new facts and ideas in an active and critical way, relating to their prior knowledge. They have an intention of understanding, engaging with, operating in, and valuing the subject. They actively seek to understand the course content, search subject material, ask questions, and look for answers. They take a broad view and relate ideas to one another. They are motivated by interest, and usually broaden their knowledge, going beyond the course requirements (Lublin, 2003). In addition to durable and holistic knowledge, they develop cognitive skills, starting from the basic, such as memorising and naming, to the most advanced skills: explaining, hypothesising, and reflective thinking. In practice, we may distinguish determinants of a deep approach to learning which depend on the teacher:

- teaching in a way that helps to keep the structure of the topic,
- teaching to make students active in responding (by asking questions, presenting problems to be solved),
- teaching by relating to students' prior knowledge, building on what they already know,
- challenging and amending students' misconceptions,
- assessing for understanding of and ability to connect to information rather than memorisation of independent facts,
- creating a positive atmosphere during class, allowing students to make mistakes and learn from them,
- focusing on depth of learning rather than on coverage,
- using teaching and assessing strategies that help to reach intended course outcomes (Biggs & Tang, 2007).

When planning constructivist classes, David Kolb's learning cycle is useful (Kolb, 1984; Kolb et al., 2001). It is the basis of the concept of experiential learning. It assumes that learning is the transformation of information and experience into useful knowledge and skills. In this process, the learner needs to go through four different stages, starting with direct experience (real or simulated), which is analysed in the reflective process and on which the learner forms principles which are applied in the last phase. It means that students are actively involved in some form of a learning event; then they reflect back on the activity on their own or in interaction with others to develop the understanding of what they have experienced. Based on the analysis of this understanding, the learners structure the information, and formulate the generalised set of principles and rules. In the last phase, they try the theories out (experimenting) to assess their validity and/or to identify the most practical approach in achieving the expected results. The above phases of Kolb learning cycle are often used by teachers as the successive stages of classes, within the framework of which specific cognitive activities are designed and appropriate teaching strategies and forms are used in order to support students' constructivist learning.

SUPPORTING STUDENTS' LEARNING IN BUSINESS EDUCATION WITH THE USE OF SIMULATIONS

Today it is hard to imagine that it is possible to reflect on the complex, diverse, and multidimensional nature of the real business world with only the use of course books and lecture slides (Reiners et al., 2015). However, business education, including entrepreneurship and management education, is still frequently criticised 'for being theory-driven and for the lack of critical thinking, creativity and innovation' (Abdullah et al., 2013, p. 95). Aram and Noble (1999) point out that business schools do not properly prepare their students for the labour market, which is a result of, among other things, inappropriate models of teaching and learning used in the education of students. They note that teachers mainly apply the content-centred approach and focus on the predictable aspects of organisational life, ignoring the paradoxical and unpredictable characteristics of the contemporary business world (Lainema & Mekkonen, 2003; Ben-Zvi & Carton, 2007). Business education is also criticised for the lack of integration of issues under study: the separation of subject content which should be combined, e.g., finance, accounting, management, or marketing (Selen, 2001; Walker & Black, 2000 as cited by Lainema & Mekkonen, 2003). By looking at a single business case from different perspectives, students could gain the holistic knowledge of economic reality and discover links and relations among the specific fields of economy and management. What would be the natural implication of adopting such a model of teaching is the development of a number of cognitive competences, such as analysing, arguing, explaining, and reasoning, as well as creativity and co-operation, discussion, negotiation or decision-making skills. These and many other competences are part of the profile of the business school graduate that is sought in the labour market (Michoń & Ławrynowicz, 2009; Buttler & Ławrynowicz, 2012). They cannot simply be developed through the content-delivery teaching.

Heinonen and Poikkijoki (2006) indicate that what is important for students in entrepreneurship education is not only to understand the essence of entrepreneurship (how to define and approach it), but also to become an entrepreneurial person (a person that sets up and runs his/her own business activity). Therefore, students' education should involve not only the pursuit of declarative and procedural knowledge, but also the development of new ways of thinking, as well as new capabilities and manners of behaviour. This is possible only owing to the designing of non-standard learning activities and having students solve complex business cases (Balan & Metcalfe, 2012; Smith & Beasley, 2011). It is thus proposed that some elements of the 'learning-by-doing' strategy (Tan & Ng, 2006) and the 'hands-on' approach to learning (Martin, 2000; Kolender et al., 2003; Gaweł & Wach-Kąkolewicz, 2016) should be applied.

New ways of thinking are often associated with creative approaches. While there are several theories of creativity, ranging from developmental or psychometric to evolutionary categories (Kozbelt et al., 2010), one particularly pertinent to the discussion is the componential theory of creativity (Amabile, 1983). The componential theory includes three intra-individual components, and one external component influencing creativity. The external element is the social environment, while the individual components are (1) domain-relevant skills, (2) creative-relevant skills and (3) task motivation. Domain-relevant skills incorporate individual knowledge, basic talent for thinking, and problem-specific technical skills. Creative-relevant skills encapsulate individual approaches to problems and solutions, depending on personality, thinking, and working styles among other items. Finally, intrinsic task motivation focuses on self-approach and attitude to a task. According to the theory, these components combine in a multiplicative fashion: if the envisaged target includes creativity, none can be completely absent (Amabile & Pillemer, 2012).

Among many teaching strategies which support students' deep approach to study in business education, the following are worth mentioning: problem-based learning; case study and simulations, which are based on solving complex, multidimensional; and real problems (Ammerman et al., 2012; Abdullah et al., 2013). These encourage the integration of knowledge from different fields and develop students' cognitive, interpersonal, social, and managerial skills.

Simulations, including electronic ones based on a complex, often dynamic scenario, provide a context which imitates reality (a system, entity, phenomenon, or process) (Lean et al., 2006), thus supporting authentic education (Reiners et al., 2015). Business games offer students the opportunity to 'learn by doing', involving them in a simulated experience of the real world. This immerses them in authentic management situations, allowing them deal with real business problems and decision-making, as well as the consequences that result (Garris et al., 2002; Martin, 2000; Vörös & Köles, 2011; Gaweł, 2014). Business games provide students with the opportunity to adopt the roles and duties of managers so that they can get involved in challenges faced by real employees in real companies and learn to work under pressure and cope with risks (Ben-Zvi & Carton, 2007). They constitute a link between abstract theoretical concepts, which can be found in course books or heard at lectures, and events taking place in the business world. Students who take part in simulations solve problems through making natural references to their prior knowledge and experience, in order to devise the best reaction to the issues posted in the simulation. They reflect on the problem, draw conclusions, try to understand the theory and embed it in the structures of their knowledge, and then apply it in practice (Ben-Zvi & Carton, 2007). In other words, simulations used properly in the teaching process are part of Kolb's experiential learning theory. They involve students cognitively and emotionally, particularly influencing their motivation and joy of learning (Garris et al., 2002). Simulations also have huge potential different fields of business and scientific disciplines are combined (Vörös & Köles, 2011), thus they help students to integrate knowledge and make it holistic as they recognise the complexity and diversity of economic phenomena and processes.

Clarke (2009), having analysed the literature on simulation, distinguishes a number of benefits that simulations bring (see: Mitchell, 2004; Gaweł, 2014a):

- motivation (enjoyment, engagement, high level of intrinsic motivation),
- problem-solving and analytical thinking skills (development of problem analysis from multiple perspectives and decision-making skills),
- transfer of knowledge (opportunities to provide and use theory into practice, a realistic risk-free learning environment that let check what the students have already learned in the class),
- decision-making and cross functional skills (learning and improving strategic management capacity, leadership skills, teamwork, etc.),
- increased retention of knowledge (students learn more effectively through active engagement by exploring, analysing, communicating, creating, reflecting, or using new information or experiences),
- adaptable learning (they enhance learning ability and help students to acquire complex skills more quickly than other learning methods),
- behavioural, attitudinal and knowledge change (positive students' changes in behaviour and attitude towards business problems and decision-making processes).

Given the above aspects, it seems that simulations as a teaching method in business education are an interesting alternative to the traditional educational strategies, as they help to fill the competence gap between the labour market requirements for graduates and knowledge acquired in lectures, and thus they can be an effective teaching tool.

TEACHING STRATEGIC MANAGEMENT WITH THE VIRTUAL SIMULATION PROJECT GAMES

The analysis in this part of the chapter is based on the experience gained during the implementation of the international project entitled Virtual Game Method in Higher Education (GAMES), project number 2014-1-PL01-KA203-003548, funded by ERASMUS+ programme, in the years 2014–2016 (Wach-Kąkolewicz & Muffoletto, 2016), which was the continuation of an earlier project within the framework of Leonardo da Vinci programme (Gaweł & Pietrzykowski, 2014).

Owing to the implementation of international projects, a team of academics from the Poznań University of Economics and Business drew up, tested, and introduced virtual strategic simulations. The outcome of the first project was the company that made and sold chocolate in selected European markets. Within the framework of the second project, which involved the simulation of a service company, four game scenarios (developed by project partners), based on the same game engine, were created: a fitness club (Poland), a car wash (Estonia), a coffee shop (Spain) and a social and health service (Finland).

The aim of the simulation is to run a company and manage it to maximise the economic profit in the end. At the beginning, students receive some capital and run virtual enterprises in teams consisting of a few members, competing in a game made up of 10 decision rounds. They make decisions related to different areas of business activity, such as research and development, marketing, operations, human resource management, and finances. In a single game, there are usually five virtual student enterprises competing against one another. The players have access to the simulation and their player panel online, though which they can make decisions at any time and place. When running a virtual company, they assume different roles, e.g. the CEO or the director of finance or marketing, dividing their duties; although it is also possible for a single player to play all these roles. Decisions made in a round affect the results obtained by the opponents as well as the business conditions in the following round. The simulation of a service company (a manufacturing company in the previous project) is a management game in which students assume the role of managers and have to solve a number of general problems related to managing an enterprise, such as decisions connected with selling and marketing services, human resource management, and finance. After each round, the participants receive information on their financial results, which allow them to continue or redefine the previous strategy (Gaweł, 2014).

In classes taught with the application of GAMES simulation, the student-centred approach, based on constructivist assumptions, was used and Kolb's cycle became the framework for designing teaching (Gaweł & Wach-Kąkolewicz, 2016). In its first phase (concrete experience), students first learn how to play the game and discover its various components, and, more importantly, they face the task of establishing a virtual enterprise and discuss the possible directions of its activity. Having adopted the role of managers, referring to their prior knowledge and experience, they carry out an analysis of the market and formulate the corporate strategy in order to make decisions. These are then entered into the respective decision areas in the player panel. The teacher acts as the facilitator, guiding students by asking questions that stimulate their decision-making process. In this way, cognitive processes are initiated through making references to learners' prior knowledge. Based on their conjectures, students formulate hypotheses connected with the functioning of their enterprise. They naturally enter social interaction, exchanging knowledge, negotiating the meaning of concepts, providing arguments for their ideas, and in the end, coming up with the final decision. The information on their financial results (after the first game round has been completed) allows students to move to the next phase of Kolb cycle, i.e. reflective observation. The economic outcome is an indicator and very important feedback for students. Depending on the result, they either pursue the same corporate strategy or they redefine it and undertake other action. Reflection is a significant element of the learning process: at this stage, students often diagnose the mistakes they have made (e.g. related to the sale of services, recruitment or motivating staff) and analyse the steps they have taken so far. They usually discuss these issues among themselves, pose further hypotheses, and ask the teacher questions, who, however, does not provide ready-made solutions, but guides students to reach conclusions. They may discuss problems face-to-face or online, e.g., through discussion forums. Blogs are interesting tool supporting the process of reflection, analysis and synthesis. Students may run these individually or in a group; documenting their decision-making processes. The application of discussion or other methods and techniques which stimulate reflection is important, because somewhat intuitive efforts are then replaced by more rational action, based on theoretical principles and theories, developed in the third phase of Kolb cycle. At the stage of abstract conceptualisation, students, with the teacher's help, work out ground rules for the strategic management of their enterprise. They actively reconstruct their knowledge, broaden and expand cognitive schemes and structures in order to apply their newly acquired knowledge in practice, implement new solutions, and develop their managerial skills in this way. The experience of new problem situations in the following rounds returns students to the first phase of Kolb cycle, which may be repeated each time new issues connected with running a virtual company and requiring specific managerial qualities arise (Gaweł & Wach-Kąkolewicz, 2016).

The process of entering the successive stages of Kolb cycle may be viewed from the perspective of the whole game rather than from the viewpoint of individual decision rounds. The first stage of concrete action involves gathering experience throughout the entire game. After it has been completed, the stage of reflective observation begins—students analyse the performance of their virtual enterprise throughout the game. The phase of abstract conceptualisation allows them to draw conclusions concerning the proper sequence of decisions and adopted and implemented strategies. At the last stage, active experimentation, students are asked to define actions that would help them to be more successful in the game, what their strengths and weaknesses were, what they found to be a success and what could be adjusted (Gaweł & Wach-Kąkolewicz, 2016).

RESEARCH METHODOLOGY

As a result of the GAMES project, four game scenarios were created. They were based on the same assumptions and the same game engine, but their subjects were different. The games were tested by project teams and were used in classes with students. After the classes, students assessed the games by filling in an electronic survey. Some of the items in the questionnaire required them to use a five-grade Likert scale: from 'I totally agree' to 'I totally disagree'. The evaluation of the game referred to the content-related value of the simulation (aspects of strategic management), the attractiveness of the game itself (the scenario and other engagement factors), learning by playing the game, and competences (those necessary to participate in the simulation and those developed thanks to the game). The respondents also identified their personality traits and other individual characteristics (including the type of player and the level of interest in and use of information technologies in their life). The survey was completed by 118 students from different fields (mostly business students) who participated in the simulation classes. Business orientation and entrepreneurship behaviour are promoted in classes with students from beyond the areas of economics and management, therefore some students from outside those disciples were included as participants in the business scenario game project. The survey was conducted in the spring of 2016 at the Poznań University of Economics and Business, the University of Huelva, the Seinäjoki University of Applied Sciences and the University of Tartu, Pärnu College.

RESULTS AND DISCUSSION

The general research report, emphasising selected elements, was presented by Öun et al. (2016). Bearing in mind the aim of this chapter, only the aspects which evaluate learning with the application of the GAMES project will be discussed here. The goal of this section of the research was to diagnose whether virtual game-based learning was evaluated as being constructivist. Basic data concerning the nationality, age, gender, and field of study are presented in Table 2.

Table 2. Respondents by nationality, age, gender and field of study

		Frequency	Percent
Nationality	Spanish (ESP)	16	13.6
	Estonian (EST)	33	28.0
	Finnish (FIN)	38	32.2
	Polish (PL)	31	26.3
Age	under 18 years	6	5
	18–23 years	82	69.5
	24–34 years	24	20.3
	35+ years	6	5.1
Gender	Female	96	81.4
	Male	22	18.6
Field of study	Business and Administration	26	22.0
	Social Work	40	33.9
	Tourism Studies	14	11.9
	Project Management	7	5.9
	International Business	31	26.3
Previously played a similar virtual game	No	70	59.3
	Yes	48	40.7

Source: Öun, Mägi and Noppel (2016, p. 92).

Students from Finland represented the largest percentage of respondents (32.2%). They were followed by students from Estonia (28%), Poland (26.3%) and Spain (13.6%). Most students surveyed were between the ages of 18–23 (69.5%) and women were the overwhelming majority (81.4%). They studied different majors: International Business (26.3%), Business and Administration (22%) and Project Management (5.9%). The remaining respondents studied non-business fields, such as Social Work (33.9%) and Tourism (11.9%), within the framework of which entrepreneurial competences and business orientation are also developed. What is particularly important as far as the detailed results of the survey are concerned, is the fact that while just over 40% of the students polled had already played a similar game before, but for almost 60% of the respondents it was the first time they had taken part in a simulation.

The research tool included indicator statements, describing the assumptions of constructivist learning, which students evaluated with regard to the simulation. To this end, a Likert scale was used. Students could choose from one answer from an option of five: totally disagree (1), disagree (2), neither agree, nor disagree (3), agree (4), and totally agree (5). Table 3 presents average evaluations of all statements with standard deviation (SD); Table 4 shows the percentage distribution for each of the possible answers; and Figure 1 presents aggregated data in three groups: (1) totally agree and agree, (2) neither agree nor disagree (3) totally disagree and disagree.

Students found learning with the use of simulations to be useful. They particularly evaluated the aspects of constructivist learning quite highly, which is reflected in the range of values from 3.36 to 3.66. The statement 'Collaborative

Table 3. Learning with the use of simulation (average values and SD)

The characteristics of constructivist learning	Average values	SD
Learners construct their knowledge in an active way	3.64	1.13
Learners use their previous knowledge in building new knowledge	3.49	1.16
Authentic tasks in a meaningful context are encouraged	3.34	1.12
Reflection on prior knowledge and the task is encouraged	3.44	1.11
Collaborative work is encouraged	3.66	1.19
Learners experience new situations and explore them in finding the right solutions	3.65	1.14
Learners get the feedback on their activity	3.37	1.21

work is encouraged' got the highest score (3.66). In this case, 58.48% of the students admitted that the game requires interaction, dialogue, and an attempt to understand different viewpoints in the decision-making process; thus, it gets learners involved in co-operation. The following statements were evaluated almost as highly: 'Learners experience new situations and explore them in finding the right solutions' (3.65) and 'Learners construct their knowledge in an active way' (3.64). According to the assumptions of constructivism, learning consists of seeking solutions to a new problem, thus active learning takes place when a learner has an opportunity to explore a new environment, becoming involved at the cognitive, emotional and behavioural level. The results show that as many as 61.86% of the students recognised the issue they had explored in the game as a new problem for them and that it made them look for appropriate solutions. At the same time, 56.78% felt that simulation encourages active learning, which helps to reconstruct prior knowledge (Table 3 and Figure 1). It must be pointed out, however, that these aspects of learning were negatively assessed by about 25% of the students (Table 3 and Figure 1).

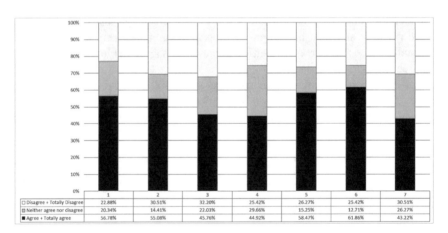

Figure 1. Learning with the use of simulation

The following statements ranked lowest: 'Authentic tasks in a meaningful context are encouraged' (3.34) and 'Learners get the feedback on their activity' (3.37). The first assumes that the learning is of situational nature and initiates problem-solving in a well-known and real context. The results show that although 32.2% of the players did not agree with this statement, 45.66% of them acknowledged that simulation imitates the (business) reality and provides students with tasks which are not separated from the real context. Although 43.22% of the players admitted that simulation-based learning gives them information on the progress they have made so far, 30.51% of the students pointed out that there was no feedback (Figure 1 and

Table 3). In this respect, it is the teacher's role to situate the game in the economic context and make it applicable. He/she should also offer support (e.g. through comments or by asking questions) in order to receive feedback on the business strategy used by students.

Table 4. Learning with the use of simulation (values in %)

	Characteristics of constructivist learning	Totally agree	Agree	Neither agree, nor disagree	Disagree	Totally disagree
1.	Learners construct their knowledge in an active way	29.66	27.12	20.34	22.88	0.00
2.	Learners use their previous knowledge in building new knowledge	24.58	30.51	14.41	30.51	0.00
3.	Authentic tasks in a meaningful context are encouraged	20.34	25.42	22.03	32.20	0.00
4.	Reflection on prior knowledge and the task is encouraged	24.58	20.34	29.66	25.42	0.00
5.	Collaboration work is encouraged	33.90	24.58	15.25	26.27	0.00
6.	Learners experience new situations and explore them in finding the right solutions	28.81	33.05	12.71	25.42	0.00
7.	Learners get the feedback on their activity	27.12	16.10	26.27	27.97	2.54

The statements with quite similar meaning—both referring to prior knowledge—obtained scores in the medium range. They were: 'Learners use their previous knowledge in building new knowledge' (3.49) and 'Reflection on prior knowledge and the task is encouraged (3.44). The importance of the use of previous competence and experience in the running of a virtual enterprise was emphasised by 55.08% of the learners, while 30.51% of respondents were of a different opinion in this respect. According to 44.92% of students, simulation-based learning encourages reflection in one's actions and on these actions, although 25.42% of the learners denied this statement. Reflection is an important stage in constructivist learning but can only be initiated when students work on their tasks and it requires teachers who support learners in this regard.

When drawing conclusions from the obtained research results, we should look at them in a universal way, treating statements as the indicators of the general variable of constructivist learning. The analysis of the results shows that more than half of the students surveyed believe that the game meets the assumptions of the constructism paradigm (52.29%). This group includes those students who have never played a game like this before. They highly valued simulation-based learning. The differences in the frequency of answers are statistically significant for all analysed statements (Table 5). For this group of students, electronic simulation appeared to be a very attractive learning method.

Table 5. Learning with the use of simulation (test chi2 results)

Characteristics of constructivist learning	chi2	df	p
Learners construct their knowledge in an active way	31.59	3	<0.001
Learners use their previous knowledge in building new knowledge	44.01	3	<0.001
Authentic tasks in a meaningful context are encouraged	37.34	3	<0.001
Reflection on prior knowledge and the task is encouraged	39.24	3	<0.001
Collaboration work is encouraged	30.56	3	<0.001
Learners experience new situations and explore them in finding the right solutions	39.25	3	<0.001
Learners get the feedback on their activity	23.17	4	<0.001

It is also worth mentioning that there was no statistically significant difference in received opinions in terms of gender, nationality or field of study.

Returning to the componential theory of creativity (Amabile, 1983), some of the survey questions may be used as proxy elements for the intra-individual and external components. Statement 2 may act as a proxy for domain-relevant skills, while statement 1 and 6 are particularly applicable to creative-relevant skills, with the highest agree and totally agree percentages among the replies. Finally, statement 3 ensures motivation for the task. As a group-based activity, statement 5 is indicative of the external component. Most of these statements received agree and totally agree replies from more than 50% of the participants (Table 6). The lowest percentage is achieved by statement 3—clearly signifying that the simulation has to be placed in the context of individual experiences and relevant business similarities should be highlighted. These results, however, support the existence of the creativity components during the simulation.

The evaluation of learning through the application GAMES project's business simulation may have been affected by a number of intervening variables, which were not taken into account in the study. One the most important determinants of the assessment of learning (as well as indirectly the evaluation of classes) is the teacher, and his/her professional competence, which was emphasised above. It should be

Table 6. Creativity in constructivist learning in business simulations

The componential theory of creativity	Characteristics of constructivist learning	Agree and totally agree (values in %)
The intra-individual components		
Domain-relevant skills	Learners use their previous knowledge in building new knowledge (2)	55.08
Creative-relevant skills	Learners construct their knowledge in an active way (1)	56.78
	Learners experience new situations and explore them in finding the right solutions (6)	61.86
Task motivation	Authentic tasks in a meaningful context are encouraged (3)	45.76
The external component		
Social environment	Collaboration work is encouraged (5)	58.47

noted that students took part in classes where the same game was used (although it was based on different scenarios), but that there were four different teachers. For most of the teachers them, it was the first class that was taught with the application of the electronic simulation method; despite teacher training offered within the framework of the project, the methodology applied to teach classes could have had an impact on the ultimate opinion on game-based learning. For many students, the simulation was just a one-off activity, during which not all assumptions of constructivist learning could be met. When games last throughout the term, the learning process is designed more thoroughly. There is more time for reflection, discussion and feedback from the teacher and other students.

CONCLUSION

This chapter focuses on and leads the reader through three kinds of an analysis: starting from theoretical assumptions, moving to practical issues, and finishing up with research results discussions. The presented theoretical assumptions of teaching students and the resulting guidelines for teachers—which concern the designing of classes—are a point of departure and explain why modern education should be based on the student-centred approach. These guidelines help teachers to understand the rationale for interactive and problem-solving learning and teaching, especially in business education, which is based not only on the knowledge of theory and rules governing economic mechanisms, but also on the skill of using them in practice. This is what activating educational strategies are used for. They immerse the student in the business reality, thus helping him or her better prepare for the labour market.

Business simulations, which have been made the core concept of this work, have huge educational potential and have become an inherent part (as a teaching strategy) of the constructivist learning paradigm, encapsulating creativity components.

As a practical example of the application of simulation in students' education, we presented virtual management simulations developed within the framework of the GAMES project. In this section of the chapter, I discussed what this specific simulation is, what its essence is and what the most important game rules are. At the same time, I wanted to show how the game may be located in Kolb's constructivist cycle, identifying the role of the teacher and students during classes. Thus, I tried to illustrate the theoretical assumptions, formulating teaching guidelines which are useful for designing and conducting classes. These may be a source of knowledge and inspiration for many teachers, in addition to being a good example of translating theoretical premises of the student-centred approach into practical activities undertaken with students.

The last part of the chapter includes the results and analysis of the study, representing a closure of the theoretical-practical-research character of the chapter. The conclusions drawn show that the presented simulation is an interesting educational tool, which was quite highly evaluated by students, especially those who have played a game of this type for the first time. The students under survey confirmed most statements constituting the constructivist assumptions with reference to simulation-based learning. Neutral and negative results show, however, that there may be some areas of the game and classes based on it that require improvement. They stimulate the reflection on the graphic and technological aspect of the game itself, its logic, and, almost importantly, the way of teaching classes with the application of simulations. They constitute a valuable source of information not only for the creators of the game, but also for the teachers who wish to conduct classes based on virtual business simulations in modern creative university.

REFERENCES

Abdullah, N. L., Hanafiah, M. H., & Hashim, N. A. (2013). Developing creative teaching module: Business simulation in teaching strategic management. *International Education Studies, 6*(6), 95–107.

Amabile, T. M. (1983). Personality process and individual differences. The social psychology of creativity: A componential conceptualization. *Journal of Personality and Social Psychology, 45*(2), 357–376.

Amabile, T. M., & Pillemer, J. (2012). Perspectives on the social psychology of creativity. *Journal of Creative Behaviour, 46*, 3–15.

Ammerman, P., Gaweł, A., Pietrzykowski, M., Rauktienė, R., & Williamson, T. (Eds.). (2012). *The case study method in business education*. Poznań: Bogucki Wydawnictwo Naukowe.

Aram, E., & Noble, D. (1999). Educating prospective managers in the complexity of organizational life. *Management Learning, 30*(3), 321–342.

Balan, P., & Metcalfe, M. (2012). Identifying teaching methods that engage entrepreneurship students. *Education and Training, 54*(5), 368–384.

Barr, R., & Tagg, J. (1995). From teaching to learning: A new paradigm for undergraduate education. *Change, 27*(6), 12–25.

Ben-Zvi, T., & Carton, T. C. (2007). From rhetoric to reality: Business games as educational tools. *INFORMS Transactions on Education, 8*(1), 10–18.

Biggs, J. (1987). *Student approaches to learning and studying.* Melbourne: Australian Council for Educational Research.
Biggs, J., & Tang, C. (2007). *Teaching for quality learning at university.* Berkshire: Open University Press.
Buttler, D., & Ławrynowicz, M. (2012). Porównanie pożądanych kompetencji absolwentów w opiniach studentów i absolwentów [A comparison of the desired competences of graduates in the opinions of students and graduates]. In A. Andrzejczak (Ed.), *Dylematy i wyzwania kształcenia ekonomistów w szkołach wyższych* (Vol. 240, pp. 52–62).
Clarke, E. (2009). Learning outcomes from business simulation exercises: Challenges for the implementation of learning technologies. *Education and Training, 51*(5), 448–459.
Entwistle, N. J., & Ramsden, P. (1983). *Understanding student learning.* London: Croom Helm.
Fink, D. (2008). Evaluating teaching: A new approach to an old problem. *To Improve the Academy: Resources for Faculty, Instructional, and Organizational Development, 26,* 3–21.
Fosnot, C. T. (Ed.). (2005). *Constructivism: Theory, perspectives, and practice.* New York, NY: Teachers College Press.
Fosnot, C. T., & Perry, R. S. (2005). Constructivism: A psychological theory of learning. In C. T. Fosnot (Ed.), *Constructivism: Theory, perspectives, and practice* (pp. 8–38). New York, NY & London: Teachers College Press, Columbia University.
Garris, R., Ahlers, R., & Driskell, J. E. (2002). Games, motivation and learning: A research and practice model. *Simulation & Gaming: An Interdisciplinary Journal, 33*(4), 441–467.
Gaweł, A. (2014). Gry strategiczne w edukacji przedsiębiorczej [Strategic games in entrepreneurial education]. *Horyzonty Wychowania, 13*(26), 303–325.
Gaweł, A. (2014a). Strategic management games from the perspective of a business trainer. In A. Gaweł & M. Pietrzykowski (Eds.), *The strategic management: Virtual game method in business education* (pp. 77–93). Warszawa: Wydawnictwo IUSatTAX.
Gaweł, A., & Pietrzykowski, M. (Eds.). *The strategic management: Virtual game method in business education.* Warszawa: Wydawnictwo IUSatTAX.
Gaweł, A., & Wach-Kąkolewicz, A. (2016). Konstruktywizm edukacyjny w nauczaniu przedsiębiorczości metodą gier elektronicznych [Constructivism in teaching entrepreneurship with the use of virtual games]. *Horyzonty Wychowania, 15*(34), 87–102.
Heinonen, J., & Poikkijoki, S. A. (2006). An entrepreneurial-directed approach to entrepreneurship education: Mission impossible? *Journal of Management Development, 25*(1), 80–94.
Kąkolewicz, M. (2011). *Uczenie się jako konstruowanie wiedzy. Świadomość, qualia i technologie informacyjne* [Learning as knowledge constructing. Consciousness, qualia and information technologies]. Poznań: Wydawnictwo Naukowe UAM.
Ketteridge, S., & Marshall, S. (Eds.). *A handbook for teaching and learning in higher education.* London: Routledge.
Kolb, D. A. (1984). *Experiential learning: Experience as the source of learning and development.* Englewood Cliffs, NJ: Prentice-Hall.
Kolb, D. A., Boyatzis, R. E., & Mainemelis, C. (2001). Experiential learning theory: previous research and new directions. In R. J. Sternberg & L.-F. Zhang (Eds.), *Perspectives on thinking, learning, and cognitive styles* (pp. 227–247). Mahwah, NJ: Lawrence Erlbaum Associates.
Kolodner, J. L., Gray, J., & Fasse, B. B. (2003). Promoting transfer through case-based reasoning: Rituals and practices in learning by design classrooms. *Cognitive Science Quarterly, 3*(2), 183–232.
Kozbelt, A., Beghetto, R. A., & Runco, M. A. (2010). Theories of creativity. In J. C. Kaufman & R. J. Sternberg (Eds.), *The Cambridge handbook of creativity* (pp. 20–47). Cambridge: Cambridge University Press.
Lainema, T., & Makkonen, P. (2003). Applying constructivist approach to educational business games: Case REALGAME. *Simulation & Gaming: An Interdisciplinary Journal, 34*(1), 131–149.
Lean, J., Moizer, J., Towler, M., & Abbey, C. (2006). Simulations and games. *Active Learning in Higher Education, 7*(3), 227–242.
Lublin, J. (2003). *Deep, surface and strategic approaches to learning.* Belfield: Centre for Teaching and Learning, University College Dublin.
Martin, A. (2000). The design and evolution of a simulation/game for teaching information systems development. *Simulation & Gaming: An Interdisciplinary Journal, 31*(4), 445–463.

Marton, F. (1975). On non-verbatim learning—1: Level of processing and level of outcome. *Scandinavian Journal of Psychology, 16*, 273–279.

Masek, A., & Yamin, S. (2010). *Fostering creativity from constructivist perspectives: A literature review*. Proceedings of the 3rd Regional Conference on Engineering Education & Research in Higher Education, Kuching, Sarawak: School of Professional and Continuing Education (UTMspace), University of Technology, Johor Bahru, Malaysia.

Michoń, P., & Ławrynowicz, M. (2009). *Trzy światy. Badanie rynku pracy w Wielkopolsce* [Three worlds. A study of the labour market in Wielkopolska]. Poznań: Wydawnictwo. Edustacja.pl Sp. z o.o.

Mitchell, R. C. (2004). Combining cases and computer simulations in strategic management courses. *Journal of Education for Business, 79*(4), 198–204.

Öun, K., Mägi, M., & Noppel, A. (2016). Learning business through simulation games. Survey among students who played developed games. In A. Wach-Kąkolewicz & R. Muffoletto (Eds.), *Perspectives on computer gaming in higher education*. Poznań: Bogucki Wydawnictwo Naukowe.

Pritchard, A. (2009). *Ways of learning: Learning theories and learning styles in the classroom*. Abingdon: Routledge.

Prosser, M., & Trigwell, K. (2014). Qualitative variation in approaches to university teaching and learning in large first-year classes. *Higher Education, 67*, 783–795.

Ramsden, P. (1988). *Improving learning: New perspectives*. London: Kogan Page.

Ramsden, P. (1992). *Learning to teach in higher education*. London: Routledge.

Reiners, T., Wood, L. C., Gregory, S., & Teräs, H. (2015). Gamification design elements in business education simulations. In M. Khosrow-Pour (Ed.), *Encyclopedia of information science and technology* (pp. 3048–3068). Hershey, PA: Information Science Reference.

Sajdak, A. (2013). *Paradygmaty kształcenia studentów i wspierania rozwoju nauczycieli akademickich. Teoretyczne podstawy dydaktyki akademickiej* [Paradigms of students' learning and supporting academics' development. Theory of teaching and learning in higher education]. Kraków: Wydawnictwo Impuls.

Smith, K., & Beasley, M. (2011). Graduate entrepreneurs: Intentions, barriers and solutions. *Education and Training, 53*(8), 722–740.

Tan, S. S., & Ng, C. K. F. (2006). A problem-based learning approach to entrepreneurship education. *Education and Training, 48*(6), 416–428.

Trigwell, K., & Prosser, M. (2004). Development and use of the approaches to teaching inventory. *Educational Psychology Review, 16*(4), 409–424.

Trigwell, K., Prosser, M., & Ginns, P. (2005). Phenomenographic pedagogy and a revised approaches to teaching inventory. *Higher Education Research & Development, 24*(4), 349–360.

Trigwell, K., Prosser, M., & Waterhouse, F. (1997). Relations between teachers' approaches to teaching and students' approaches to learning. *Higher Education, 37*(1), 57–70.

Vörös, T., & Köles, B. (2011). *Management education in a globalizing world: The use of simulations* (pp. 256–261). Proceedings of The 2nd International Conference on Society and Information Technologies (ICSIT), Orlando, FL.

Wach-Kąkolewicz, A. (2016). Constructivist approach in teaching in higher education. In A. Wach-Kąkolewicz & R. Muffoletto (Eds.), *Perspectives on computer gaming in higher education* (pp. 11–20). Poznań: Bogucki Wydawnictwo Naukowe.

Wach-Kąkolewicz, A., & Muffoletto, R. (Eds.). (2016). *Perspectives on computer gaming in higher education*. Poznań: Bogucki Wydawnictwo Naukowe.

Anna Wach
Department of Education and Personnel Development
Poznań University of Economics and Business
Poznań, Poland

JOAKIM JUHL AND ANDERS BUCH

7. THE ROLE OF EDUCATION IN ACADEMIC ECOSYSTEMS

INTRODUCTION

The social purpose of universities and academic work has been subject to multiple interpretations (Bush 1945; Gibbons et al., 1994; Nowotny, Scott, & Gibbons, 2001), most of which focus on the production of knowledge and, more recently, on its commodification (Etzkowitz & Leydesdorff, 2000). By presenting a means for sustained governmental funding, the introduction of mass higher education is typically associated with the massive expansion of scientific research. Despite their intrinsic ties, higher education and scientific research are also often seen as 'uneasy bedfellows' because they compete for the same institutional resources (Nowotny et al., 2001). In this view, education presents a risk of hampering universities' widely perceived core obligation to generate and commercialise research. While the strong focus on knowledge production emphasises the role of research activity, it also contributes to a marginalised conception of the role of education as being just a derivative reproductive mechanism determined by research activities.

In this chapter, we wish to add nuance to the ways in which we understand the dynamics of the *academic ecosystem* and its (de)stabilising institutional mechanisms within the university. In line with the scope of expanding the widely perceived meaning and value of academic practice, we preliminarily define the 'academic ecosystem' in the broadest possible way, including *both* research and educational practices, in order to avoid prejudiced conceptions that risk unwarranted demarcation and delimitation. Instead, by outlining the development of the Design & Innovation program (D&I) as an example, we wish to illustrate how education poses the potential to affect academic institutions' direction of research, and thereby come to play a significant role in determining the developments within academic ecosystems. In conclusion we draw attention to research approaches that potentially can investigate the academic ecosystem further.

In 2002, the Technical University of Denmark (DTU) launched the D&I engineering program. The innovative program introduced anthropological field studies and creative synthesis methods to the otherwise tradition-bound Danish flagship for engineering research and education. DTU typically emphasised mathematics and physics as foundational for their shaping of engineers and gave these disciplines primacy as content of the basic courses that introduced students to engineering through the important 1st year. D&I took a different approach and

© KONINKLIJKE BRILL NV, LEIDEN, 2019 | DOI:10.1163/9789004384149_007 focused on studying the problems to be solved—before deploying technical tools to design the solutions. Instead of modelling its structure on academic disciplines, and introduce problems as they manifested from within these, D&I introduced problem-based learning (PBL) to DTU. With its curricular content organised around practical problems, the D&I program presented an alternative to conventional mono-disciplinary engineering education.

Since the D&I program did not follow the conventional hierarchy and model of any particular scientific discipline, the program's development and implementation pose the question of how we can conceptualise relationships between scientific research, academic disciplines, and higher education. If D&I did not emerge primarily from within the intellectual landscape of scientific disciplines, then how can we account for its origin and how can we conceptualise the program's implications for the role of education in the academic ecosystem?

The argumentation of the chapter first contextualises some of the main historical events that characterise how science and academic institutions have been seen as valuable to society. Following this we introduce the Danish sociopolitical context around DTU within which the D&I was developed. This leads to the analysis of D&I's curricular composition and how it sat against DTU's educational traditions and institutional setup. We conclude the chapter with a discussion of the implications of seeing the academic ecosystem as 'ecologies of practices'.

SCIENCE AND SOCIETY

This chapter draws inspiration from Sheila Jasanoff's (2004) notion of co-production that assumes society, as we know it, to be a product of its knowledge production and dissemination processes, which, likewise, are inseparable from the society they aid in the creation of. Jasanoff's co-production provides us with an initial interpretative framework for thinking about how societies' knowledge processes are normatively linked up in 'academic ecosystems'. Co-production has proven to be productive for understanding reciprocal relations between societal and scientific transformations (Jasanoff, 2015). Yet the framework has not previously been utilised to understand the specific role of education within academic ecosystems. Although co-production can link to, and situate, microsociological observations, the framework is mainly developed on basis of macro-level analyses of societal and scientific transformation. In order to better understand the role of education within academic work practices, we therefore draw additional inspiration from practice theory.

Kemmis et al. (2014) have suggested that transformations in education should be studied by focusing on the mundane educational practices as they unfold on a day-by-day basis. In this perspective, the 'academic ecosystem' can be studied as an 'ecology of practices'. In this view, the academic ecosystem is constituted by a multitude of practices (e.g. teaching practices, leadership practices, administrative practices, student practices, research practices) that are situated and interwoven in complex ways. By focusing on the concrete 'doings' and 'sayings' and 'relatings' of actors in their sociomaterial contexts in university settings, we can attain a clearer view of how scientific research and education are reproduced and/or transformed. The practice theoretical perspective thereby adds to our analyses of higher education by enabling us to draw a more finely grained picture of its heterogeneous practices, and how these are co-produced with the contemporary society in which they take place. More specifically, this combination of perspectives aids our understanding of how variously situated educational practices relate to research practices in the academic ecosystem.

For the purpose of this chapter, we use co-production and practice theory as resources for reflecting on how academic science and higher education have been and are conditioned by particular sets of ideas and rationales about what science is, and how concrete research and educational practices shape academic ecosystems. In conclusion, we reflect upon the notion of 'academic ecosystem' to evaluate its merits and problems. In the following, we will briefly examine the historical highlights since World War II that mark the development of shared visions of the place of academia in society.

Basic Science in Post-War America

The great focus on science and technology as the engines for economic progress came as a consequence of the efforts in military controlled research and development during World War II. Post WWII, the definition of social purpose for science and technology came to be integral to the mission to secure progress, wealth, and prosperity. Technology, the fruits of scientific breakthroughs, would, due to market-mechanisms, be harnessed into new products and services which were seen as raising the living standard across all levels of society. Policy innovation, successfully promoted by the distinguished MIT engineer and wartime hero Vannevar Bush, and other collaborators of the famous 1945 report: *Science—The Endless Frontier*, was to continue public funding of science for the peaceful purposes of fostering technological innovation, economic growth, health, and prosperity.

> New products, new industries, and more jobs require continuous additions to knowledge of the laws of nature […] This essential, new knowledge can be obtained only through basic scientific research. (Bush 1945, p. 1)

> The Government should accept new responsibilities for promoting the flow of new scientific knowledge and development of scientific talent. (Bush 1945, chapter 6, p. 1)

The result, that many have since called 'the social contract' (Jasanoff, 2011), entailed that the government would provide the necessary funding and agenda setting terms for science and, in return, the nation would receive a steady flow of technological inventions and technically trained personnel through the elite educational system that was set up around world-leading research. In contrast to the wartime efforts, the new funding regime promoted this research on scientists' own conditions and left its practical application to private industry.

While the social contract of the American post-war era resonated with prominent visionaries' depictions of science as being conducted by morally 'disinterested' individuals for 'communalist' purposes (Merton, 1942) within a self-governing 'republic of science' (Polanyi, 1962), unsatisfied expectations of returns within society slowly eroded the patience of the model's political supporters. As a consequence of the great expenditures of pursuing science's 'endless frontiers', new policies formed through the late 1970s and culminated in the 1980 Bayh-Dole Act that authorised federal grantees to patent results derived from public money.

Where the post-war attitude towards science heralded it for its conquests and portrayed its leaders as the heroes who held the key to the future, the 1980 Bayh-Dole Act represented a stark shift in the widely held 'sociotechnical imaginary' (Kim & Jasanoff, 2009) that underwrote science's perceived social purpose. Defined as 'collectively held, institutionally stabilised, and publicly performed visions of desirable futures, animated by shared understandings of forms of social life and social order attainable through, and supportive of, advances in science and technology' (Jasanoff, 2015, p. 4), the sociotechnical imaginary turned from seeing science as a social resource that was best nurtured through political insulation to instead seeing science as an unrealised potential, the social accountability of which depended on its economic impact. The later vision spoke not about training scientific talent, but of promoting successful business entrepreneurs.

Danish Post-War Academia

On the other side of the Atlantic, similar expectations of science emerged after World War II. In post-war Denmark the expectations were expressed on grounds that centred on practical application and value in the reconstruction of Danish society. In 1940 plans had already been drafted for the technical-scientific research council (TVF), but the war postponed its realisation to 1946. The new council attained resources from Denmark's national budget for 'concrete research tasks' and managed Marshall-funding, as well as other international funds, for 'technical-scientific objectives' (Forskningsministeriet, 2013). Through the 1950s Danish public planning focused on expanding the industrial sector, which meant that technical fields of research were given priority in order to reinforce the transition from agriculture to industry with technically trained labour.

But the government's investments in techno-scientific research did not suffice in the public eye. On February 2nd, 1951, approximately 10,000 students, professors, and high-level administrators from the majority of Danish colleges joined together in front of the government building in a mutual demand for better conditions for higher education and research. Existing student scholarships and research grants from the private Carlsberg foundation had become increasingly insufficient, and students and academics requested better governmental support. The public request resonated with the emergence of a new sphere for science policy, which in 1952 resulted in the founding of the state science fund (SAF) and the youth educational fund (UU).

The youth educational fund offered economic aid to all Danes over the age of 18 who undertook education and was the predecessor of the current Danish SU-system, which was first formally established in 1970. The mission remained unchanged over the years: to compensate for social inequality by ensuring that 'no skilful students would have to abandon higher education on the basis of absent economic possibilities' (Syrelsen for Videregående Uddannelser, 2017). The youth educational fund marked the emergence of a widely held rationale and position within Danish political culture that regarded the promotion of social equality to be of primary importance.

Famously expressed at the 1960 election by the social democrat Viggo Kampmann, who won the election, the political climate of the late '50s and early '60s Denmark was characterised by an economic upturn and a growing public desire for social welfare:

> Now it goes up. The automatic increase in income means that taxes are flowing in. We know to seize this historical chance. These funds should not be paid back as tax cuts but [should] be used to get the population the goods that the majority desires. We want to build universities and colleges. We want to build social institutions. We want to support art and culture. We want to increase the standard within all areas. (Gaardmand, 1993, p. 72)

The establishment of SAF and UU initiated the integration of universities within the Danish public sector. Although their initial funding was extremely modest, their founding marks an important milestone in the Danish articulation of social purpose for science. Universities became directly dependent on, and accountable to, the Danish government and the political climate in which it operated. Universities' student recruitment became an extension of the state's social responsibilities and was obligated to encompass additional social layers in order to combat 'social heritage' through wider dissemination of higher education. As part of the public sector, scientific research had to justify itself by benefitting the majority of the Danish population.

The increased inrush of a more diverse student population enlarged and empowered Danish universities but also lead to a confrontation between the new student generation's expectation of influence and the traditional norms and academic hierarchy in which only professors had influence. In May 1968, the great youth rebellion occupied Copenhagen University as a culmination of increased public pressure to change the Danish university system. Formal responses later arrived in the shape of the 1970 and the 1973 statutes that implemented democratic decision-making principles, where students and non-academic staff each obtained 25% of the seats at universities' decision-making bodies. In addition, the 'konsistorium', the longest living and highest-level decision-making body at Danish universities, was opened up by supplementing its faculty members with students and non-academic staff. The new governance structure was later called the 'collegiate system'.

Mode-2 Science

In the early 1990s, analysts of scientific conduct in Europe observed a shift away from the Vannevar Bush era's university based and disciplinary 'Mode 1' knowledge production. The new tendency that Michael Gibbons et al. (1994) termed 'Mode 2' knowledge production took place within its context of application rather than at universities and entailed a mix of approaches rather than one mono-disciplinary methodology. As a consequence, 'Mode 2's authors noted that the assessment method by which science was evaluated had to be reconsidered in order to encounter a new and more interwoven fabric of science that besides intellectual merit had to address questions about the purpose of its research, the marketability of its results, and the social accountability of its enterprise. In other words, a science that would be answerable to society rather than detached from it, as proponents of Mode 1 (Merton, 1942; Bush, 1945; Polanyi, 1962) had suggested. In the view of its authors the new mode of knowledge production included the following characteristics:

- Knowledge is increasingly produced in contexts of application (that is, *all* science is to some extent 'applied' science),
- Science is increasingly transdisciplinary; that is, it draws on and integrates empirical and theoretical elements from a variety of fields,
- Knowledge is generated in a wider variety of sites than ever before, not just universities and industry, but also in research centrer, consultancies, and think tanks,
- Participants in science have grown more aware of the social implications and assumptions of their work (that is, they have become more 'reflexive', just as publics have grown more conscious of the ways in which science and technology affect their interests and values).

By turning its performance criteria toward impact in society, Mode 2 challenged traditional Mode 1 disciplinary demarcations by reorganising scientific knowledge production around non-academic domains of application. Maintaining its modus operandi around 'science' and the 'production site' of knowledge, later reflections on Mode 2 by several of its original authors touched upon Mode 2's effects on dynamics surrounding higher education within the academic ecosystem:

> More seriously, mass access [to higher education] and high-quality research have come to be driven by, and to address, different value systems. But this may partly be explained by the persistence of traditional—'Mode 1'— accounts of research. Within the context of 'Mode 2', these tensions are reduced, and new synergies are apparent between the democratization of higher education and the wider social distribution of knowledge production. (Nowotny et al., 2001)

While differences between the value system of mass higher education and that of traditional high quality 'basic' science had become a growing source of tension, Mode 2 reduced this tension because of its more mundane and 'applied' orientation. Although the value systems of Mode 2 and mass higher education appear more compatible, this does not tell us much about how the dynamics of the academic ecosystem operate under a Mode 2 informed governance paradigm. How, for instance, does a Mode 2 inspired education like the D&I program emerge within a tradition-bound, discipline-oriented technical university like DTU? What does the emergence of D&I tell us about the relationship between scientific research and higher education? In order to respond to these questions, in the following we will describe the sociopolitical context in which DTU found itself during the time of D&I's development. After that, we turn our analytic gaze to D&I's curricular composition and what it meant in context of the academic ecosystem in which it operated.

DTU AND DANISH ACADEMIA REFORMED

In the late 1990s, DTU, the Danish epicenter for technical research, faced severe economic problems and found itself entangled in a revitalised political game regarding the institution's future. Declining numbers of students and budgets that heralded returning rounds of severe cutbacks—and potential bankruptcy—threatened the once highly distinguished and politically sacred institution. In the late 1990s, DTU's Konsistorium was confronted with a difficult choice: either face severe cutbacks or accept a confidentially negotiated deal between the then DTU president, Hans Peter Jensen, and Minister for research, Birte Weiss. This deal would, in effect, turn the public institution into an autonomous organisation. DTU would undergo a reorganisation that replaced its top-down heirarach collegiate system with appointed leaders, a president, and an executive board with a majority of external members—predominantly appointed from the private sector. While the settlement resolved DTU's financial situation, it also meant the end of academics' self-governance.

Eventually, public universities and higher education were brought in line with Denmark's substantial New Public Management restructuration of its public sector that had continued throughout the 1990s. In 2001, the newly elected Liberal Party's message to Danish universities and their employees was clear: *From Research to Invoice* was the mantra through which the newly appointed Minister of Science, Technology and Development, Helge Sander, would transform the costly public universities into revenue generating cogwheels in the new public management era of public privatisation.

The first move was to instate the researchers' patent law in 2001, which enabled universities to patent publicly supported research. Later the same year came the DTU-law that in effect gave DTU's president almost complete autonomy and unrestricted authority to rule the institution. Amongst the reform's initiatives, the most controversial and publicly disputed aspect was regarding university's leadership. Not only was the democratic collegiate system with its elected leaders replaced with a new system of commissioned leaders, but the 'konsistorium', which had remained the highest-level decision-making body at Danish universities since the founding of Copenhagen University in 1479, was replaced in the reform's efforts to 'professionalise' Danish universities.

The follow-up came in 2003 with the publication 'Time for transformation of Denmark's universities' which carried the subtitle 'Strengthened leadership, increased freedom, stable economy' (Regeringen, 2002). This introduced the remaining Danish universities to the possibility of undergoing wide-ranging reorganisation similar to the implemented changes at DTU. The Minister of Science, Technology and Development announced the reform as being the most substantial transformation of the Danish scientific system since the opening of Copenhagen University. The reform's official objectives were to 'open up' the university system 'outwards to society' and improve universities' 'decision-making competence'.

The reforms marked a significant reconfiguration of Denmark's moral space for science. Inward-looking self-assessment by intellectual peers that valued integrity was replaced with professional administrations that strove for financial rewards that could secure the survival of their self-sustaining institutions. In effect, the new economic space in which academic institutions and their employees operated had become significantly more dependent on how the surrounding society perceived its value and utility. Research groups now found themselves in a radically new institutional setup where the basis for legitimacy was no longer obtained by electing leaders that would be sympathetic to their intellectual projects. Instead formal responsibilities towards educational programs and the ability to attract students, external grants, and industrial income became increasingly paramount to researchers' and teachers' professional survival.

The reforms turned Danish universities into economically autonomous institutions and exchanged universities' collegial self-governing system of employee-elected leaders with executive boards consisting primarily of external members from industry (Carney, 2006). The 'bibliometric research indicator'—a Danish ranking system for international journals—became a counting system for measuring, comparing, and distributing public funds between universities based on their publication scores (Jensen, 2011). Another example was the introduction of 'recruitment panels' consisting of industry leaders whose advice and interest became part of Danish higher education's recurring accreditation.

In line with Mode 2 thinking, the reformed economic space for Denmark's academic ecosystem had become significantly more dependent on its perceived value and utility to the surrounding society. In the face of declining student numbers, DTU's new autonomous status emphasised its necessity to generate income in order to live up to its function as an economically self-sustaining organisation. As we will describe in the following, there was a flipside to this tense economic situation in that it necessitated fundamental changes that would otherwise be difficult to sanction in the highly tradition-bound educational culture. New measures for attracting students gained renewed institutional legitimacy.

HIGHER EDUCATION AND THE ACADEMIC ECOSYSTEM: THE CASE OF D&I

Shortly after the DTU law was passed, a group of researchers and teachers commenced the development of an entirely new engineering program that introduced new curricular and pedagogical structure, and new inter-faculty collaboration. In 2002, roughly one year after the DTU law, the new D&I engineering program was launched. The program presented an objection against the ways in which engineering previously had been thought and taught at DTU.

> The curriculum represents a radical innovation in engineering curriculum. Not least as it includes new disciplines covering sociotechnical analysis and new approaches to design synthesis as well as integrates open ended project assignments in cooperation with companies and other actors in society. (Jorgensen et al., 2011, p. 1)

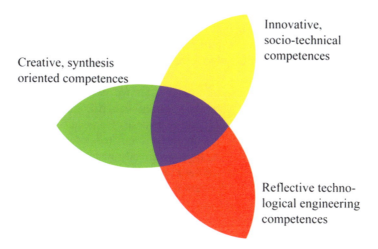

Figure 1. Multidisciplinary composition of the design & innovation curriculum (Jorgensen et al., 2011)

Including what the program's teachers saw as the necessary competences needed for engineers to practice design in professional settings, the above Venn diagram (Figure 1) illustrates the core structure of D&I's curricular composition. The composition is based on three equally important basic knowledge and skill components: 'reflective technological engineering competences' (dark grey), 'creative, synthesis oriented competence' (medium grey), and 'innovative sociotechnical competences' (light grey). This was described as 'the multidisciplinary approach to engineering applied in the design & innovation program at DTU giving equal importance to the social and the technical sciences' (Jorgensen et al., 2011, p. 11).

Besides the noteworthy introduction of creative content including sketching and decision-supporting synthesis methods, the inclusion of social scientific content primarily from Science and Technology Studies (STS) was perhaps the program's most contentious supplement to the distinguished and tradition-bound engineering institution. Making social science available to engineering students was not in itself controversial. However, making social science an accredited core part of the curriculum of an engineering program was a significant breakthrough for the institutionalisation of the research group responsible for D&I program. As a result, social scientific teaching and research acquired formal representation within DTU's activities and responsibilities.

Making Room for D&I

Rather than buying into the prevailing trend of large common courses that were delivered to hundreds of students from several engineering programs, D&I's mathematical and technical content was rethought from the ground up to fit its multi-disciplinary and collaborative vision. While generic courses enabled large lecture hall classes and thus 'effective' use of researchers' teaching obligations, the idea behind the D&I program was instead to scale down and focus on creating an intimate relationship between teachers and students. By means of a restricted cap on the size on student admission and the use of 'studios', known from design and architect schools, for lecturing and group work, the program was effectively sat up to ensure protection against generic engineering courses. Instead of large lecture halls in which a few teachers could cover course requirements of hundreds of students, the studio solutions ensured that resources would be more directly attached to the teachers who controlled the program. The composition of the Design & Innovation program thus represented a counter-move from the performing level against the centralisation of power within Danish higher education.

Despite D&I's deviation from the dominant scheme of standardised mathematical and technical courses, and its implications for centralised resource politics, the condition of DTU's student enrolment meant that radical means gained more tolerance than usual. While the DTU law paved the way for centralising power within the newly implemented one-string administration, the same political context was, paradoxically, also responsible for emphasising universities' dependence on their researchers' and teachers' capacity to invent new innovative curricular and teaching approaches that would improve upon income generating student admission numbers.

Making Identity by Reframing Engineering

An important motivation for the management of the university to provide the new education in D&I was the interest in attracting more and new types of students who presented better high school graduation scores, but who were not already attracted by traditional engineering curricula. D&I achieved not only recruitment of almost 50% of its students from groups who explicitly would not have sought admittance to any of the traditional engineering programs, it also succeeded to attract almost as many female as male students (Jorgensen et al., 2011, p. 4).

The ability to open up 'engineering', extend its appeal beyond what attracts the usual profile, and recruit students that would otherwise not have chosen an engineering program was paramount to DTU's future. Although D&I's aspirations to strengthen the position of reflexive social sciences at DTU were controversial, they were also a timely answer to DTU's critical situation.

Besides its unique curricular composition, D&I also built on a radically different pedagogical approach to engineering education than was previously present at existing DTU programs. Because of low admission rates, Danish engineering programs have traditionally had no access restriction. While other DTU engineering programs' courses 'front-leaded' their first semesters with mathematics and physical sciences, D&I instead focused on projects and group collaboration, through which students acquired both technical skills *and* competencies to apply them within the social context of group work. In effect, fewer students dropped out and D&I soon attained higher completion rates than any other DTU program.

> The students seem to have embraced the new curriculum and the number of students' abandoning the education is very low. (Jorgensen et al., 2011, p. 8)

While most other engineering programs had plenty of empty seats to fill every year, D&I, from its initial year, had to reject more applicants than the program could accept. As a result, admission to D&I required the highest level high school grades of any engineering program of its time in Denmark.

Innovation through Users

Whilst common interpretations of *innovation* in business terms centre on economic goals and market growth, the D&I program represented an interpretation that was inspired by the notion of 'domestication' as portrayed in the Social Construction of Technology (Pinch & Bijker, 1987). Here, innovation is about users' adoption of technology and adaption within use-practices. In contrast to market analyses that assess sales potentials and design marketing strategies at the macro-level by constructing consumer categories and market segments from sales data, D&I investigated users' adaption of technology at the micro level in order to define goal specifications for engineering design.

> The synthesis oriented competences of the DTU design & innovation program has therefore attempted to include user investigations and involvements as a basic mindset from the very first semester. Further the re-design activities of the second semester builds on studies of the use and problems related to existing

products and technologies to provide the students with toolsets and approaches to tackle the demand side of products, services and systems. (Jorgensen et al., 2011, p. 5)

Whereas business' conception of innovation tends to separate the 'demand side' from technology development, D&I presented an alternative and third interpretation of innovation, whereby users' needs and adoption of technologies were seen as integral to the development of technology. By combining social science methods to investigate use-practices, technical analytical knowledge, and design synthesis competencies, D&I was setup to produce a new kind of holistic knowledge. Grounded in the epistemological principle of 'design synthesis', D&I students drew together representations that contained knowledge from different disciplinary approaches into new holistic design insights (Juhl & Lindegaard, 2013). These insights in turn presented new potentials for innovation.

Maintaining Education, Institutional Tumult, and Declining Support

Another significant feature of the Design & Innovation program was that the program had two faculties behind it. The program was based on a new form of collaboration between ten experienced researchers and teachers from two different faculties. Both faculties invested heavily in developing the program's curricular content;

> The starting point for the development of a new engineering curriculum in design & innovation was based on the work of a group of ten devoted and experienced teachers of engineering design and social science subjects based in the departments of 'Mechanical Engineering' and 'Manufacturing Engineering and Management'. (Jorgensen et al., 2011, p. 8)

Since no single faculty could cover the entire curriculum, the institutional re-engineering behind D&I demonstrated what was special and vulnerable about the program. The two department faculties made coordination more demanding because it had to transcend intra-departmental concerns at the risk of getting caught up in inter-departmental politics.

DTU's operation as an autonomous economic agent within a competitive environment meant that control over resources had become increasingly valuable political capital. Top-down decisions to redefine departments' areas of responsibility often clashed with bottom-up experiences from university employees, who felt that their professional identities and institutional legitimacy were jeopardised by the institution's repetitive attempts to position itself within the ever-more competitive intellectual landscape of academia.

For the two faculties contributing to D&I, the political tumult was felt as the group responsible for teaching engineering design, and mechanical engineering went through several departmental relocations. First the group was moved from the department of Mechanical Engineering to Manufacturing Engineering and

Management, and subsequently when that department changed name to Management Engineering, the group moved back again to Mechanical Engineering.

When new programs are created and new institutions build the need for cooperation and the value of coherent curricula is obvious and resources often channeled to satisfy this task. When programs mature and the research career motives of the faculty supported by the measures of individual success in academic activities increasingly shadow for the tedious and often complex tasks of maintaining the coordination and continued improvement of the teaching program. Though many engineering universities claim to value curriculum and teaching improvements reality demonstrates that research activities are valued even higher. (Jorgensen et al., 2011, p. 11)

Once the D&I program became everyday-business, the conditions for its inter-faculty collaboration transitioned from a status of 'special project', which received extra resources for its development, to a status of 'regular maintenance', where effectiveness was the operator.

When new teachers were ascribed to existing teaching duties that had been painstakingly developed and negotiated to fit the program's unique demands, the extra resources that had been available to the previous teachers' development did not transfer to the new teachers. As a result, some of the original pedagogical groundwork slowly eroded and the coherent and holistic idea behind the program became increasingly difficult to fulfil.

While many of the teachers involved in D&I saw the program's development as a necessary move to secure new positions as well as their own research areas at DTU, they soon realised that the resources that they had hoped for were slowly but steadily redirected to other institutional priorities. At a university where the ability to attract industry funding for new laboratory equipment meant that the university provided the real estate for the new laboratories, the price was paid by those who had to be moved in order to free up the required space. To D&I this was felt when real estate that used to be classrooms and group workspaces was withdrawn in order to house newly funded laboratories and private workshops. Slowly, but steadily, the conditions that used to support D&I's trademark pedagogic approach were recast to a degree, which to the program's teachers was increasingly felt to be a straitjacket.

In 2012, after 10 years of successful program building, 26 researchers, including most of the social scientist and teachers who built D&I, collectively left DTU for another academic institution. In an interview on national television, several of the senior researchers expressed that the working conditions had become too hostile for them to continue their work at DTU. Despite that many of the researchers involved were responsible for significant contributions to building and maintaining what had become the most successful educational program in DTU's history (Uddannelses-og Forskningsministeriet, 2012), the teachers feared that the declining resources jeopardised their teaching and research, and, ultimately, threatened their future at the university.

While the exit of 26 researchers was an unprecedented event in Danish academia that entered national newspapers and primetime television, not a single word was mentioned regarding the departing researchers in DTU's own two news magazines. To establish that nothing significant had taken place, the acting DTU president, Anders Bjarklev, replied in an interview that:

> We have about 4000 researchers and research-related employees, and many of them work with sustainability and innovation, thus the quality certainly won't suffer.

Although Mode 2 inflected sociotechnical imaginaries created conditions for researchers to become educational entrepreneurial and, in that way, build legitimacy for their research, neoliberal governance structure meant that such epistemic legitimacy ultimately had little clout in the greater picture of institutional branding and commercial interests. To DTU, the identity and quality of D&I went beyond the individuals who were engaged in the program's development. Scientific researchers and teachers were considered resources, and as such, they were replaceable.

CO-PRODUCTION OF EDUCATION AND KNOWLEDGE IN ACADEMIA

The D&I case exemplifies how higher education can assume a role in the de- and restabilisation processes of academic ecosystems and universities' institutional spaces. The D&I program's development draws attention to the contingencies and situated nature of how new educational curricular framings of can legitimate scientific knowledge productions within academic institutions. In this case, both the scientific knowledge production and the higher educational program resonate with the predominant focus on technology-driven commercial innovation. While the neoliberal take on the principles of Mode 2 justifies knowledge production by its economic impact, we also witness a 'bottom up' counter move from educators who seek to define innovation in terms that adhere to more traditional academic values and practices: visions of holistic engineering; sociotechnical reflectivity; and processes of user-driven innovation reflect a sociotechnical imaginary that associates new moralities, ethics, and meanings with the authoritative principles of innovation in higher education. This modified perspective does not decouple but coexists with the dominant sociotechnical imaginary of innovation. As the entrepreneurs of the D&I program envisioned a new take on innovation, they modified the overarching neoliberal narrative of knowledge production via more traditional academic Mode 1 values and practices in education. In this modified imaginary, business is no longer seen as confined to operate within the market, but more broadly as sociotechnological engagement with citizens, consumers, and users. within a broader notion of society— or in other words, Mode 2 inflected conceptions of domain specific 'applicability'.

This observation helps us to conceive of higher education, not merely as a second order consequence of research, but as a main element that can both adopt and adapt formal directions of research, including its institutionalisation. The Mode 1–Mode 2 axis' focus on modalities in knowledge production seems unable to properly reflect education's role in academic ecosystems. This point is underpinned by Hessels and van Lente's (2008) review of the literature on knowledge production. The role of 'education' is absent in the reviewed literature. This omission calls for a conceptual reconstruction of the academic ecosystem in which it is possible to include knowledge dissemination through higher education and consider its importance to the ways in which knowledge work is undertaken within contemporary universities.

Researching Academic Ecosystems as Ecologies of Practices

But how is it possible to combine overarching sociotechnical imaginaries about knowledge production, as manifested in the Mode 2 narrative, with mundane everyday educational practices as they unfold at universities? Kemmis and Smith offer an Aristotelian take on practice in which moral virtue informs actors' reasoning and decision-making as a disposition towards doing something well and for the good for the world.

> It [Praxis] is action that is *morally-committed, and oriented and informed by traditions in a field.* It is the kind of action people are engaged in when they think about what their action will mean in the world. (Kemmis & Smith 2008, p. 4, emphasis in original)

The moral component of 'praxis' thus inflects a socially distributed character by invoking agency of culturally situated 'practice traditions' containing value dispositions about what 'good' means. Where sociotechnical imaginaries according to their definition are 'widely held', their situated meanings are not evident before we study how they are enacted in local practices and interconnected within different (and maybe competing) practices.

We suggest that the study of transformative processes in academic ecosystems pay due attention to both research *and* educational practices, and consider their complex situated interplay. In practice theory Stephen Kemmis and his associates have suggested studying educational systems as 'ecologies of practices', i.e. 'how different practices coinhabit and coexist in a site, sometimes leaving residues or creating affordances that enable and constrain how other practices can unfold' (Kemmis et al., 2014, p. 43). Practice theory thus offers a range of theoretical resources and methodological inroads to study education and academic practices that avoid reifying sociotechnical imaginaries as overarching structural tenets of the academic system, while also guarding against conceptualising imaginaries as purely individual (mental) convictions (e.g. Kemmis et al., 2014; Mahon et al., 2017; Grootenboer et al., 2017). Instead, the practice theoretical approach understands sociotechnical imaginaries as they manifest in the normativised doings, sayings, and relatings that constitute academic activities. This framework enables scholars to study the constituents of the academic practices—and their interplay—in detail, and investigate what mechanisms are active in transforming academic ecosystems.

Our findings regarding how D&I came into existence and developed at DTU indicate that accounts of the academic practices and their dynamics should focus more on education, and avoid the constraints of prevailing narratives and their inherited emphasis on scientific knowledge production, which tend to include notions of performance criteria that have little room for what higher education has to offer. As a result, higher education is often presented as being at odds with high quality research output, rather than being seen as an alternative output of equal merit. Taking a practice perspective enables us to think of the interplay of academic ecosystems, in terms of knowledge circulation and dissemination, as important and productive outputs that are often more beneficial to society than cutting-edge research itself. As opposed to the research-centred Mode 2 perspective, the practice theoretical approach to the study of academic ecosystems entails a more symmetrical distribution of attention between research and educational practices.

In the introduction, we framed our discussion by invoking the metaphor of 'academic ecosystems' without defining its boundaries. The metaphor has helped us to envision how academic practices and sociotechnical imaginaries, surrounding both research and education, are interlinked within the institution of the university. We must, however, take caution not to be misguided by the metaphor. The scholarly tradition of systems theory has made strong claims as to how (social) orders are established and change as *systems* (cf. Pickel, 2011). Scholars of the practice theory tradition are, on the other hand, more cautious and prefer to frame discussions of the hanging together of practices by invoking the term 'nexus of practices' (cf. Hui et al., 2017). We suggest that envisioning universities as academic ecosystems, understood as nexuses that include multiple practices—and thus also educational practices—gives us more nuanced accounts of transformations in academia than the dominant Mode 2 perspective.

REFERENCES

Bruun Jensen, C. (2011). Making lists, enlisting scientists: The bibliometric indicator, uncertainty and emergent agency. *Science Studies, 24*(2), 64–84.

Bush, V. (1945). *Science, the endless frontier* (2nd ed.). Washington, DC: United States Office of Scientific Research and Development.

Carney, S. (2006). University governance in Denmark: From democracy to accountability? *European Educational Research Journal, 5*(3–4), 221–233.

Etzkowitz, H., & Leydesdorff, L. (2000). The dynamics of innovation: From national systems and "mode 2" to a triple helix of university–industry–government relations. *Research policy, 29*(2), 109–123.

Forskningsministeriet. (1998). *Betænkning om forskningsrådgivning*. Retrieved from http://www.fsk.dk/fsk/publ/betnk1287

Forskningsministeriet. (2013). *Betænkning om forskningsrådgivning. 3. Forskningsrådgivning I Danmark—1940–1989*. Retrieved from http://archive.is/iS32R

Gaardmand, A. (1993). *Dansk Byplanlægning, 1938–1992*. Copenhagen: Arkitektens forlag.

Gibbons, M., Limoges, C., Nowotny, H., Schwartzman, S., Scott, P., & Throw, M. (1994). *The new production of knowledge: The dynamics of science and research in contemporary societies*. London: Sage Publications.

Grootenboer, P., Edwards-Groves, C., & Choy, S. (Eds.). (2017). *Practice theory perspectives on pedagogy and education. praxis, diversity, and contestation*. Singapore: Springer.

Hessels, L. K., & van Lente, H. (2008). Re-thinking new knowledge production: A literature review and a research agenda. *Research Policy, 37*, 740–760.
Hui, A., Schatzki, T., & Elizabeth, S. (2017). *The nexus of practices: Connections, constellations, practitioners.* London: Routledge.
Jasanoff, S. (2004). *States of knowledge: The co-production of science and social order*. London: Routledge.
Jasanoff, S. (2011). *Designs on nature: Science and democracy in Europe and the United States*. Princeton, NJ: Princeton University Press.
Jasanoff, S. (2015). Future imperfect: Science, technology, and the imaginations of modernity. In S. Jasanoff & S.-H. Kim (Eds.), *Dreamscapes of modernity: Sociotechnical imaginaries and the fabrication of power.* Chicago, IL: Chicago University Press.
Jorgensen, U., Lindegaard, H., Brodersen, S., & Boelskifte, P. (2011). *Foundations for a new type of design-engineers*. DS 68-8: Proceedings of the 18th International Conference on Engineering Design (ICED 11), Impacting Society through Engineering Design, Vol. 8: Design Education, Lyngby/Copenhagen, Denmark.
Juhl, J., & Lindegaard, H. (2013). Representations and visual synthesis in engineering design. *Journal of Engineering Education, 102*(1), 20–50.
Kemmis, S., & Smith, T. J. (2008). Praxis and praxis development. In S. Kemmis & T. J. Smith (Eds.), *Enabling praxis: Challenges for education*. Rotterdam, The Netherlands: Sense Publishers.
Kemmis, S., Wilkinson, J., Edwards-Groves, C., Hardy, I., Grootenboer, P., & Bristol, L. (2014). *Changing practices, changing education*. Singapore: Springer.
Kim, S.-H., & Jasanoff, S. (2009). Containing the atom: Sociotechnical imaginaries and nuclear power in the United States and South Corea. *Minerva, 47*(2), 119–146.
Mahon, K., Francisco, S., & Kemmis, S. (Eds.). (2017). *Exploring education and professional practice: Through the lens of practice theory*. Singapore: Springer.
Merton, R. K. (1942). The normative structure of science. In R. K. Merton (Ed.), *The sociology of science: Theoretical and empirical investigations*. Chicago, IL: University of Chicago Press.
Nowotny, H., Scott, P., & Gibbons, M. (2001). *Rethinking science: Knowledge and the public in an age of uncertainty*. Cambridge: Polity Press.
Pickel, A. (2011). Systems theory. In I. C. Jarvie & J. Zamora-Bonilla (Eds.), *The Sage handbook of the philosophy of social sciences*. London: Sage Publications.
Pinch, T. J., & Bijker, W. E. (1987). The social construction of facts and artifacts: Or how the sociology of science and the sociology of technology might benefit each other. *The Social Constructions of Technological Systems: New Directions in the Sociology and History of Technology, 17*, 1–6.
Polanyi, M. (1962). *Personal knowledge: Towards a post critical philosophy*. London: Routledge.
Regeringen. (2002). *Tid til forandring for Danmarks universisteter: Styrket ledelse, Øget frihed, Stabil økonomi*. Retrieved from http://ufm.dk/publikationer/2002/filer-2002/tid-til-forandring.pdf
Syrelsen for Videregående Uddannelser. (2017). Retrieved from http://www.su.dk/om-su/historien-om-su/
Uddannelses- og Forskningsministeriet. (2012). *Den Koordinerede Tilmelding 1977–2012 HOVEDTAL 2012.* Retrieved from https://ufm.dk/uddannelse-og-institutioner/statistik-og-analyser/sogning-og-optag-pa-videregaende-uddannelser/grundtal-om-sogning-og-optag/kot-hovedtal/hovedtal2012.pdf

Joakim Juhl
Department of Planning
Aalborg University Campus Copenhagen
Copenhagen, Denmark

Anders Buch
Department of Learning and Philosophy
Aalborg University Campus Copenhagen
Copenhagen, Denmark

BENTE ELKJAER AND
NIELS CHRISTIAN MOSSFELDT NICKELSEN

8. EXPLORING UNIVERSITIES AS 'ORGANISATIONS THAT MAY LEARN'

INTRODUCTION

'The rise of the all-administrative university' is part of the title of a book published by American scholar Alan Ginsberg (Ginsberg, 2011), in which he describes how (North American) universities are in the process of changing, owing to an explosively expanding number of administrative staff, at the expense of academic staff. Rebecca Boden and Susan Wright (2010) have documented a similar increase in both the number of administrative staff and the related expenditure on university administration, compared to research funding, at Danish universities. Boden and Wright measure the relative increase in administrative expenditures between 2005 and 2009 to an equivalent expenditure on associate professors:

> Put simply, if administration had been pegged at the same proportion of total expenditure as in 2005, then in 2009 Danish universities would have had an additional 415.6 million Kroner to spend on frontline services such as teaching and research. Again, assuming an annual salary of 557,000 Kroner, this is equivalent to 746 'lektor' posts. (Boden & Wright, 2010, p. 6)

Along similar lines, Jan Holm Ingemann (2015) provides a vivid description of his experience with the development at Danish universities, and he concludes that a large number of administrative staff are employed to control, evaluate, and assure the quality of his teaching; and to a large extent, he and the other professors must provide the input for the work of the *administrative* staff (Ingemann, 2015, p. 15, our translation and emphasis). It is arguable that the relative number of administrative staff at universities has been on the rise, and one may look at this development as taking something (research and teaching) away from academic staff. However, it may be more correct to say that the increase in the number of administrative staff is the result of new and more tasks being assigned to contemporary universities, owing to their increasingly strategic role in society (Ramirez & Christensen, 2013). The increasing number of students and the globalisation of universities have also created a need for more administrative staff. These reasons for the expansion of administrative staff do not alter the feeling among university academics of being subject to handling systems, which provide information related to teaching and research activities for administrative staff, as Ingemann (2015) hinted. However, we may continue to regard this development as a loss for academics, or we may examine universities as organisations—particularly, as learning organisations—consisting of many staff members working together, engaged in their work, and open to opportunities to learn. However, looking more closely at universities as organisations, and 'organisations that may learn' (Argyris & Schön, 1996), is not quite so simple: what does it mean?

In our research, we work from an understanding of organisational learning as a combination of the field of organisation studies, with the fields of education and learning. However, none of these fields are clear-cut, and each comprises multiple perspectives, theories, and concepts. We are inspired in our work by American pragmatism, particularly John Dewey's work (Elkjaer & Simpson, 2011), in our understanding of both organisational studies and learning. This means that we work with an understanding of organisational learning in which the creation of an environment conducive to problem-solving related to the work practices at hand is pivotal (Brandi & Elkjaer, 2013; Elkjaer, 2003, 2004; Farjoun, Ansell, & Boin, 2015). Below, we will elaborate what this means when we look at the tasks and practices of universities, as well as of the experiences of university professors. Before doing so, we introduce a reading of the literature on universities in light of organisation studies and theories. This introduction is made through a reading of texts on universities as organisations, starting with the classic understanding of their being 'loosely coupled' (Weick, 1976) and 'organised anarchies' (Cohen, March, & Olsen, 1972), and moving to a contemporary reading of texts on universities as more tightly coupled organisations, owing to their similarity to business enterprises, as the result of public sector reforms (Brunsson & Sahlin-Andersson, 2000). This development is mainly described in terms of questions of mission, management, and control, and through the concepts of identity, hierarchy, and rationality. We argue that this is not particularly helpful when organisational learning is at stake. This is the reason we propose conceptual development related to tasks, practices, and experiences, in order to understand the energies and passions that may drive organisational learning at universities. The background for our proposal to more closely examine the work practices at hand is a reading of contemporary research in the field of organisation studies, in which it is possible to distinguish two concurrent developments. One calls for a focus on organisation studies as a 'practical science' through the notion of 'core task' or 'primary purpose' (du Gay & Vikkelsø, 2016). Another is inspired by the 'practice turn' in the social sciences, which claims that the 'practice' is the unit of analysis (e.g. Corradi, Gherardi, & Verzelloni, 2010; Newton & Riveros, 2015; Nicolini, 2012). We suggest that both 'task' and 'practice' are helpful for understanding universities as organisations, but in order to address universities as 'organisations that may learn' (Argyris & Schön, 1996), it is important to include not just the experiences of those who do research at universities, but also those who teach, administer, and manage. This is the background against which we propose pragmatism, and particularly the pragmatist concepts of experience and inquiry in order to inspire research on universities as learning organisations (Dewey, 1925 [1981]).

EXPLORING UNIVERSITIES AS 'ORGANISATIONS THAT MAY LEARN'

This chapter first introduces the changing roles of universities, particularly those concerning questions of loosely and more tightly coupled organisations. We argue that it is necessary to examine the tasks, practices, and experiences of everyday working life at universities, because in many cases contemporary university tasks involve both administrative and academic staff. We introduce these notions in order to consider universities 'from below', rather than maintain an overarching focus on management and control. This is a difficult task, because the university is discursively constructed in a way that reverberates primarily around the latter, which we emphasise through the narrative of the previous rector of Aarhus University. However, we maintain that in order to tell the full story, and to provide ideas and the impetus for supporting universities as learning organisations, we need to include a focus on the organisational practices, and on what people do and how they interact, because this is where everyday organisational learning happens. First, we consider the changing role of universities, in order to set the scene.

THE CHANGING ROLES OF UNIVERSITIES

Francisco Ramirez and Tom Christensen (2013) analyse the developments at Oslo and Stanford universities with reference to the new roles that contemporary universities now play in society:

> From 1990 to 2010 there was an increase of 73% in the number of people working in *the central administrative apparatus* of the University [of Oslo]. [...] [The] largest growth is in the departments with an external focus, whether related towards international activities, research resource provision, student affairs and communication. These changes move the university toward a more socially embedded status with greater student service orientation. (2013, p. 703, emphasis added)

With the help of our previously-mentioned Danish colleague, Jan Holm Ingemann (2015), the experience of being employed for many years at universities may be described as a gradual transformation from being a member of academia to being an employee in a knowledge concern, and from enjoying relative autonomy to being subordinated to a greater degree to hierarchical structures (Ingemann, 2015, p. 15, our translation). This is much in line with the changing role of universities in society over the last 10–15 years, where we have witnessed new ways of managing universities (Carney, 2006; Deem, 2001; Halvorsen & Nyhagen, 2011; Wright & Ørberg, 2008), greater emphasis on external funding, and on performance measurements (Rasmussen & Staugaard, 2012; Wright, 2011).

The relations between the state and higher education institutions, and the consequences of the changes in modes of governance have been widely addressed in research into the changing roles of universities (see also Whitley & Gläser, 2014). So far, intra-organisational dynamics have not been addressed in any detail. This has led to a call for an organisational perspective on higher education research by opening the 'black box' of universities as organisations, and providing insight into how its main activities—teaching, research, and services, are carried out (Fumasoli & Stensaker, 2013). However, there is a history of studying universities as organisations, and in the next section, we introduce the former and the newer models of universities (or educational institutions) as organisations.

Revisiting Classic Views on Universities as Organisations

When Michael Cohen, James March, and Johan Olsen (1972) applied the term 'garbage can' to a model of decision-making, it reflected an understanding of universities as 'organised anarchies'. Organised anarchies are characterised by (1) problematic preferences, (2) unclear technologies, and (3) fluid participation. Cohen et al. (1972) write that these properties of organised anarchy have been frequently identified in studies of organisations:

> They are characteristic of any organisation in part—part of the time. They are particularly conspicuous in public, educational, and illegitimate organisations. (p. 1)

Karl Weick's (1976) notion of organisations as loosely coupled systems used educational institutions as his research cases (Weick, 1976, p. 1). Loose coupling means that there is internal responsiveness between organisational functional units, yet they also each exhibits identity, physical and logical separation.

> Loose coupling also carries connotations of impermanence, dissolvability, and tacitness all of which are potentially crucial properties of the 'glue' that hold organisations together. (Weick, 1976, p. 3)

Douglas Orton and Karl Weick (1990) later revisited the notion of organisations as loosely coupled systems in order to clarify and augment Weick's earlier work. In the joint work of Orton and Weick (1990), it is stressed that the idea of organisations as loosely coupled is a methodology to deal with organisational processes, rather than a characteristic of an organisational form. The concept of loosely coupled organisations is an awareness of the need to 'study structure as something that organisations do, rather than merely as something they have' (Orton & Weick, 1990, p. 218).

Despite Orton and Weick's call for the study of processes, we still find a significant amount of organisational 'form' when studying the more recent research on universities as 'more tightly coupled' organisations (Pinheiro & Stensaker, 2014). That is, we find several organisational characteristics that help identify universities as organisations.

Contemporary Views on Universities as Organisations

Nils Brunsson and Kerstin Sahlin-Andersson (2000) have been an inspiration for presenting universities as more tightly coupled organisations (see also Seeber et al.,

2015), with their identification of recent public sector reforms as attempts to turn the sector into 'more complete' organisations. Brunsson and Sahlin-Andersson argue that reforms intended to establish identity, hierarchy, and rationality may be interpreted as attempts to construct organisations as 'organisatory reforms' (Brunsson & Sahlin-Andersson, 2000, p. 730). They argue that seeing something as an organisation means endowing it with an identity, emphasising its autonomy, defining its boundaries and its collective resources. With regard to organisational hierarchy, Brunsson and Sahlin-Andersson refer to the way in which coordination 'is achieved by an authoritative centre that directs the actions of the organisational members' (Brunsson & Sahlin-Andersson, 2000, p. 726). Universities accomplish this by attributing achievements to the unit, the university, or the research institute, rather than to the individual researcher.

The third aspect of Brunsson and Sahlin-Andersson's characterisation of public reform as a way to turn public institutions into business organisations is primarily the organisational claim to rationality, in the sense that organisations are expected to be intentional, that is, goal-oriented. The demand for organisational rationality also calls for the rational justification of past actions. Objectives and actions are assumed to be connected in a systematic way; organisations are expected to account for their actions with the help of preset objectives. For example, contract-like agreements may be drawn up between the central government and the universities, in which particular objectives and expected results are specified for each university (Brunsson & Sahlin-Andersson, 2000, p. 729).

Georg Krücken and Frank Meier (2006) follow much the same lines as Brunsson and Sahlin-Andersson when they speak of the university as an 'organisational actor' in which they

> try to evoke the image of an integrated, goal-oriented entity that is deliberately choosing its own actions and that can thus be held responsible for what it does. (p. 241)

Krücken and Meier (2006) discuss the 'organisational turn' in higher education, and suggest that universities as organisations are replacing the relationship between the academic professional and the state, which leaves little room for institutional management. They discuss four elements in their organisational university model First, there is organisational accountability, mainly through the establishment of evaluation procedures. Second, there is the tendency for each public institution to define their own organisational goals through mission statements in which the organisational self is established and openly presented to others for example through web-pages and other forms of communication. Third, there is the ongoing elaboration and expansion of formal technical structures around these goals. Fourth, there is the transformation of management into a profession (Krücken & Meier, 2006, p. 243). These changes at universities have resulted in their being described as more tightly coupled organisations as opposed to the classic descriptions of universities. This development of universities towards exhibiting tighter coupling has made it possible for Pinheiro and Stensaker (2014) to describe a new model of universities, from research universities to entrepreneurial ones:

> As an organisational archetype, the entrepreneurial university is characterised by the adoption of new structural arrangements aimed at enhancing internal collaborations (*coupling*) and fostering external partnerships (*bridging*). Its distinctive features include: a diversified funding base and the reallocation of resources around strategic areas; a strengthened central steering core (formal leadership structures); a focus on inter- and multi-disciplinary collaborations across teaching and research; technology transfers and collaborative partnerships along an extended development periphery and changes in governance structures like the inclusion of external parties in university boards. (p. 501, original emphasis)

The above section has attempted to sketch the development of universities when viewed through the lens of organisation studies, which results in the various models for understanding universities as organisations., From this we can conclude that it is no longer possible to see universities as catering exclusively to research and teaching, because they have become a much broader element of society, with their 'third mission' tasks ('knowledge exchange').

To illustrate the argument developed in this paper, we present an account of Aarhus University, provided by the rector who initiated the 'most comprehensive transformation in the history of Aarhus University' (Holm-Nielsen, 2013, p. 73). The account is supplemented with comments from other internal and external sources to provide a range of voices regarding the development of this transformation, and we should add that my co-author and I were part of the events, as a low-level manager and an associate professor.

AN ACCOUNT OF ORGANISATIONAL CHANGES AT AARHUS UNIVERSITY

Lauritz B. Holm-Nielsen held the position of rector at Aarhus University from 2005–2013. (rector from 2005–2013 Holm-Nielsen, 2013). His account describes the changes at Aarhus University as a preparation for the future challenges to higher education and the new roles of universities. For Holm-Nielsen, the point of departure is that universities 'feel the pressure of increased competition', and that this poses challenges in terms of how Aarhus University might 'maintain its position among the elite universities of the world' (Holm-Nielsen, 2013, p. 74). Holm-Nielsen's response to these challenges was to initiate what he called an 'academic development process' (2013, p. 74). The former rector describes the process as

> the largest organizational restructuring process in the history of Aarhus University [with] the objectives of removing organizational barriers to change and innovation, merging research and teaching cultures that work with related

issues, and improving conditions for research that cut across disciplines and research areas. (2013, p. 74)

Government policies in Denmark had paved the way for these changes by assigning more autonomy to universities, demanding more accountability in exchange. Additionally, the Danish University Act of 2003 converted universities into self-governing institutions administered by university boards, of which external stakeholders made up the majority. Holm-Nielsen describes the changes as follows:

> In short, the reform has contributed to more professional leadership, where the decision-making capacity and the conditions for strategic prioritization have been significantly improved. (2013, p. 76)

Mergers of government research institutions with universities, and the consolidation of 12 separate universities to eight new ones, also took place. In 2006–2007, Aarhus University integrated two former universities, the Aarhus School of Business and the Danish School of Education, and two national government research institutions for the environment and agriculture (see also Johansson, 2013).

Holm-Nielsen explains that Aarhus University has departed from the Humboldtian tradition of education, research, and knowledge exchange, and now builds on a 'quadruple helix' model (2013, p. 79), which rests on four equally important missions: education, research, talent development, and knowledge exchange. The internal organisational structures were changed during this process, from nine faculties to four, and from 55 departments to 26. Holm-Nielsen further explains:

> The primary objective of this restructuring has been to create larger academic environments that can more easily achieve critical mass and thus make possible more academic specialization. At the same time, internal barriers that hinder collaboration across academic boundaries have been greatly reduced, creating the right conditions for more interdisciplinary research. (2013, p. 82)

A new management model was implemented to tie together the university across the departments, which were turned into rather large units. The four deans were included in the executive management team and each made responsible for one of the core missions (education, research, talent development, and knowledge exchange). Finally, the university administration was centralised, so it could work closely together with the executive management.

The main impetus for the changes to Aarhus University's management and structure is found in the model of global competition created by a ranking regime of all universities worldwide. The result is fewer faculties and departments, as well as a more unified management structure; that is, decisions are centralised and the University's internal hierarchy is strengthened (Johansson, 2013). The administrative staff are also centralised into functional units (e.g. AU Studies, Human Resources, and Information Technology), which are headed by assistant general managers, and include fewer administrative staff members directly connected to the departments (Paldam, 2015). This separates academic and administrative staff, because they no longer interact on a day-to-day basis. Problems concerning teaching and research are often addressed entirely through email or telephone communication. In his analysis of the changes at Aarhus University, economics Professor Martin Paldam writes:

> Nobody in the A-staff [academic staff] wanted a large unified anonymous administration in a distant building. We want a flexible administration that is easy to communicate with. Clearly the whole idea of a unified central administration is a silly, harmful idea seen from the interests of society, the students and the A-staff. Also, it has made the work of the B-staff (administrative staff) more mechanical and dull. (2015, p. 145)

The question that emerges is whether it is possible to go beyond management and structures, to the actual tasks and practices of contemporary universities. We do not claim to have all the answers, but we aim to present the conceptual elements related to the tasks and practices as means for future research to identify the learning aspects of universities as organisations.

In the next section, we turn to organisational research, theories, and concepts that address organisations 'from below', from the organisation of the interactions of human beings and their tasks, practices, experiences, and learning opportunities.

CORE TASKS AND THE DIFFICULTY OF DEFINITION

Recently, some organisational scholars have called for a revival of the idea of organisational studies as a 'practical science' (du Gay & Vikkelsø, 2014), because they claim that despite the financial crises, 'the voice of organisation studies has been noticeably absent from the heart of the public debate on this and related matters of concern' (du Gay & Vikkelsø, 2014, p. 737). We would add that this voice has also been absent from the debate on the changes to universities, which has—as we hope we have demonstrated above—been more concerned with university management than with the everyday organising processes of the work practices at hand.

One way to revive organisation studies as a practical science is through the notion of 'the primary task' or the 'organisational purpose', which refers to the necessity of developing an understanding of the practical work undertaken in an enterprise (du Gay & Vikkelsø, 2014). Only through this understanding is it possible to discuss an enterprise as an 'organisational reality' or a 'cooperative system' (du Gay & Vikkelsø, 2014, pp. 745–747). However, the concept of 'task' is highly contested in organisation studies (Vikkelsø, 2015), where critics agree 'that a practical understanding of organisations as task systems is both simplistic and dangerous' (Vikkelsø, 2015, p. 424). This contradicts the classic organisational theorists, such as Chester Barnard (1956), who argue that the 'existence of a collective "task" or "purpose", something that unites the members of the organisation in concerted action for a shorter or longer period, and which may be explained and discussed among them' (here from Vikkelsø, 2015, p. 424) is what distinguishes an organisation from a more haphazard grouping of people.

Vikkelsø (2015) argues that organisations may have more than one primary task, but that it is around the primary task(s) that the organisation is made to serve as an organising body of work and persons. She also argues that tasks regarded as core objects make it possible to investigate organisations such as schools and universities as practical endeavours, instead of 'mere containers for processes inside and above them' (Vikkelsø, 2015, p. 432). In other words, following a task makes it possible to acquire knowledge about the organising and learning processes specific to the situations at hand.

Identifying the core tasks of university scholars' work practices is difficult, as Christine Musselin notes (Musselin, 2007). Musselin argues that teaching and research are 'complex processes, which are difficult to grasp' (Musselin, 2007, p. 71), therefore they are difficult to prescribe and to reproduce. 'Books entitled "how to prepare a thesis" provide fine tricks but they cannot explain how to write a thesis in the way technical notices tell us how to use a mobile phone' (Musselin, 2007, p. 72). Musselin argues that this also holds for teaching. Online courses may be seen as a rationalised way to teach, however there is still a lot of work requiring a tutor or teacher that needs to be available to students in order for this kind of teaching to result in successful learning. Musselin also argues that there are 'ambiguous relationships between tasks and results'; that is, between the influence of 'what' and 'how' is taught to outcomes of students' learning. Finally, there is no touchstone that defines good or poor research. Nevertheless, Musselin concludes:

> In many ways, research and teaching thus possess certain characteristics that are not shared by other work activities. This specificity should not be overestimated (as it often was the case in the past) and the recent trends in rationalizing, measuring, assessing academic activities showed that they indeed can partially be affected by these processes. Nevertheless they also strongly resist such changes and this is due to their special features. (2007, p. 74)

Despite the difficulty of identifying the tasks of university scholars, following the tasks and purposes of university work as a whole may bring us closer to changes in the actual work practices than sticking with a more general understanding that focuses on changes in relations between policy and management. However, we also believe that having the concept of 'practice' more explicitly include aspects other than the task of the 'situations at hand' and, in that sense, may be an inspiring conceptual tool. It is to this conceptual introduction of practice that we now turn our attention.

THE CONCEPT OF PRACTICE

An overall dividing line between the concepts of practice is whether practice is understood as an empirical object ('a doing') or a particular perspective for seeing and understanding phenomena. When practice is a perspective, 'practice' refers to a relational ontology in which 'doings' and 'doers' ('knowns' and 'knowings') are inseparable, and following from that, practice as a way of seeing includes another epistemology, another way of asking questions (Corradi et al., 2010). Paul Newton and Augusto Riveros (Newton & Riveros, 2015) work from what they term an 'ontology of practices' when they focus on educational administration. They define the empirical field as a set of practices in which agency and structure are mutually constituted. That is, the connection between leadership and organisation needs to be established, and 'a study of leadership is a study of organization, since separation of actors and contexts are irrelevant' (Newton & Riveros, 2015, p. 336). Therefore, leadership is a set of practices situated in a social and material context.

Davide Nicolini (2012), a proponent of practice theory, argues that an enterprise is better understood as a 'fluid scene that unfolds in front of us in terms of multiple practices carried out at the same time' (Nicolini, 2012, p. 2), rather than as a functional system with clear boundaries towards other organisational systems. He argues that organisations are both the site and the result of work practices, in other words, 'bundles of practices' (Nicolini, 2012, p. 2). In Nicolini's universe of practice theory, activity, performance, and work are foregrounded, and structure and process are understood as recursive processes. Thus, Nicolini says that first and foremost practice theories are:

> inherently relational and see the world as a seamless assemblage, nexus, or confederation of practices—although not all having the same relevance. (2012, p. 3)

Second, practice theories emphasise the role of the body and material things in all social affairs. Third, agency and agents are inherent in practice theories as the carriers of practices, 'a body/mind who "carries", but also "carries out" social practices' (Nicolini, 2012, p. 4). Fourth, knowledge confers a form of mastery, which is demonstrated by one's capacity to carry out social and material activity.

> Knowledge is thus always a way of knowing, shared with others, a set of practical methods acquired through learning, inscribed in objects, embodied and only partially articulated in discourse. (Nicolini, 2012, p. 5)

Fifth, all practice-based approaches foreground

> the centrality of interest in all human matters, and therefore put emphasis on the importance of power, conflict, and politics as constitutive elements of the social reality we experience. (Nicolini, 2012, p. 6)

The consequence of studying organisations with Nicolini's approach to practice theory is that one studies practices, not practitioners, as the units of analysis. We may ask 'what sort of agency and 'actor-ship' is made possible by these specific situations' (Nicolini, 2012, p. 7). Practice theories do more than describe what people do, practices are 'meaning-making, identity-forming, and order-producing activities' (Nicolini, 2012, p. 7). Cognition and sense-making also emerge from an organisation's practices, they do not stem from the mind of an individual. Sense-making is always located in material and discursive activity, bodies, artefacts, and habits. Practice theories are relational theories, and they ask not only 'how?', but also 'why?'

We have introduced the concept of 'doings' by means of tasks and purpose, and following practice-theory, we have gone beyond the mere doings to see them as part of practice, in the sense of connecting 'doings' and 'doers' as situated parts of context. However, the consequences of this collapsing in practice theory of the tasks and the human beings doing the tasks, is that human beings tend to disappear as intentional beings. It is difficult to apply the explicit conceptual tools of practice theory to answer questions such as, 'Why do human beings, such as university scholars and administrative staff, fulfil their tasks and carry out their practices?' 'Why do some put more energy and passion into doing their tasks/carrying out their practices than others?' We believe that the pragmatist notion of 'experience' more explicitly includes intentionality as well as situatedness (i.e. not all intentionality can be expressed). In many ways, one may see the two notions—practice and experience—as being alike, because they draw on the same ontology, but 'experience' more explicitly describes what persons bring to situations, and how and why work practices alter through the notions of the uncertain situation and inquiry as ways to 'remake' the situation. This is also a way to connect the notion of organising to the notion of learning.

TURNING TO PRAGMATISM

Despite the resemblance of practice theory to pragmatist philosophy, the latter is rarely mentioned in the literature on the former (Nicolini, 2012; Reckwitz, 2002; Schatzki, 2001). However, in the following passage from John Dewey's *The Need for a Recovery of Philosophy* (1917 [1980]), it is rather evident that practice and experience are much the same:

> experiencing means living; and that living goes on in and because of an environing medium, not in a vacuum. [...] Experience is primarily a process of undergoing: a process of standing something; of suffering and passion, of affection, in the literal sense of these words. [...] Experience is no slipping along in a path fixed by inner consciousness. [...] Since we live forward; since we live in a world where changes are going on whose issues means our weal or woe; since every act of ours modifies these changes and hence is fraught with promise, or charged with hostile energies—what should experience be but a future implicated in the present! (pp. 7–9)

Dewey clearly situates human beings in their social and material worlds in an entwined way (see also Sandberg & Tsoukas, 2011). However, Dewey explicitly includes emotions (passion, affection) and the future (living forward, promise), and as one contemporary pragmatist philosopher says, with reference to Dewey's *Experience and Nature* (1925 [1981]), 'To be human is to be engaged in practices' (Boisvert, 2012, p. 109). We believe that engagement, commitment, and passion are needed when addressing work practices at universities, which is why the notion of experience in pragmatism is more appealing to us than the notion of practice in practice theory: it explicitly includes human beings by way of human experience.

For the pragmatists, meaning and meaning-making derive from lived experience, where human beings interact with their environments in an entangled manner, and on a continuous basis. Pragmatism regards concepts as 'tools for action', and, as such, is instrumental in coping with situations and events, which may lead to a (re)construction of meaning and action through experimental work with concepts. However, all educational aspirations begin with the sense that 'something is not right'. As human beings we are embedded in the world, and as participants (and not spectators) we have experiences, which are not just our own personal experiences, but experiences that come from being enmeshed in the world. In other words, experience is ontological and based on the transactional relation between person and world. When you only have an epistemological orientation toward experience, it means that it is possible to exclude situations in which knowledge is not the primary content or purpose. It also means that you become unable to see that having an experience is also an emotional and aesthetic affair, and not solely a 'knowledge affair'.

When 'experience had' leads to learning experiences and knowledge, it provides the ability to act in a mindful ('intelligent') way, using the present and past to anticipate the future. Another Deweyan concept, inquiry, is a method for systematically acquiring knowledge from experience. Dewey's concept of inquiry is connected to his notion of experience, because inquiry is an answer to a felt ('emotional') encounter with a conflict in experience; for example, a habit that no longer works in a beneficial way, or becomes invalid, and needs to be changed. Inquiry begins with an emotionally felt difficulty, or an uncertain situation, and is a method for resolving this conflict of experience. When something is experienced with the 'stomach', or an emotional response is exhibited as part of a situation, inquiry is a way to help define experience in a cognitive sense and create meaning out of emotional turmoil. To do so, it may be necessary to activate former similar experiences by experimenting with various possible ways of attributing meaning to the situation at hand, and, through that, transform the emotional experience into something that may be comprehended as a cognitive and communicative experience. This is how an emotional experience becomes a reflective one; it becomes a learning experience, and may lead to knowledge, which in turn can inform experience in any future similar emotionally difficult situations.

Returning to our query of universities as 'organisations that may learn, the notion of experience maintains the focus on the tasks and practices of university work, the relational connection between the doings and the doers. The notion of experience focuses on universities as organisations including human beings and their passions. The notion of experience also links to learning through inquiry, as a way to rebalance uncertain situations. We suggest that redirecting the understanding of universities from organisations comprising complex tasks and practices to organisations involving different experiences and passions for work and learning, may be a way to understand universities as (potential) learning organisations. This perspective on universities may also help us to understand why they (still) work, despite tighter controls and more elaborate management hierarchies. In other words, the concept of experience may help to open the black box of 'intra-organisational dynamics', in which we may see both management and research, and a multiplicity ofty persons continuously learning in universities while engaging in the plurality of tasks involved in the performance of the core task of contemporary universities.

DISCUSSION

The way we have looked at universities as organisations in this paper may be regarded as connected to the concepts of work and organisation of the Chicago school of sociology, also termed 'interactionism'. This school of thought draws on pragmatist philosophy and includes notions of actions and interactions. Abbott (2009) provides a thorough historical account of this school of sociology, and mentions its various contributions to organisation studies (see also Fisher & Strauss, 1978). The Chicago school of sociology understands organisations as being less like entities, and more like organising processes. The interactionists present a consistent vision of social organisation and disorganisation as ongoing processes, and an understanding of change rather than stability. Abbott argues that we live in

> a world of rapid turnover and change in organizations, a world of continuous organizational restructurings and financial prestidigitation, of networks and arm's length relationships, a world in which the employment and production structures that were laboriously built by scientific management and human relations have been deconstructed through outsourcing and offshoring, a world that deals with its human relations problems by denying and outrunning them. It is a world much better fitted to the ecological and processual 'organizing' theory of the Chicago School than to the organization theory we have inherited from the Warnerians and Mertonians. (2009, p. 419)

Another perspective on the heritage of the Chicago school of sociology discusses how the conceptualisation of organisations is replaced by 'the relationships among individuals and how people create meaning and social relations' (Hallett, Shulman, & Fine, 2009, p. 488). This leads Hallett et al. to emphasise the value of the interactionist approach to organisational research as that of 'the constitutive role of people in organizations', hence the term, 'peopling organizations', in contrast to organisations as 'disembodied structures' found in institutional theory, for example (Hallett et al., 2009, p. 488). The classic interactionists did not theorise about the organisation, but analysed work and work settings. They drew on pragmatist philosophy, and were not 'simply interested in ideas for their own sake, but as a means to promote social change' (Hallett et al., 2009, p. 490).

To understand organisations as constituted by the mutual interplay of tasks, practices, experiences, human beings, and learning, the interactionists tell us to focus on actions and interactions. This understanding helps us to see how the processes of actions and interactions organise work in social arenas/worlds in which participants' commitment is the central tenet. In the understanding of the interactionists, social worlds organised into social arenas form the locus of analysis. These social worlds are not defined a priori as social units or structures bounded by space or formal membership, but by demonstrating commitment to organisational actions and interactions, which is evident through discourse and action (Becker, 1970; Clarke, 2003; Shibutani, 1955).

In our work, we both connect and add to the work of the interactionists. We connect through the notion of seeing organisations as processes of actions and interactions among a plurality of staff members, and we add by including the notion of practice as the (wider) locus of these processes. This makes it possible to see why some discourse and actions can be exerted or kept at bay through different power games and positions beyond the actual actions and interactions. For example, see how actions and interactions are embedded in national politics of the distribution of research money and the way 'quality assurance' is performed, which may install competition that may both inhibit and facilitate potentials for organisational learning. We also connect through emphasising human beings and human experience, as well as human commitment, and we add by linking commitment to passions (or the opposite) towards work, making us capable of explicitly including a notion of inquiry and learning triggered by emotional uncertainties within experience. For example, previous experiences of obscure organisational changes leading nowhere may lead to a continued lack of passion for work, and as such inhibit organisational learning potential to unfold. Finally, we connect through our focus on work, and we add by addressing this as part of the organisational tasks (or primary purposes), because this inevitably includes the organisation as a whole. This makes it possible to, for example, include the changing role of universities due to their expanding tasks, and to work from that 'reality' rather than an out-of-touch fantasy of the universities' role in contemporary societies.

CONCLUSION

We began our exploration of universities as 'organisations that may learn,' inspired by the works of Chris Argyris and Donald Schön (1996), by identifying the problems of contemporary universities, as observed in research that focuses on new forms of management and control within universities, and in light of the new societal–strategic role ascribed to contemporary universities. This has resulted in a new constellation of staff, with more administration compared to academic staff. We situated this development in a more elaborate debate on universities' new role in society, and with the help of classic organisation studies, described the development of universities from loosely to more tightly coupled organisations.

We highlighted the organisational concepts used to describe this process: identity, hierarchy, and rationality, as well as professional management. We provided an illustration highlighting the management rationale for this development, using Aarhus University as a case. We identified the analyses of this as developing within a management paradigm, rather than examining the work, the doings, and the doers at universities, and introduced the notions of 'task' and 'practice'. In order to connect this to the idea of universities capable of learning, we expanded our conceptual toolbox to include the pragmatist notions of experience and inquiry, which include human passions and ways of becoming knowledgeable through inquiry and learning. Finally, in our discussion we connected, as well as added to, the Chicago school of sociology. Our additions include situating actions and interactions in the notion of practice to embed these in a wider context, and, through the notions of passions for work, to include the emotional uncertainties as triggers for organisational learning, as well as by the notion of task to include the university as a whole. The latter makes it possible to see that the changing role of universities in societies reverberates around the expanded tasks of contemporary universities.

We propose that including practices, passions, and tasks as pivotal conceptual reference points makes it possible to transcend the focus of university research beyond administration, management, and control in favour of an inclusion of the experiences of the participants. Additionally, through the experiences of the participants, these conceptual reference points may also act as a pathway to organisational learning and provide ways to see universities as 'organisations that may learn'.

REFERENCES

Abbott, A. (2009). Organizations and the Chicago school. In P. S. Adler (Ed.), *Sociology and organization studies* (pp. 399–420). Oxford: Oxford University Press.
Argyris, C., & Schön, D. A. (1996). *Organizational learning II: Theory, method, and practice*. Reading, MA: Addison-Wesley Publishing Company.
Barnard, C. I. (1956). *The functions of the executive*. Cambridge, MA: Harvard University Press.
Becker, H. S. (1970). *Sociological work: Method and substance*. Chicago, IL: Allen Lane.
Boden, R., & Wright, S. (2010). *Follow the money: An interim report on Danish university funding prepared for dansk magisterforening* (Working Papers No. 16). Copenhagen: Danish School of Education.
Boisvert, R. (2012). Whither pragmatism? *The Pluralist, 7*(3), 107–119.
Brandi, U., & Elkjaer, B. (2013). Organisational learning: Knowing in organising. In M. Kelemen & N. Rumens (Eds.), *American pragmatism and organization: Issues and controversies* (pp. 147–161). Dorchester: Gower.
Brunsson, N., & Sahlin-Andersson, K. (2000). Constructing organizations: The example of public sector reform. *Organization Studies, 21*(4), 721–746.
Carney, S. (2006). University governance in Denmark: From democracy to accountability? *European Educational Research Journal, 5*(3–4), 221–233. doi:10.2304/eerj.2006.5.3.221
Clarke, A. E. (2003). Situational analyses: Grounded theory mapping after the postmodern turn. *Symbolic Interaction, 26*(4), 553–576.
Cohen, M. D., March, J. G., & Olsen, J. P. (1972). A garbage can model of organizational choice. *Administrative Science Quarterly, 17*(1), 1–25.
Corradi, G., Gherardi, S., & Verzelloni, L. (2010). Through the practice lens: Where is the bandwagon of

practice-based studies heading? *Management Learning, 41*(3), 265–283.
Deem, R. (2001). Globalisation, new managerialism, academic capitalism and entrepreneurialism in universities: Is the local dimension still important? *Comparative Education, 37*(1), 7–20. doi:10.1080/03050060020020408
Dewey, J. (1917 [1980]). The need for a recovery of philosophy. In J. A. Boydston (Ed.), *The middle works of John Dewey, 1899–1924* (Vol. 10, pp. 3–48). Carbondale & Edwardsville, IL: Southern Illinois University Press.
Dewey, J. (1925 [1981]). Experience and nature. In J. A. Boydston (Ed.), *The later works of John Dewey, 1925–1953* (Vol. 1, pp. 1–326). Carbondale & Edwardsville, IL: Southern Illinois University Press.
du Gay, P., & Vikkelsø, S. (2014). What makes organization? Organizational theory as a 'practical science'. In P. Adler, P. du Gay, G. Morgan, & M. Reed (Eds.), *The Oxford handbook of sociology, social theory, and organization studies: Contemporary currents* (pp. 736–758). Oxford: Oxford University Press.
du Gay, P., & Vikkelsø, S. (2016). *For formal organization: The past in the present and future of organization theory*. Oxford: Oxford University Press.
Elkjaer, B. (2003). Organizational learning with a pragmatic slant. *International Journal of Lifelong Education, 22*(5), 481–494.
Elkjaer, B. (2004). Organizational learning: The 'third way'. *Management Learning, 35*(4), 419–434.
Elkjaer, B., & Simpson, B. (2011). Pragmatism: A lived and living philosophy. What can it offer to contemporary organization theory? *Research in the Sociology of Organizations, 32*, 55–84.
Farjoun, M., Ansell, C., & Boin, A. (2015). PERSPECTIVE—Pragmatism in organization studies: Meeting the challenges of a dynamic and complex world. *Organization Science, 26*(6), 1787–1804.
Fisher, B., & Strauss, A. L. (1978). The Chicago tradition and social change: Thomas, Park and their successors. *Symbolic Interaction, 1*(2), 5–23.
Fumasoli, T., & Stensaker, B. (2013). Organizational studies in higher education: A reflection on historical themes and prospective trends. *Higher Education Policy, 26*(4), 479–496.
Ginsberg, B. (2011). *The fall of the faculty: The rise of the all-administrative university and why it matters*. Oxford: Oxford University Press.
Hallett, T., Shulman, D., & Fine, G. A. (2009). Peopling organizations: The promise of classic symbolic interactionism for an inhabited institutionalism. In P. S. Adler (Ed.), *The Oxford handbook of sociology and organization studies: Classical foundations* (pp. 486–509). Oxford: Oxford University Press.
Halvorsen, T., & Nyhagen, A. (Eds.). (2011). *Academic identities—Academic challenges? American and European experience of the transformation of higher education and research*. Cambridge: Cambridge Scholars Publishing.
Holm-Nielsen, L. B. (2013). Making a strong university stronger. In Q. Wang, Y. Cheng, & N. C. Liu (Eds.), *Building world-class universities: Different approaches to a shared goal* (pp. 73–87). Rotterdam, The Netherlands: Sense Publishers.
Ingemann, J. H. (2015). Fra professorvælde til regnearkstyranni. *Tidsskrift for Arbejdsliv, 17*(4), 11–24.
Johansson, L. (2013). *Universiteter under forandring: En historisk konkret analyse af den faglige udviklingsproces på Aarhus Universitet* (Speciale). København: Aarhus Universitet.
Krücken, G., & Meier, F. (2006). Turning the university into an organizational actor. In G. S. Drori, J. W. Meyer, & H. Hwang (Eds.), *Globalization and organization: World society and organizational change* (pp. 241–257). New York, NY: Oxford University Press.
Musselin, C. (2007). Are universities specific organisations? In G. Krücken, A. Kosmützhy, & M. Torka (Eds.), *Towards a multiversity? Universities between global trends and national tradition* (pp. 63–84). Bielefeld: Transcript.
Newton, P., & Riveros, A. (2015). Toward an ontology of practices in educational administration: Theoretical implications for research and practice. *Educational Philosophy and Theory, 47*(4), 330–341. doi:10.1080/00131857.2014.976927
Nicolini, D. (2012). *Practice theory, work, and organization: An introduction*. Oxford: Oxford University Press.
Orton, J. D., & Weick, K. E. (1990). Loosely coupled systems: A reconceptualization. *Academy of Management Review, 15*(2), 203–223.
Paldam, M. (2015). The public choice of university organization: A stylized story of a constitutional

reform. *Constitutional Political Economy, 26*(2), 137–158.
Pinheiro, R., & Stensaker, B. (2014). Designing the entrepreneurial university: The interpretation of a global idea. *Public Organization Review, 14*(4), 497–516. doi:10.1007/s11115-013-0241-z
Ramirez, F. O., & Christensen, T. (2013). The formalization of the university: Rules, roots, and routes. *Higher Education, 65*(6), 695–708.
Rasmussen, P., & Staugaard, H. J. (2012, October 25–26). *Nordisk Netværk for Professionsforskning*. Professionalisering, decentralisering og styringsmaskering: Paper til Nordisk Konference om professionsforskning, NORPRO, Århus, Denmark.
Reckwitz, A. (2002). Toward a theory of social practices: A development in culturalist theorizing. *European Journal of Social Theory, 5*(2), 243–263. doi:10.1177/13684310222225432
Sandberg, J., & Tsoukas, H. (2011). Grasping the logic of practice: Theorizing through practical rationality. *Academy of Management Review, 36*(2), 338–360.
Schatzki, T. R. (2001). Introduction: Practice theory. In T. R. Schatzki, K. Knorr Cetina, & E. Von Savigny (Eds.), *The practice turn in contemporary theory* (pp. 1–14). London: Routledge.
Seeber, M., Lepori, B., Montauti, M., Enders, J., de Boer, H., Weyer, E., Bleiklie, I., Hope, K., Michelsen, S., Mathisen, G. N., Frølich, N., Scordato, L., Stensaker, B., Waagene, E., Dragsic, Z., Kretek, P., Krücken, G., Magalhães, A., Ribeiro, F. M., Sousa, S., Veiga, A., Santiago, R., Marini, G., Reale, E. (2015). European universities as complete organizations? Understanding identity, hierarchy and rationality in public organizations. *Public Management Review, 17*(10), 1444–1474. doi:10.1080/14719037.2014.943268
Shibutani, T. (1955). Reference groups as perspectives. *The American Journal of Sociology, 60*(6), 562–569.
Vikkelsø, S. (2015). Core task and organizational reality. *Journal of Cultural Economy, 8*(4), 418–438.
Weick, K. E. (1976). Educational organizations as loosely coupled systems. *Administrative Science Quarterly, 21*(1), 1–19.
Whitley, R., & Gläser, J. (2014). *Organisational transformation and scientific change: The impact of institutional restructuring on universities and intellectual innovation* (Vol. 42). Bradford: Emerald Group Publishing.
Wright, S. (2011). Universitetets performancekrav: Viden der tæller. In K. M. Bovbjerg, S. Wright, J. Krause-Jensen, J. B. Krejsler, L. Moos, G. Brorholt, & K. L. G. Salamon (Eds.), *Motivation og mismod: Effektivisering og stress på offentlige arbejdspladser* (pp. 211–235). Aarhus: Aarhus Universitetsforlag.
Wright, S., & Ørberg, J. W. (2008). Autonomy and control: Danish university reform in the context of modern governance. *Learning and Teaching, 1*(1), 27–57. doi:10.3167/175522708783113550

Bente Elkjaer
Danish School of Education
University of Aarhus
Aarhus, Denmark

Niels Christian Mossfeldt Nickelsen
Danish School of Education
University of Aarhus
Aarhus, Denmark

BENGT-ÅKE LUNDVALL

9. CREATIVE AND INCLUSIVE UNIVERSITIES IN THE GLOBALISING LEARNING ECONOMY

The more any quantitative social indicator is used for social decision-making, the more subject it will be to corruption pressures and the more apt it will be to distort and corrupt the social processes it was intended to monitor.
– Donald T. Campbell (1976)

INTRODUCTION

How can universities respond to current challenges emanating from the growing role of knowledge and learning in global competition?[1] First, changes in the global knowledge landscape imply that universities in Western countries need to give more attention to creativity. Second, the new kind of polarisation of societies where economic inequality is combined with the opening up of cultural gaps between creative metropoles and regional peripheries requires that universities give more attention to inclusion.

The chapter draws upon different bodies of research. It reflects my research on innovation systems and the learning economy (Lundvall, 2016) and combines it with 'intellectual trespassing' into research on creativity. It attempts to link concepts and literature that normally appear in separate domains. While 'creativity' gives associations to the exceptional individual, 'inclusion' points toward the societal level. The research-based literature on creativity has little to say about the social dimension while the literature on social inclusion has little to say about creativity. Combining disparate and distant elements may lead to new insights and new action.

In the first part the focus is on the role of creativity in teaching, research, and third mission. The second part deals with how universities can respond to the polarisation of Western societies while also reflecting knowledge-based and global competition. The chapter ends with a discussion of university strategies that combine the promotion of creativity with social inclusion.[2]

DOES THE CURRENT RESPONSE TO GLOBALISATION UNDERMINE
THE CREATIVITY OF UNIVERSITY RESEARCH?

One important outcome of the globalisation process is that the knowledge gap between OECD-countries and major Asian economies such as China and India has been reduced over the last couple of decades. This change in the global knowledge landscape has put the issue of creativity in research on the policy agenda in Europe (see, for instance, Blau, 2006) as a source of competitiveness for developed economies. As global competitors close the knowledge gap something 'extra' is needed to remain competitive. In this part I discuss how the response of governments and universities to globalisation and knowledge-based competition has changed the mode of knowledge production at universities. Based on discussion of insights from creativity research, it is argued that the predominance of global ranking systems and the single-minded focus on bibliometric indicators as performance criteria undermine creativity.

Universities in Global Competition

National policies for higher education and research have responded to the more intense global competition by setting new ambitious objectives for universities and required that those objectives be expressed on simple quantitative scales. To highlight excellence in research in global rankings has become a major policy concern.[3] Excellence in research attracts elite scientists and students who can contribute to the competitiveness of the national innovation system. Universities have become important players in a game where national economies engage in global knowledge-based competition (Hazelkorn, 2011).

Each individual university has an interest in raising its position in national and international rankings. In order to get its share of public funding, a university needs to show that it is competitive in terms of teaching, research, and fund raising from private sources. A high ranking also makes it possible for a university to increase its income through student fees and contracts with business enterprises. Increasingly universities have become directly involved in domestic and global competition with each other.

As part of this process governments have supported, and local university administrations have implemented, new forms of management where the emphasis is upon the use of standardised indicators measuring the output from universities. The focus is on indicators that can be made comparable across the world, and one aim is to raise the universities' position in global rankings.

One specific consequence is that the number of publications in journals and patterns of citation have become the predominant performance indicator at all levels, spanning from the national university system, the single university, the department, the research group, and down to the individual scholar.[4]

Under certain circumstances a move towards measurable outcome may be 'progressive'—for instance explicit criteria can serve to expose hidden male dominance and gender-biased recruitment at universities. Another example is when old established institutions that rely on historical reputation get challenged by new universities that perform better than the old ones.

But when the global ranking exercises become more widespread, and the ranking philosophy permeates all activities at the university, the negative consequences take the upper hand (see the introductory classical citation from Campbell, 1976). When one or a few success indicators are used over a time period, they will always have perverse effects on the activities that are benchmarked. One example is from the Soviet era, when the measuring production and growth in Soviet Union was in terms of weight. Not surprisingly, it led to products that were heavier than they were useful.

In the case of universities, an extreme focus on bibliometric performance has several perverse effects. Other activities such as interaction with society and fostering students are given lower priority. Cut-throat individual competition now operationalised and visualised in numbers of papers and citations undermines knowledge sharing within and across research teams.

And while there is little doubt that the incentive system has worked well in the sense that it has raised 'the productivity' of scholars (on average each scholar now produces more scientific papers per annum than before), it has also led to a standardisation of research publications and to a bias in research activities. The format of the standard scientific article gives little room for radically new ideas and for developing new theory.[5]

When the new incentive system is implemented in universities, where research is organised in scientific disciplines defining legitimate borders of research fields, and defining what is acceptable in terms of methods, this leads to an overproduction of trivial scientific papers and to a systematic neglect of research issues that cannot easily be transformed into articles fitting the standard format.

Professors are tempted to advise PhD students to stick to safe fields of research where there is sufficient data to apply standard methods. Researchers can raise their own ranking by producing almost identical papers again and again.[6]

Defining Creativity in Research

Most definitions of creativity refer to an idea or artefact that is useful as well as new and original. In the case of scientific research there are specific problems with such definitions. An important insight from creativity research is that creative thinking and action will meet resistance (Sternberg & Lubart, 1995), since it destabilises ongoing activities and undermines positions of powerful people. This is true also for scientific work. Even if they are highly relevant, radical new ideas and research results will often not be accepted without a long time-lag

I, therefore, define creative activities in science as activities that result in new ideas and methods without adding the conditionality of usefulness. Newness can refer to the problem studied, to methods used, and to results from the research. Especially interesting is creativity that results in new theory and new theoretical perspectives. From time to time such changes may result in a shift in scientific paradigm. The great majority of scientific publishing involves incremental change rather than paradigmatic change. In fact, it can be argued that scientific training, where scientists learn to follow the conventions of a specific discipline, aims at ensuring that they do not deviate too radically from the mainstream. While the individual researcher is expected to add something new in each scientific paper, the emphasis is on continuity rather than novelty.

There is a voluminous scientific literature on individual creativity stretching from life stories of individuals who are generally regarded as creative people, brain studies, and attempts to measure creativity through testing (Sternberg, 1999; Helson, 1986; Weisberg, 1983). One insight from this research is that creativity is domain specific. The artist, the music composer, and the author are all constantly engaged in creating something that is unique. The scientist, the engineer, and the skilled worker will depend on creativity when confronted with more or less unforeseen and complex problems.

Product developers in R&D-departments, software developers, architects, and designers may be seen as operating in between the world of creative art and the world of creativity in material production.[7]

The idea that more creativity is always a good thing is too simplistic. Most meaningful economic, social, and intellectual processes need to combine creative thinking and action with skilful routine behaviour and application of established knowledge. This is certainly the case for research. In what follows I nonetheless assume that more creativity in research would be a good thing. This is based upon the observation that there is an overproduction of publications presenting trivial results and a scarcity of contributions opening up new insights that can be used to solve social problems and bolster technical and social innovations.

Teresa Amabile on Creativity

Teresa Amabile is widely cited in the research on creativity (Amabile, 1982, 1986). Her contributions are of special interest for the discussion here since her work links the analysis of individual creativity to the creativity of teams and to innovation in organisations (Amabile, 1988; Amabile & Pratt, 2016).

Amabile's original model was developed based on interviews with scientists and marketing experts (Amabile, 1988). It links a process of individual and team creative thinking to a process of innovation at the level of the organisation.

At the level of the individual she found that three types of factors contribute to creativity:

- Domain specific skills,
- Creativity relevant skills,
- Intrinsic task motivation.

One provocative and interesting result of her studies is the emphasis on motivation, particularly her argument that extrinsic motivation has a negative impact upon creativity. The following quotes are from Amabile (1988):

> Motivation is the component of individual creative performance that has been most neglected by creativity researchers, theorists, and practitioners. Yet, in

some ways, this may be the most important component. No amount of skill in the domain or in methods of creative thinking can compensate for a lack of appropriate motivation to perform an activity.

Thus, motivation may simply be the most straight forward component to address in attempts to stimulate creativity. Relatively subtle changes in the work environment can make possible substantial increases in individual creativity.

The negative impact of extrinsic motivators appears in the interview study as the 'externally motivated' factor: being motivated primarily by money, recognition, or other factors aside from the work itself, responding primarily to restrictions and goals set by others, being competitive and jealous of someone else's success. Each of these elements describes an extrinsic motivation, and each was linked to low creativity in the stories told by our interviewees. (p. 133)

In a very ambitious research survey on creativity and innovation covering the period 2002–2013 and almost 300 papers, Anderson, Potnicic, and Zhou (2014) revisit the issues raised in Amabile's 1988 model. They conclude that in general her analysis of the importance of intrinsic motivation has been supported by more recent research.

On the basis of a meta-study covering more than 80 empirical studies, Cerasoli, Nicklin, and Ford (2014) show that both intrinsic and extrinsic incentives affect 'performance'. But they also show that, while extrinsic incentives have a positive impact upon quantitative variables, when it comes to *quality*, intrinsic motivation is the most important factor. They also find that when extrinsic incentives are combined with stricter managerial control they have a negative impact upon quality.

Amabile and Pratt (2016) have developed a new and extended version of the model that Amabile introduced 1988. One important change is that they now recognise that extrinsic incentives, under certain circumstances, can reinforce intrinsic motivation. This might be the case when there is a pro-social motivation—when the individual finds work meaningful because the individual and the team's contribution is seen as useful for society. This, arguably, goes beyond scholars' efforts to produce more publications and citations.[0]

Synergy between extrinsic and intrinsic incentives may also be present when extrinsic incentives take the form of information rather than control, and when the information takes the form of giving recognition on dimensions valued by individuals.

This points to the possibility that bibliometric indicators as basis for evaluating success may have stimulated creativity at the level of individuals and teams at an early stage. But the more bibliometric performance becomes dominant and the more it permeates the university system, the more likely that a negative impact upon the originality and relevance of research may take the upper hand.

A Case Study—on the Limited Creativity of Creativity Studies

As mentioned, the Anderson, Potnicic, and Zhou (2014) survey is very ambitious, covering almost 300 scientific papers on innovation and creativity in organisations. They identify six theoretical frameworks in this subfield of psychology and organisational studies (one of which is Amabile's model from 1988). With one exception (ambidextrous theory) they are all contributions from around 1990.

Andersen et al. (2014) end the survey article with the observation that, in spite of the many new publication from the period (2002–2013), there has been little progress in terms of new theoretical understanding of the phenomena. Zhou (2006), demonstrating that creativity may thrive under different conditions in Asia than in the United States, is presented as an exception. Most of the surveyed papers test specific hypotheses derived from classical contributions.

Here some citations from the concluding part of their paper (Andersen et al., 2014, p. 1318):

… we are struck by the relative lack of theoretical advances.

… a whole morass of valuable empirical studies has appeared over the last decade.

… some of the most influential theories in the field have been around for 20–30 years or even longer.

For a sub-field whose raison d'être is to advance understanding of how new and innovative ideas flourish and are implemented this is both paradoxical and perplexing …

It is not immediately clear to us why this is the case.

Based on my experience with research on innovation, entrepreneurship, and organisational learning, I would expect to find similar patterns in many other fields of research. One root cause of the lack of theoretical advance is the academic incentive system; where it has become more important to be productive than creative.

Another factor is 'tribalism' in research where scholars interact within a group defined by a discipline, sub-discipline, or a narrowly defined inter-disciplinary field. It is striking that the literature survey on creativity and innovation in organisations mentioned above made no reference to scholarly work in what others refer to as 'innovation studies', as developed by sociologists, economists, and business economists (Fagerberg et al., 2012). A similar survey within this field would probably show that the systematic neglect goes both ways.

Recent Trends in Incentivising University Research and Lessons from Creativity Research

The research by Amabile and others on creativity shows that most interesting forms of creativity are knowledge based. The skills are crucial for the creativity of artists, designers, and engineers. But not all forms of knowledge lead to creative thinking and action. The incentive system is crucial for the creative use of knowledge. Creativity thrives when individuals and teams are driven by enthusiasm and passion. The combination of management control and extrinsic incentives undermines creativity. Therefore, we would expect a major negative impact from the current use of numbers of articles and citations as the dominant measure of performance.

When extra weight is given to publication in specific 'high-quality' journals, the room for creativity is narrowed down even further. Bibliometric studies show that the focus on 'high quality journals' in connection with ranking of institutions systematically disfavours interdisciplinary research as compared to single discipline research (Rafols et al., 2012).

HOW CAN UNIVERSITIES COPE WITH GROWING INEQUALITY AND WIDENING CREATIVITY GAPS?

Universities financed by tax payers' money have a wider responsibility than fostering a creative class and promoting creative research in general. The ongoing polarisation of societies has, as illustrated by the recent presidential election in the United States, 'Brexit', and growing nationalism in Europe and other parts of the world, wider consequences in terms of undermining the open society. It may be seen as a challenge that points to the need to give creativity a direction. To engage in inclusive development may actually stimulate creativity. One interesting result from Amabile's most recent research discussed above is that individuals and teams are more creative when they experience that the activities that they engage in are meaningful.

One major factor behind populism and nationalism is growing inequality, combined with a growing cultural gap between 'the creative class' and the rest of the population. Universities are at the frontline in fostering the core of the creative class and they need to find ways to combine creativity with social and cultural inclusion.

To illuminate this problem, I will first use the concept the globalising learning economy to link global competition to growing income inequality (Archibugi & Lundvall, 2006). As a second step I will use the work by Richard Florida (2002) on the creative class to see how growing income inequality gets combined with a growing creativity gaps between regions within high income countries.

The Learning Economy, Globalisation and Growing Inequality

The tendency toward polarisation in labour markets, where the gap in terms of job opportunities and income between those with higher education and the rest becomes wider, can be tracked back at least to the middle of the 1980s (OECD, 1995). According to the OECD Job's Study, the two main factors explaining growing inequality were new technology (especially information technology) and international trade (especially outsourcing of activities to low wage countries).

In Lundvall and Johnson (1993) we proposed The Learning Economy as an alternative interpretation and we pointed to how the combination of new technology and more intense, global competition leads to acceleration in the rate of change, giving new importance to the capacity to learn at all levels of society.

Seen in this perspective polarisation reflects that educated workers are better prepared to engage in learning and that they get more generous access to training and learning within organisations in the private and public sector (known as the Matthews-effect).[9] Another factor behind growing income inequality is the prevailing form of globalisation where unregulated financial markets make it possible for the very rich to harvest most of the gains from globalisation. Finance capital has developed strategies that exploit the competition between national governments in a context of global transactions and weak global governance. This takes the form of international competition in establishing tax havens and lowering taxes.

Welfare systems, education systems, and labour markets mediate the impact of globalisation at the national level. In some countries the costs of globalisation are carried directly by individuals and families while in others more or less ambitious welfare states aim at compensating the victims of globalisation. Investments in workplace training and life-long learning may counter the polarisation effect. But income inequality has increased in all OECD-countries. Recently it has grown most significantly in egalitarian Nordic welfare states: Denmark, Finland, Iceland, Norway, and Sweden.

If the governance of the learning economy is left to market forces, these will tend to open up learning divides between regions and between social classes in national systems. Growing inequality is problematic not only from a normative perspective where social cohesion is seen as a positive characteristic of society. The economies that perform well in terms of growth and innovation are those where there is wide participation in organisational learning. Increasing inequality undermines the learning capability of organisations, regions, and countries (Lundvall, 2002).

What Role for the University in the National Learning System?

How the national education system responds to increasing inequality has to do with both the overall structure of the system and how learning is organised in schools (Lundvall, Rasmussen, & Lorenz, 2010).

Education systems where students can postpone their choice between 'practical' and 'academic' branches of the school system will work against stratification. Systems with good provision of vocational education and training programs will counterbalance the hierarchical bias and short-term perspective in much workplace training. Systems that are open in the sense that there are alternative ways to reach the highest level of education, and where adults who originally have had little education or training can join education programs and, in principle, reach the highest level, will be reflected in a more egalitarian culture than systems aiming at picking and isolating the elite at an early stage.

Universities may play a more or less positive role in this context. The most obvious implications are first, that teaching should aim at stimulating the capacity to learn and second, that universities need to combine youth education with life-long education programs. A less obvious implication is the need to design the knowledge infrastructure, including the universities and labour market institutions so that they give privileged access to skill upgrading for the low-skilled, semi-skilled, and narrow-skilled whose skills become obsolete in the globalising learning economy (Lundvall, 2013).

To increase the openness of universities in terms of recruitment, and in terms of their interaction with other components of the national education system, is one important response to the growing inequality. The trend toward elitism and sharp distinctions between teaching programs with theoretical and practical activities contribute to polarisation. Universities where research explicitly aims at solving societal problems and graduate programs include significant elements of practice, including periods of practical work, can enhance both the learning capacity of students and the relevance, quality, and creativity of research. Below I will give special attention to how universities may respond to regional polarisation.

The Creative Class

As we saw above, most research on creativity has focused on the individual, while scholars such as Amabile and her colleagues have thrown light on how individual creativity relates to creativity in teams and to organisational innovation. But even in her work, the organisation is treated as closed and there are few references to the wider setting in terms of regions and nations.

Richard Florida's publication of *The Rise of the Creative Class* (2002) was one of the first to give attention to what constitutes the basis for, and impact of, creativity at the levels of regions and nations. In a series of empirical studies Florida and his co-authors have argued that the presence of the creative class provides a key to explain differences in terms regional development (Florida, Mellander, & Stolarick, 2007; Mellander & Florida, 2006).

In Florida (2002), he states that the distinguishing characteristic of the creative class is that its members engage in work creating meaningful new forms. He refers to a 'super-creative core' producing new forms or designs that are readily transferable and widely useful. This group includes occupations such as scientists, poets, and architects. Beyond this core, Florida includes a diverse group of creative professionals within the creative class, who engage in creative problem-solving, drawing on complex bodies of knowledge to solve specific problems.

Florida's notion of the creative class is economic and based on the kinds of work activities or jobs that different occupational categories typically undertake. Consistent with this, he groups occupations in three classes: the creative, the service, or the working class. The creative class is defined to include most management occupations, professionals, and selected categories of technicians and assistant professionals. Florida (2002, p. 75, 330) estimates that in the United States the creative class increased from 3 million workers or 10% of the workforce in 1900 to 38.3 million or 30% in 1999.

Florida's message to policy makers is that there are positive opportunities in creating framework conditions in cities and regions that are attractive for the creative class. Prominent among these are values such as tolerance and diversity. Old industrial cities with conservative values and institutions will lose out to new ones that offer a diversified and multi-ethnic culture. Important components of the regional creative centres are universities. And universities are also important because they foster the core of the creative class.

Creative Work

Florida's way of measuring the size of the creative workforce has a number of limitations. As Florida's discussion of the creative factory emphasises (Florida, 2002, p. 52), creativity can extend down from the firm's management and technical services to the shop floor, and highly creative firms typically seek to mobilise the knowledge and skills of the entire workforce. To define the work of operators, sales and service staff, and craft workers as non-creative is at odds with a vast literature on 'learning organisations' that emphasise the collective learning and creativity at the workplace.

In a period where there is a growing focus upon polarisation between social groups and regions, it is useful to change the focus toward who is actually doing creative work. This is what we did in Lorenz and Lundvall (2010) where we used survey data to compare the organisation of work in 27 EU-member countries. The analysis demonstrated that not everybody who belongs to the creative class according to Florida's definition do 'creative work' while many service employees and workers actually do creative work.

The other important result was that the rate of participation in creative work was very different across the 27 EU-countries studied. Creative workers are most present in the Nordic countries and the Netherlands, and least present in the South and East of Europe. There are intermediate levels of creative work activity in the continental European nations and the United Kingdom.

This is important since it demonstrates that national institutional characteristics determine to what degree ordinary workers are included in a creative society. We found that countries with high degrees of income inequality have low degree of participation in creative work among ordinary workers, while flexicurity in labour markets (a combination of mobility in labour markets along with income security) has a positive impact.

In Lundvall, Rasmussen, and Lorenz (2010) we show that the frequency of creative work and discretionary learning in a national economy tends to be positively correlated with the education system and, more specifically, with its openness—to what degree individuals at all levels can enter the system during their life-cycle and end up as graduates. We also give some indications of how pedagogical methods can contribute to or hamper the capacity to learn and to cope with uncertainty.

Florida on the Formation of Creative Mega-regions

More recently, Florida has added a global perspective to his analysis of the creative class. He argues that global competition tends to lead toward the formation of a small number of mega-regions at the world level. Florida (2006) refers to one or two dozen mega-regions built around clusters of knowledge institutions. A major characteristic of those mega-regions is the presence of world leading universities. On this base Florida argues that nations and regions need to engage more strongly in attracting and developing world class universities.

But it is possible to use the insights from Florida's work for a different purpose. His analysis helps explain why the increasing income inequality becomes overlaid by a cultural polarisation reflecting the concentration of creative activities in certain regions and impoverishing other regions in terms of creativity. It could also be used to inspire strategies that counter these tendencies.

Florida is correct in assuming that processes of knowledge creation and knowledge use tend to become more and more transnational. New technologies make it possible to produce and use knowledge in global networks. At the same time, knowledge production is an activity characterised by strong centripetal forces and this leads toward concentration in the global and national knowledge landscape. The result is the concentration of knowledge production in a small number of specific regions located in Europe, the US, and Asia.

One factor behind this development is that it is attractive for scholars to operate in proximity of other lead scholars. This has to do with the fact that all forms of knowledge, including science, have important 'personal' and 'tacit' components that can be shared only through face-to-face communication. An interesting illustration is that Noble Prize winners in science tend to point to personal interaction with other senior scholars as being the most crucial inspiration for their major breakthroughs (Zuckerman, 1977).

The current form of globalisation tends to produce a combination of social polarisation and growing cultural and knowledge-based divides between centre and periphery. This is reinforced by the fact that metropolitan areas offering tolerance and diversity tend to attract the members of the so-called creative class. If left to market forces this leaves the periphery impoverished in terms of cultural capital and creativity.

As consequence, low-skilled, semi-skilled, and narrow-skilled workers living in the periphery experience a double alienation reflecting both economic and cultural factors. The current cultural and political gap between metropolitan areas deeply involved in global exchange of ideas such as New York and San Francisco on the one hand and regions in the US Midwest, where globalisation mainly results in the closing down of old industries, may be seen in this light.

One important implication is that the location of knowledge production and of cultural institutions and activities has become a burning issue. While economic geography has been mainly concerned with factors that determine the location of job creation, the focus now moves toward factors that determine the location of organisations and infrastructure that contributes to knowledge production, knowledge diffusion, and creativity.

UNIVERSITY STRATEGIES FOR COMBINING CREATIVITY AND INCLUSION

The transformation of universities has been described in terms of a movement from Humboldtian to Entrepreneurial Universities (Benner, 2011). In the Humboldtian University the focus is on doing basic research and on training a small number of elite students primarily for posts in the public sector or in research.[10] In contrast, the entrepreneurial university has strong connections to the private sector, large numbers of students, less strict borders between disciplines, and operating in a much more diversified knowledge infrastructure, sometimes referred to as Mode 2 production of knowledge (Gibbons et al., 1994).

An interesting question is if a third model might be possible, where the focus is more on social entrepreneurship and social inclusion than on market-oriented activities. Arocena and Sutz (2017) have discussed an alternative that they refer to as a 'developmental university', aiming at contributing to social well-being, peace, democracy, and sustainability in social, environmental, and economic dimensions, through stimulation of creativity and innovation and with roots in the region where it operates. They take historical inspiration from the Land University tradition in the US, from the Latin American movement for university, and from modern experiences with regional dispersion of university activities in Norway and Sweden (Arocena & Sutz, 2016). In this last section I discuss how universities can combine creativity with social inclusion in education, research, and in their interaction with society.

Table 1 presents ideas on how universities can develop strategies that contribute to creativity and inclusion. It makes a distinction between education, research, and the third mission, and adds ideas for what university administrators could do. It looks at initiatives aiming at, respectively, creativity and inclusion and it gives examples of how the two dimensions can be combined in concrete action.

Education should prepare students for the learning and creative economy. Pedagogical methods that make it possible to use theories and methods in the context of real, complex, and unstructured problems and grading systems that do not always ask for 'the right answer' contribute to this. Universities need to allocate more resources to 'life-long learning'. Combining theoretical studies with elements of practical work reduces the gap between universities as creative islands and the rest of society.

When it comes to inclusion, education programs should be made more accessible for students with non-academic backgrounds both in economic terms and through the introduction of coaching and mentorship programs that make the entrance into

Table 1. A university strategy for creativity and inclusion

	Creativity	Inclusion	Creativity & Inclusion—examples
Education	Problem based Theory & Practise Life-long	Access Outreach Open university	Let students from different study programs form groups that engage in studying and finding solutions to major societal problems.
Research	Diversity in Staff Meeting places Problem oriented Competing teams Prizes	Research agenda New partnerships	Develop new sets of success indicators for research where the focus is upon collective break-through results in tackling major societal challenges.
Third Mission	Students as ambassadors Define lead users in social domains	Relocate research and education activities toward periphery Build networks with social dimension	Open up the university through a combination of face to face and internet based interactions with a wide set of diverse users as members of new community. Establish problem catalogues for research and educational projects through this community.
University administrators	Stimulate all Initiatives from below	Develop a culture and mission that gives a strong emphasis on inclusion	Define the university as a major change agent in society. Combine focus on 'global excellence' with 'local relevance'.

academic environments less difficult. Group work may be organised in such a way that it gives room both for individual and collective creativity. Besides the regular study programs, universities may offer 'open university' education for occasional or part-time students

Study programs should give opportunities to collaborate with students from other programs. Letting interdisciplinary study groups focus upon societal problems enhances incentives for creativity and give students more meaningful learning experiences.

Research is more creative when scholars in research teams have different backgrounds in terms of culture, gender, and education. Creating meeting places at universities where scholars belonging to different research teams can meet stimulates the development of new ideas. To overcome the barriers between disciplines, there should be more emphasis on problems and less on disciplines when setting up the organisation of the university. Competition between teams working on a similar set of problems stimulates creative efforts and so does the use of 'prizes' as incentives.

Research can be inclusive in terms of the research agenda and in terms of the problems addressed. But inclusiveness can go further and include new partners and participants in research. Universities need to reduce their subjugation to current simplistic benchmarking and move toward full development plans taking into account their specific context. Such plans should include diverse objectives and refer to corresponding indicators of success. In the current era, some of the indicators that should be given special attention relate to outreach to peripheral regions and disfavoured social groups. In a rapidly changing context, development plans should be revised at least every five years and the success indicators should be reviewed and changed in order to avoid the potential for long term use to 'distort and corrupt the social processes it was intended to monitor' (cf citation from Campbell, 1976).

Both in the triple helix and the entrepreneurial university discourse the focus of the third mission is collaboration with industry or state. To stimulate creativity there is a need to develop a broader user interface. Connecting to lead users in terms of grassroots organisations that work for change in society would be useful in opening up new research questions. Students should be seen as important ambassadors for the university and letting students use their project work to engage with diverse users outside university would stimulate creativity.

The inclusion dimension of the third mission relates to physical location. The internet offers new opportunities for long-distance interaction but, as we have seen above, the physical location of activities remain of great importance. To establish physical locations in a wider set of places in the periphery, where research results can be presented and where part-time or full-time study programs can be offered, would help reduce the 'creativity gap'.

Establishing the university as a node in a diverse, community-based network of citizen organisations, and perhaps even formalising it into a network of university correspondents with privileged access to university activities, would have a positive effect both on creativity and inclusion. Such a network could be instrumental in the development of the problem catalogues for education and research.

Finally, the management and administrators can contribute to creativity by, not hindering, but stimulating new initiatives from the staff. They should (by setting good examples) foster a culture where creativity and inclusion are seen as important positive values. On this basis they should develop a mission for the university that combines the two. They need to balance between the current efforts to become a 'world class university' and the equally important goal to become a university with strong and deep roots in a socially and culturally cohesive society.

CONCLUSION

In this chapter I have discussed the societal role of universities in the light of ongoing changes in the world economy and with reference to the growing social, political, and cultural splits within western societies. I combined two perspectives—the perspective of creativity and the perspective of inclusiveness. While it is highly relevant to put more emphasis upon creativity in education and research, it is equally important for universities to avoid becoming islands of creativity isolated from the domestic periphery. The major challenge is to enhance creativity in research and education through changes that make universities more inclusive. There is a need for creativity in setting up new forms of inclusive interaction with society, and there is a need for different indicators of success than those that currently corrupt major functions of the university.

NOTES

[1] The chapter is based upon key-note lecture with the same title at the Aalborg conference on Creative Universities October 14, 2016.
[2] We define the *creative university* as an institution that stimulates research that open up new understanding of the world, fosters graduates who are able to cope with new problems while learning from doing so and establishes new kinds of relationships with diverse social groups. We follow Arocena and Sutz (2017, p. 62) in their definition of the *inclusive university* as referring to generalising access for students with focus on underprivileged groups, a research agenda that covers important societal problems and an interaction with and active involvement of people from all segments of society.
[3] Ranking of universities was first developed in the US as a service to students and parents who wanted to make informed choices. With growing mobility of researchers and students it spread internationally and today according to Hazelkorn (2011) there are more than 50 national ranking lists and 8 global ones.
[4] To be employable it is necessary for the individual scholar to produce a certain number of articles and citations and to be regarded as star scientist and get the extra privileges that follow from such status you need to be highly productive in these respects.
[5] The standard format does not invite radical new ideas. It is a short text where a substantial part should refer to earlier research. Based upon these references the author should point out what is new in the article and then move on to hypotheses, testing, results and conclusions.
[6] The global ranking has other negative side effects as well. It reinforces the dominance of English as Lingua Franca of universities and hereby it disfavours the participation of whole continents when it comes to academic networking. It also reinforces the regional concentration of knowledge production since a high ranking tends to attract further resources. In this part of the chapter I focus upon the negative effect of global rankings and the related focus on quantitative indicators on creativity in research.
[7] This literature is dominated by studies of creativity in the US and some other western countries. Only recently it has been considered that 'creativity' may take on different meanings and play a different role in different parts of the world.
[8] On the other hand, it implies that moving toward an inclusive university where the common goal is to create a more cohesive society can stimulate creativity among scholars.
[9] In Lundvall (2002) we find a strong 'Matthews's effect' in the distribution of training opportunities in Danish firms. Employees with higher education were offered opportunities to attend courses much more frequently than were workers with short formal education.
[10] These institutions had a dominant role in knowledge production and they were conservative and authoritarian (dominated by old white men). Perhaps the German universities remain closest to this ideal. The Humboldtian universities were not highly creative and definitely not inclusive.

REFERENCES

Amabile, T. M. (1982). Social psychology of creativity: A consensual assessment technique. *Journal of Personality and Social Psychology, 43*, 997–1013.
Amabile, T. M. (1988). A model of creativity and innovation in organizations. In B. M. Staw & L. L. Cummings (Eds.), *Research in organisational behaviour* (Vol. 10, pp. 123–167). Greenwich, CT: JAI Press.
Amabile, T. M. (1996). *Creativity in context*. New York, NY: Westview Press.

Amabile, T. M., & Pratt, M. G. (2016). The dynamic componential model of creativity and innovation in organizations: Making progress, making meaning. *Research in organizational behaviour, 36*, 157–183.

Anderson, N., Potočnik, K., & Zhou, J. (2014). Innovation and creativity in organizations: A state-of-the-science review, prospective commentary, and guiding framework. *Journal of Management, 40*(5), 1297–1333.

Archibugi, D., & Lundvall, B.-Å. (Eds.). (2001). *Europe in the globalising learning economy.* Oxford: Oxford University Press.

Arocena, R., & Sutz, J. (2017). Inclusive knowledge policies when ladders for development are gone: Some considerations on the potential role of universities. In B. Göransson & C. Brundenius (Eds.), *Universities, inclusive development and social innovation.* Cham: Springer International Publishing.

Benner, M. (2011). In search of excellence? An international perspective on governance of university research. In B. Göransson & C. Brundenius (Eds.), *Universities, inclusive development and social innovation.* Cham: Springer International Publishing.

Blau, J. (2005). Europe seeks greater creativity in basic research. *Research Technology Management, 48*(3), 2–3.

Brundenius, C., Göransson, B., & de Melho, J. M. C. (Eds.). (2017). *Universities, inclusive development and social innovation.* Cham: Springer International Publishing.

Cerasoli, C. P., Nicklin, J. M., & Ford, M. T. (2014). Intrinsic motivation and extrinsic incentives jointly predict performance: A 40-year meta-analysis. *Psychological Bulletin, 140*(4), 980–1008.

Campbell, D. T. (1976, December). *Assessing the impact of planned social change.* Hanover, NH: The Public Affairs Center, Dartmouth College.

Fagerberg, J., Fosaas, M., & Sapprasert, K. (2012). Innovation: Exploring the knowledge base. *Research Policy, 41*, 1132–1153.

Florida, R. (2002). *The rise of the creative class.* New York, NY: Basic Books.

Florida, R. (2006). The flight of the creative class: The new global competition for talent. *Liberal Education, 92*(3), 22–29.

Florida, R., Mellander, C., & Stolarick, K. (2008). Inside the Black box of regional development human capital, the creative class and tolerance. *Journal of Economic Geography, 8*, 615–649.

Gibbons, M., Limoges, C., Nowotny, H., Schwartzman, S., Scott, P., & Trow, M. (1994). *The new production of knowledge: The dynamics of science and research in contemporary societies.* London: Sage Publications.

Göransson, B., & Brundenius, C. (2011). *Universities in transition: The changing role and challenges for academic institutions.* Ottawa: Springer.

Hazelkorn, E. (2011). *Rankings and the reshaping of higher education: The battle for world wide excellence.* Dublin: Center for Social and Educational Research, Dublin Institute of Technology.

Helson, R. (1996). In search of the creative personality. *Creativity Research Journal, 9*, 295–306.

Lorenz, E., & Lundvall, B.-Å. (2010). Accounting for creativity in the European Union: A multi-level analysis of individual competence, labour market structure, and systems of life-long learning. *Cambridge Journal of Economics, 34*(1), 1–26.

Lundvall, B.-Å. (2002). *Innovation, growth and social cohesion: The danish model.* Cheltenham: Edward Elgar.

Lundvall, B.-Å. (2013). The 'new new deal' as a response to the Euro-crisis. In B. Benner (Ed.), *Before and beyond the global economic crisis: Economics, politics and settlement* (pp 151–172). Cheltenham: Edward Elgar.

Lundvall, B.-Å. (2016). *The learning economy and the economics of hope.* London: Anthem Press.

Lundvall, B.-Å., Rasmussen, P., & Lorenz, E. (2010). Education in the learning economy: A European perspective. *Policy Futures in Education, 6*(6), 681–700.

Ministry of Education. (1997). *National kompetenceudvikling.* Copenhagen: Ministry of Education.

OECD. (1994). *The OECD jobs study.* Paris: OECD Publishing.

Rafols, I., Leydesdorff, L., O'Hare, A., Nightingale, P., & Stirling, A. (2012). How journal rankings can suppress interdisciplinary research: A comparison between innovation studies and business & management. *Research Policy, 41*(7), 1262–1282.

Reddy, P. (2011). The evolving role of universities and their contribution to innovation and development. In B. Göransson & C. Brundenius (Eds.), *Universities in transition* (pp. 25–52). New York, NY: Springer.
Sternberg, R. J. (Ed.). (1999). *Handbook of creativity*. Cambridge: Cambridge University Press.
Sternberg, R. J., & Lubart, T. I. (1995). *Defying the crowd: Cultivating creativity in a culture of conformity*. New York, NY: The Free Press.
Weisberg, R. (1993). *Creativity: Beyond the myth of genius*. New York, NY: W.H. Freeman.
Zhou, J. (2006). A model of paternalistic organizational control and group creativity. *Research on Managing Groups and Teams, 9*, 75–95.
Zuckerman, H. (1977). *Scientific elite: Nobel laureates in the United States*. New York, NY: The Free Press.

Bengt-Åke Lundvall
Department of Management and Business Studies
Aalborg University
Aalborg, Denmark

MICHAEL A. PETERS AND PETAR JANDRIĆ

10. PEER PRODUCTION AND COLLECTIVE INTELLIGENCE AS THE BASIS FOR THE PUBLIC DIGITAL UNIVERSITY

INTRODUCTION[1]

During the past few decades, the traditional concept of the university has been permanently (and probably irreversibly) altered. Universities are now 'engines of innovation' for 'fast capitalism' dealing in 'fast knowledge', 'fast publishing' and 'fast teaching' (e.g. Massive Open Online Courses—MOOCs) where 'knowledge' (confused with information) is seen as having a rapidly decreasing half-life (Hayes & Jandrić, 2017; Peters, 2015a). We have passed the bedding-down stage of neoliberal universities that occurred with the transformation of the public sphere during the Reagan–Thatcher decades of the 1980s and 1990s. We have passed the stage of the adoption of principles of New Public Management (NPM) (Olssen & Peters, 2005) and the emulation of private sector management styles to enter an era of universities in the service of finance capitalism where universities, increasingly reliant on student fees (especially international students) and independent research funds, serviced by high-speed networks and MOOCs, operate as a part of global finance culture. While these developments have brought about significant changes in political economy of the university, information and communication technologies have simultaneously brought about new affordances for (and new restrictions to) human creativity (Peters & Jandrić, 2018a).

Building on historical models of the university from mid-twentieth century until today developed in our earlier works (Peters & Jandrić, 2018a; see also Peters & Heraud, 2015), and examination of practices of a number of online educational institutions, this chapter develops the model of 'the creative university as digital public university'. It argues for a conception of the 'creative university' that embraces user-centered and open-innovation public ecosystems based on the shared ethos underlying 'co-creation', 'co-production', and 'co-design'. These new platforms emphasize and utilize theories of collective intelligence and commons-based peer production. By contrast to the historically enduring models of German idealism and Romanticism that emphasize individual creativity anchored in the passions and dark inchoate forces of the subconscious, the model of peer production and collective intelligence is a product of social, networked, and rich semiotic environments in which everything speaks. This chapter outlines these contrasting ideals and articulates the latter ideal as a philosophy for the public digital university.

© PHILOSOPHY OF EDUCATION SOCIETY OF AUSTRALASIA, 2018
DOI:10.1163/9789004384149_010

M. A. PETERS & P. JANDRIĆ

THE COLLECTIVE NATURE OF CREATIVITY

Ancient philosophers did not have today's concept of creativity. In *The Republic*, Plato (360 BC) describes artistic creation as imitation of nature. Aristotle generally agrees with Plato, yet he acknowledges that the act of creation is not purely rational and compares the act of creation with madness. The first Western concept of creativity was derived from the Biblical stories of creation. For Christians, creativity is the property of God, which can only be discovered and/or imitated by people. Since the dawn of Christianity, the modern concept of creativity took almost two millennia to emerge in its present form (Sternberg, 1999).

The Enlightenment defined creativity in two main ways. First, philosophers of Enlightenment argued that Reason was the basis of all science. In this view mathematics and logic became paradigmatic forms, and they established the culture of the objective. Thus, for Voltaire,

> God has given us the principle of universal reason just as he has given feathers to birds and furs to bears, and this principle is so constant that it continues to exist despite all the passions which fight against it; despite the tyrants who wish to drown it in blood; despite the impostors who would employ superstition to bring it to naught. (Voltaire, 1759)

The second, Romanticist vision claimed that art, music, poetry, and literature were the paradigmatic expression of creativity. In this vision, which established the culture of the irrational, Fichte writes: 'Heed only yourself: turn your gaze away from all around you, and inwards towards yourself; this is the first demand that philosophy makes of its apprentice. Nothing outside you matters but solely you yourself' (Fichte, 1794).

The quotes by Voltaire and Fichte illustrate an important general principle: the Enlightenment view to creativity is based on logic and reasoning, while the Romanticist view to creativity is based on feeling and intuition. However, the history of human thought cannot be described in black and white, and the space between these extremes contains many shades of gray. In the context of epistemology, today's science and technology studies (STS) recognize that knowledge is always a combination between logic, reasoning, feeling, and intuition—and heavily shaped by various social forces (see, for instance, Fuller, 2006). Speaking of creativity, however, the essential battle between reason and unreason remains until present— Romantic worldview is still with us, even though it exceeds its intellectual defense.

A good example of one-sided view to creativity is Howard Gardner's influential and heavily contested theory of multiple intelligences and creativities. According to Gardner,

> we are all able to know the world through language, logical-mathematical analysis, spatial representation, musical thinking, the use of the body to solve problems or to make things, an understanding of other individuals, and an understanding of ourselves. (Gardner, 2011, p. 12)

Gardner's seven creativities are based on the paradigm of individual psychology and deeply Americentric. The theory of multiple intelligences holds on to the past liberal arts values as the means to resist the digital onslaught. In this stereotype, the great creatives of our times are those who produce applications (such as Steve Jobs and Mark Zuckerberg) rather than those who produce infrastructures (such as Tim Berners Lee). Two decades ago, Richard Barbrook and David Cameron linked such views to creativity and the ideology of neoliberalism, and dubbed it 'the Californian ideology' (Barbrook & Cameron, 1996). More recently, Jandrić's analysis of the history of computing shows that infrastructures, as necessary preconditions for applications, are just as responsible for innovations as the individual creative genius (Jandrić, 2017). Individual creativity cannot be thought of without social creativity, and each individual act of creativity is also an act of collectivity.

Using a different approach, Peters (2009) also firmly opposes Gardner's psychologization of creativity. He analyses Banaji, Burn, and Buckingham's construction of the idea of creativity as the series of ten 'rhetorics of creativity', and concludes that it represents one of the best reviews of creativity in the field of education. The ten 'rhetorics of creativity' are:

1. Creative Genius
2. Democratic Creativity and Cultural Re/Production
3. Ubiquitous Creativity
4. Creativity for Social Good
5. Creativity as Economic Imperative
6. Play and Creativity
7. Creativity and Cognition
8. The Creative Affordances of Technology
9. The Creative Classroom
10. Art, Creativity and Political Challenge (Banaji, Burn, & Buckingham, 2006).

According to Peters, the ten 'rhetorics of creativity' are underpinned by a balanced combination of the Enlightenment views to creativity and the Romanticist views to creativity. He argues that 'while the rhetorics approach is not made clear, the review usefully identifies cross-cutting themes as a basis for future research' and asks the following questions:

1. Is creativity an internal cognitive function or an external socio-cultural or economic phenomenon?
2. It it a ubiquitous human activity or a special faculty?
3. Is it inevitably 'pro-social' or can also be dissident or even anti-social?
4. What the implications are for a creative model of teaching and learning? (Peters, 2009, p. 50).

Peters answers these questions by developing two distinct accounts. The dominating account is the 'personal anarcho-esthetics', which is based on the romantic, irrational, and individualistic view to creativity; the minor, but rapidly developing account of 'the design principle' is based on logic of collaboration and peer production (Peters, 2009, p. 40). In *The Digital University: A Dialog and Manifesto* (Peters & Jandrić, 2018a) we relate personal anarcho-esthetics to the notion of *homo economicus*, and the design principle to the notion of *homo collaborans*. Without undermining the importance of psychology, this conclusion transfers questions pertaining to creativity from the realm of individualist approaches into the realm of social sciences.

Based on these conclusions, we defend a different paradigm of creativity as a sum of rich semiotic systems that form the basis of distributed knowledge and learning. This view sees creativity as enabled or permitted by the new digital infrastructures of human culture in twenty-first century—primarily technical infrastructure, code, and content. It is based on Wittgenstein's conception of language games developed in *Philosophical Investigations* (2001) and *On Certainty* (1975)—by making new rules, it creates a new game. In *The Digital University*, we describe this paradigm in more detail:

> In contrast to the individualistic Romantic model of creativity, the 'collective design paradigm' is both relational and social. It is more recent and tends to emerge in intersecting literatures of sociology, economics, technology and education surfacing in related ideas of 'social capital', 'situated learning', and 'P2P' accounts of commons-based peer production.
>
> In this model, innovation and creativity are seen as products of social and networked environments—rich semiotic environments in which everything speaks. This collective view of creativity is seen as a product of 'systems design'—platforms for collective awareness—that allows a high degree of interaction and rests on principles of distributed knowledge and collective intelligence. (Peters & Jandrić, 2017)

This view describes the logic of creativity in and for the age of digital reason. It avoids some problems associated with earlier theories, most notably the artificial divorce between reason and feeling and various problems arising from managerialist approaches. This view also introduces an array of new problems, primarily those related to collective construction of knowledge, some of which will be explored in the rest of the chapter. In order to explore these issues, we will first link the developed views to creativity with past and present ideas of the university.

THE IDEA OF THE UNIVERSITY: A HISTORICAL OVERVIEW

In *The University in Ruins* (1996) Bill Readings claims that the contemporary idea of the university is based on three important building blocks: the Kantian idea of reason, the Humboldtian idea of culture, and the technological idea of excellence. For Kant, it was the idea of reason which provided an organizing principle for the disciplines, with 'philosophy' as its home. Reason is the founding principle of the

Kantian university: it confers a universality upon the institution and, thereby, ushers in modernity. The Kantian university displaces the Aristotelian order of disciplines of the medieval university based on the seven liberal arts, to substitute a quasi-industrial arrangement of the faculties. The Kantian university has no content apart from the free exercise of reason and the self-critical and self-legislating exercise of reason.

For the German idealists, from Schiller through Schleiermacher to Fichte and Humboldt, the unity of knowledge and culture, exemplified best in the organicity of ancient Greek culture, has been splintered and lost. It can be reintegrated into a unified cultural science and research through *Bildung*, the formation and cultivation of moral subjects. In *The Digital University*, we show that many features of the contemporary university stem directly from Humboldt's view to the university as a public good (Peters & Jandrić, 2018a, Chapter 19). Public goods are non-excludable and non-rivalrous—their consumption does not reduce availability to others (e.g. language, security, knowledge). Understood as a public good, the university contributes to development of 'political sphere' for rational debate and deliberative democracy, fostering of democratic citizenship, growth of general 'civic intelligence', and also determining the 'public interest'.

For Readings (1996, Chapter 2), the technological idea of excellence replaces the ideology of national culture with the ideology of the marketplace. Through dubious practices such as the UK's Research Excellence Framework (popularly known as the REF), the vague notion of excellence, thus, becomes an important currency within the contemporary university. Readings' critique by and large corresponds to wider critiques of the neoliberal university and its focus to excellence provides an important input for further research of practices such as NPM.

Depending on focus, universities can be classified into various models. In *The Digital University* (Peters & Jandrić, 2018a, Chapter 19), we develop three main contemporary models of the relationships between digital technologies and the university—'the functionally integrated digital university', 'the information model of the digital university', and 'the open model of the digital university'—and we argue that the open model is best suited for the age of the digital reason. In regards to the understanding of the university as a public good, in this chapter, we identify two conflicting mainstream models: the 'Public' University circa 1960–1980, and the 'post-historical' university.

The 'Public' University circa 1960–1980 saw its public mission in the historical purpose 'to educate citizens in general, to share knowledge, to distribute it as widely as possible, and to produce it in accord with publicly articulated purposes (as well as on the assumption of eventual public benefit)' (Calhoun, 2006, p. 19). However, such correspondence does not immediately imply the Humboldtian nature of the 'Public' University. According to Foucault,

> the thread that may connect us with the Enlightenment is not faithfulness to doctrinal elements, but rather the permanent reactivation of an attitude—that

is, of a philosophical ethos that could be described as a permanent critique of our historical era. (Foucault, 1996, p. 312)

Thus, one of the main missions of the 'Public' University circa 1960–1980 is social critique.

The 'post-historical' university is much less, if at all, focused to social critique. Based on neoliberal ideology fostered by (but not limited to) the discourses of globalization and technological excellence, we call it the Global Service University. This model shifts core commitment of the university from 'the quest for universal truth' to 'quality assurance' in the discourse of excellence, where neoliberal managerialism becomes the dominant model of knowledge performance. Structural transformation toward the 'knowledge economy' is based on production of knowledge, investment in human capital, and diffusion of ICTs requiring 'management'. Neoliberal knowledge management rests on principles of *homo economicus* (assumptions of individuality, rationality, and self-interest) that are radically at odds with distributed knowledge systems (Peters & Jandrić, 2018a, Chapter 19).

TOWARDS THE CREATIVE UNIVERSITY AS DIGITAL PUBLIC UNIVERSITY: THE CASE OF DENMARK

Inspired by Olssen (2005), Degn and Sorensen develop the matrix of four different visions of the university, 'thus focusing on how ideational/normative conceptions shape the legitimate organizational forms' (2015, p. 939) (Figure 1). 'The community of scholars' vision is based on legacy of the Enlightenment and *Bildung*; 'the representative democracy' vision sees the university as a battlefield of internal converging interests; the 'university as the political instrument' vision is driven by university's service to the society at large; and 'the service enterprise' vision is driven by university's service to the (capitalist) marketplace.

Until 1970, Denmark had two universities: University of Copenhagen and Aarhus University. The 2003 University Act closed down Senate and Faculty Councils and introduced an external governance system with new boards of governors with an external majority, and the new 2011 University Act streamlined the managerial system. Using the matrix of four different visions of the university (Figure 1), Degn and Sorensen show that

> Denmark thus seemed to follow the path of NPM-reforms set out in other European countries and Australasia and pursue the political goal of strengthening the strategic capacity and competitiveness of the HEIs by increasing the formal autonomy of the institutions, granting them status of self-governing institutions and placing the overall responsibility for the performance of the institutions with a board comprising a minority of collegial representatives (staff and students) and a majority of external stakeholders

(e.g. business representatives). This change in governance structure is seen in many countries across Europe [...]. (Degn & Sørensen, 2015, p. 933)

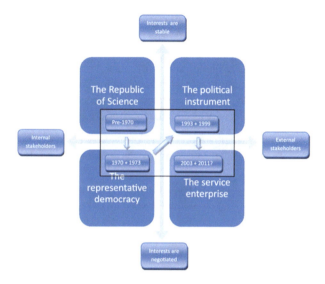

Figure 1. Four visions of the university (Degn & Sørensen, 2015, p. 40)

Some aspects of this change include:

1. Limited devolution to improve central government control.
2. Performance management culture—incentives, monitoring and contestable funding.
3. Contractualism—(principal-agency theory) *ex ante* performance specification.
4. Strategic planning.
5. Decentralisation of production and management decision-making resources.
6. Financial management system based on accrual accounting—"fiscal responsibility".
7. Competitive tendering and contracting out.

In an earlier work, Peters (2013) shows that NPM has by and large failed to address own growing problems and contradictions—many of which are echoed in the above list. Therefore, he concludes that the cutting edge of change has moved on to Digital Era Governance (DEG) which reintegrates concerns into government control, holistic (or joined-up) government and digitalization. DEG draws on principles of open government and utilizes the Web and digital storage to focus on transparency and better communication within government. It fosters digitalization of administrative processes, and reconnection with citizens. In this way, the digital university becomes a basis for the vision of the new public university, which recognizes that model of peer production and collective intelligence is a product of social, networked, and rich semiotic environments in which everything and everyone speaks.

The case of Denmark shows strong connections between models based on understanding of the university as a public good (the 'Public' University circa 1960–1980, and the 'post-historical' university) and models based on relationships between digital technologies and the university ('the functionally integrated digital university', 'the information model of the digital university', and 'the open model of the digital university'). Therefore, we use it as real-life inspiration for development of the new model which integrates the 'Public' University and 'the open model of the digital university': 'the creative university as digital public university'. This model is based on:

1. User-centered and open-innovation public knowledge ecosystems.
2. Shared ethos underlying 'co-production', 'co-creation', 'co-design' and 'co-responsibility'.
3. New platforms to utilize collective intelligence and commons-based peer production.
4. Focuses on the links between openness and creativity; design and responsibility; DEG.
5. Radical openness, interconnectivity and interactivity—shift from industrial broadcast media (one to many) to new social media (many to many).

PRACTICAL ATTEMPTS AT THE CREATIVE UNIVERSITY AS DIGITAL PUBLIC UNIVERSITY

There are many attempts at creating 'digital', 'public', and 'creative' universities. Yet, these popular buzzwords often mean different things to different people and in different contexts. Therefore, we need to take a brief look at different contemporary practices and examine their correspondence to our model.

In their promotional video, University College Cork promotes itself as Ireland's Digital University through following claims:

- Technology is a fundamental component of a twenty-first university.
- Flexible adaptive learning experience.
- Preparing students for a digital world.
- Teachers provide students with all their material online.
- Students can use devices to access knowledge anywhere at any time.
- Students can access services online 24/7 (University College Cork, 2016).

This model is clearly digital and open; yet, it lacks to mention important themes such as peer production, interconnectivity, collaboration, and creativity.

Started in 2003, the UNPIdF project was launched to establish seventeen Digital Universities across France. The recent brochure for Paris Île-de-France Digital University (UNPIdF, 2017) lists the following mission goals:

- to help the universities of Paris and Île-de-France define and implement their digital and online development policy;

- to make it easier for institutions to expand their digital services and facilities by optimizing means and resources;
- to give impetus to new services and keep up with technological developments;
- to help students and staff get to grips with digital and online tools and services (UNPIdF, 2017).

Similarly to University College Cork, the UNPIdF project also strongly focuses to digitalisation and openness; by and large, however, collaboration, creativity and the logic of peer production seem to be absent from their activities.

Similar developments can also be found in the private and corporate sectors. For instance,

> Digital University, Inc. provides online training and education to professionals in the financial industry. It offers a range of online bank and credit union courses on various topics, including accounting and finance, compliance and regulation, member service, financial products, human resources, international finance, lending, management and supervision, sales and marketing, and teller training. The company provides regulatory compliance training on federal regulations, customer service issues, and back-office and management skills. It also offers Digital PlusLMS, a learning management system with complete customization for financial institutions; Compliance Center that helps its clients'. (Bloomberg, 2017)

At the Digital University, Inc. the focus is again predominantly on the digital.

Looking at various teaching and learning practices, it is also useful to examine key policy documents. One such document, a report of the UCSD research cyberinfrastructure design team entitled "Blueprint for the Digital University"

> provides the rationale and design for a campus-wide research cyberinfrastructure (RCI) that will meet federal mandates for research data preservation, improve UCSD's academic competitiveness, and achieve economies-of-scale savings through centralization of core infrastructure elements, while at the same time recognizing the diverse and distributed nature of UCSD's research enterprise. (UCSD, 2009)

The proposed infrastructure consists of six elements: colocation facilities, centralized disk storage, digital curation and data services, research cyberinfrastructure network, condo clusters, and cyberinfrastructure expertise (ibid). This policy document focuses on digital openness and collaboration, and recognises the logic of peer production and collaboration. However, it seems to stop just short of understanding the relationships between openness, collaboration, and creativity.

Some institutions work at the intersections between education and business. For instance, in 2008 Peter Diamandis and Ray Kurzweil founded the Singularity University which serves both as an educational institution and a business incubator.

> Singularity University is a global community using exponential technologies to tackle the world's biggest challenges. Our learning and innovation platform empowers individuals and organizations with the mindset, skillset, and network to build breakthrough solutions that leverage emerging technologies like artificial intelligence, robotics, and digital biology. With our community of entrepreneurs, corporations, development organizations, governments, investors, and academic institutions, we have the necessary ingredients to create a more abundant future for all. (Singularity University, 2017)

The Singularity University is strongly oriented toward the logic of peer production and creative collaboration. However, its ethos is completely neoliberal or 'post-historical', and places neoliberal knowledge management embodied in the figure of *homo economicus* at the centre of its activities.

Some online universities seem to embody the logic of the creative university as digital public university almost completely. For instance, the Digital University of America promises education and degrees without any charge, and it offers a unique approach to curriculum:

> You will follow a COURSE of STUDY that will take you on a CHRONOLOGICAL JOURNEY from the BEGINNING of CIVILIZATION to the PRESENT. This march through time will review the contribution of Great Individuals, their ideas and concepts, Great World Events, and Great Philosophical and Scientific Ideas—along with the impact these revelations and innovations had on civilization and are still having today. When you finish this Course of Study, you will know a lot about everything and much more about your Major Subject. (The Digital University of America, 2016)

In theory, the promise of the Digital University of America seems almost too good to be true. In practice, however, a closer examination of their website reveals a dubious pedagogical model, a lack of community, a non-transparent business model, and a complete lack of quality control and certification. The Digital University of America is a university only by the name—in reality, it is just a (probably) well-intended website.

Another project based on similar principles is the University of the Commons:

> The University of the Commons creates opportunities for learning, camaraderie, and critical thinking by and for the diverse San Francisco Bay Area community. Activities include classes, lectures, workshops, seminars, exhibitions, teach-ins, and art and activist interventions. The University of the Commons aims to inspire participants to evolve more equitable and just societies and live more empowered and fulfilling lives. All activities are free of charge. (The University of the Commons, 2017)

Unlike the Digital University of America, the University of the Commons has a clear business model (volunteers from the ranks of teachers, artists, activists, scholars, writers, and others) and its website displays some online and face to face activity. The University of the Commons is definitely public and open; yet, it does not seem to recognise the importance of peer production and collaboration.

In Bangladesh, the cabinet approved a draft on "Digital University, Bangladesh Act 2014", which proposed establishing of "a specialized public university on information and communication technology with a main objective to expedite the pace of development through qualitative improvement of the IT education in the country" at Gazipur Hi-tech Park. (Bangladesh Awami League, 2017). This attempt is strongly oriented to technology; in spite of its public nature, it strongly fosters neoliberal views to knowledge creation and dissemination.

One of the most famous successful private companies offering online education is Coursera.

> Coursera was founded in 2012 by two Stanford Computer Science professors who wanted to share their knowledge and skills with the world. Professors Daphne Koller and Andrew Ng put their courses online for anyone to take—and taught more learners in a few months than they could have in an entire lifetime in the classroom.
>
> Since then, we've built a platform where anyone, anywhere can learn and earn credentials from the world's top universities and education providers. (Coursera, 2017)

In 2017, Coursera has reported an astounding number of over 2000 courses and 24 million learners (ibid). Many Coursera courses are free, but obtaining credentials requires payment. Through peer-graded assignments and other options, Coursera seems to acknowledge the logic of peer production and its relationships to creativity. However, its business model is commercial and only partially open; despite availability of huge amount of material, Coursera is very far from being public.

Another hugely successful private online education company is the Khan Academy, which has delivered more than one billion lessons between 2006 and 2017.

> Khan Academy offers practice exercises, instructional videos, and a personalized learning dashboard that empower learners to study at their own pace in and outside of the classroom. We tackle math, science, computer programming, history, art history, economics, and more. (Khan Academy, 2017)

The Khan Academy is a non-profit organization, and its lessons and videos are freely available to anyone. Yet, individual consumption of lessons is far from peer production and collaboration, and most of lessons are designed as learning supplements. The Khan Academy it is not a university, yet it supports the logic of the creative university as digital public university.

In *Preparing for the digital university: A review of the history and current state of distance, blended, and online learning,* Siemens, Gašević, and Dawson (2015) claim that educational technology has gone through three distinct generations of development and now a fourth is emerging:

Generation 1—Basic technology use: Computer-based Training (CBT) and websites.

Generation 2—Enterprise systems: learning management systems (LMS) and content management systems (CMS).

Generation 3—Fragmentation and diversification: social media, e-portfolio software and MOOC providers, integrated vendor/publishers.

Generation 4—Distributed and digitally shaped technologies: adaptive learning, distributed infrastructures, and competency models. (Siemens, Gašević, & Dawson, 2015)

In terms of technology, all examined institutions and companies use basic websites and enterprise systems (Generation 1 and Generation 2). More serious practices typically undergo at least some fragmentation and diversification (Generation 3), while only a few examined cases (such as UCSD and the Singularity University) have clearly entered Generation 4. In relation to understanding of the university as a public good, examined institutions and companies exhibit a wide range of business models and approaches. However, only a few examined cases (such as University College Cork and Paris Île-de-France Digital University) seem to be genuinely public. By now, we have not managed to find an institution or company that would meet both criteria for 'the creative university as digital public university'—a public institution which belongs to Siemens, Gašević and Dawson's Generation 4. However, this overview does indicate various developments in that direction—hopefully, we will soon witness the birth of a true 'creative university as digital public university'.

PEER PRODUCTION, COLLECTIVE INTELLIGENCE, AND DEMOCRACY

The age of the computer is commonly discussed through the discourse of pervasiveness, totality, performativity, surveillance, control, efficiency, and decentralization of information; taken together, these developments can be understood as circuits of cybernetic capitalism. In order to stress the simultaneously technological and non-technological nature of these developments, Peters has coined the expression 'the epoch of digital reason' (Peters, 2015a; Peters & Jandrić, 2017).

Recent research in computational brain science shows that the epoch of the digital reason reaches deeper than the relationships between humans and their tools. Western's inter-disciplinary Computational Brain Science (CBS) team shows that 'just as groups of people interact differently depending on context, parts of the brain also work together differently at different times. […] The brain works the same way, with different parts functioning together at different times' (Western's Computational Brain Science's, 2017). This indicates that many features of the epoch of digital reason might be ingrained deeply in human nature, and calls for stronger integration of traditional academic disciplines.

Increasingly, the abstract, internalist, individualist computer-based model of consciousness and cognition has given way to the model of embodied cognition or what has come to be called the 4 E's: Embodied, Embedded, Extended, and Enacted. In this view,

> cognitive processes are not restricted to structures and operations instantiated in the brain, but incorporate wider bodily structures and processes. These wider bodily structures and processes in part constitute—are constituents of—cognitive processes'. (Rowlands, 2010, p. 57)

To an extent, therefore, brain science indicates that the Internet can be understood as a form of a networked mind.

Similar developments can be found in many traditional academic disciplines. In the field of economy, for instance, Tapscott identifies 12 overlapping themes "which differentiate the new economy from the old. The new economy is:"

> (1) a knowledge economy, based on human capital and networks, (2) a digital economy, (3) virtualized, (4) a molecular economy, (5) a networked economy, integrating molecules into clusters which network with others for the creation of wealth, (6) eliminating middlemen, (7) being created by the new media, a convergence of the computing, telecommunications, and content industries, (8) an innovation-based economy, (9) blurring the gap between producers and consumers, (10) immediate, (11) a global economy, and (12) causing discord. (Tapscott, 1997)

This list of examples from various fields could be continued almost endlessly. However, the presented cases from brain science (small-scale; focused to the individual) and economy (large-scale; focus to the collective) clearly indicate that recent developments in diverse traditional disciplines are slowly but surely arriving to (various definitions of) the concept of collective intelligence.

Collective intelligence is a popular term that has come recently into view because technology-enabled Internet applications have accelerated and reconfigured new networks of research, sharing, and collaboration based on the driving logic that everyday problems can be solved through the democratic coordination of large groups of engaged people who become better informed and less biased in arriving at collective group-think solutions. According to Pierre Lévy, collective intelligence

> is a scientific, technical and political project that aims to make people smarter with computers, instead of trying to make computers smarter than people. So, collective intelligence is neither the opposite of collective stupidity nor the opposite of individual intelligence. It is the opposite of artificial intelligence. It is a way to grow a renewed human/cultural cognitive system by exploiting our increasing computing power and our ubiquitous memory. (in Peters, 2015b, p. 261)

Collective intelligence is but one dimension of a new collectivity based on an increased global interconnectivity that can be seen as both a cultural and evolutionary development of human intelligence that makes explicit the social basis of language and consciousness. In this sense, this new collectivity is the basis of embedded networks of collective intelligence, collective responsibility, collective governance, and collective action. As such, collective intelligence is the evolving cultural infrastructure (like the invention of alphabets and writing) for the national systems of higher education.

Systems without central control are very common in nature; insects and animals providing models of 'self-organization' in the way that they socialize in flocks, schools, swarms, etc. However, not all collective behavior is collective intelligence. Peters and Heraud define the following types of collective intelligence:

1. Biological—'swarm intelligence', social insects.
2. Political—epistemic democracy.
3. Administrative, public policy—co-creation and co-production of public services, peer production.
4. Cognitive—the embodied mind (extended, embedded, enacted), social cognition.
5. Technological—AI, machine learning, genetic algorithms, learning analytics, open-source software.
6. Evolutionary—'global brain', 'noosphere' (Peters & Heraud, 2015; for more information see Peters & Jandrić, 2015, 2017).

As of recently, all these fields have undergone significant development. However, as yet, there is no general theory of collective behavior.

According to Sumpter, 'humans are inherently social animals, whose activities exhibit many of the elements of co-operation and conflict found in other animal societies' (2006, p. 12). There is a great deal of variety in epistemic approaches to democracy but that they are all derived from the value of free public discourse that epistemologically guides political practice. There are no right answers independent of the political process, but overall it is best conceived as a collective way of coming to know and what to do. Similar approaches form the basis of our current epistemologies. For Peirce, the idea of truth is that consensus reached in the long run by a community of inquirers. Peirce takes scientific inquiry to be justified not because it is infallible but because it is self-correcting in the long-term (Burch, 2014).

The new orthodoxy is that we are entering the new age of digitally enabled peer production that is democratizing economics, politics, and culture with the participation of citizen-amateurs and the open sourcing of journalism, science, library science, and fields of cultural production. According to Kreiss, Finn, and Turner, this orthodoxy is based on five claims:

1. Pursuing psychologically gratifying labor within peer production is an unqualified good;
2. Peer networks are an egalitarian and efficient means of producing information goods;

3. Peer production necessarily realizes ethical relationships between collaborators;
4. Peer production is equally suited to all domains of social activity;
5. Peer production is nonmarket and nonproprietary (Kreiss, Finn, & Turner, 2011, p. 244).

Benkler, Shaw and Hill assert that "peer production is the most significant organizational innovation that has emerged from Internet-mediated social practice" (2015, p. 2). They define peer production as a form of collective intelligence that:

> set and execute goals in a decentralized manner; harness a diverse range of participant motivations, particularly non-monetary motivations; and separate governance and management relations from exclusive forms of property and relational contracts (i.e., projects are governed as open commons or common property regimes and organizational governance utilizes combinations of participatory, meritocratic and charismatic, rather than proprietary or contractual, models). (ibid., pp. 2–3)

These approaches and definitions open up a myriad of questions regarding the relationships between peer production, collective intelligence, the (higher education) marketplace (see Jandrić et al., 2017), and knowledge dissemination (Peters & Jandrić, 2016; Peters et al., 2016). In *The Sharing Economy: The End of Employment and the Rise of Crowd-Based Capitalism* (2016) Arun Sundararajan sums up these questions as follows: 'Will we live in a world of empowered entrepreneurs who enjoy professional flexibility and independence? Or will we become disenfranchised digital laborers scurrying between platforms in search of the next wedge of piecework?'

These questions provoke a wide spectrum of answers. On the (neo-)liberal side of the spectrum, in *Platform Revolution: How Networked Markets Are Transforming the Economy—And How to Make Them Work for You*, Parker, Van Alstyne, and Choudary answer by claiming that 'education is perhaps the prime example of a major industry that is ripe for platform disruption. Information-intensive? Check. In fact, the fundamental product being sold by schools, colleges, and universities is information of various kinds' (2016, p. 263). On the communitarian side of the spectrum, the series of Platform Cooperativism conferences presents itself as 'a coming-out party for the cooperative Internet, built of platforms owned and governed by the people who rely on them' (Platform Cooperativism, 2015; see also Taylor & Jandrić, 2016).

Technologically, both answers are equally viable—the logic of peer production can both reinforce and transform, the current logic of platform capitalism. However, contemporary university should not remain neutral in these challenges (Jandrić, 2013). Imbued in the Humboldtian tradition of *Bildung*, and more recent developments in digital democracy (see Peters & Jandrić, 2017), 'the creative university as digital public university' firmly stands with the communitarian responses to the problem of platform capitalism. It is only by fostering economic and social equality, that 'the creative university as digital public university' can sustain and develop free public discourse that epistemologically guides political practice of democracy.

TOWARDS THE CREATIVE PUBLIC DIGITAL UNIVERSITY

The open-science economy (OSE) is a rapidly growing sector of the global knowledge economy utilizing open-source models and its multiple applications (e.g. open access, open archiving, open publishing, open repositories) in distributed knowledge and learning systems. This rich-text, highly interactive, user-generated OSE has seen linear models of knowledge production give way to more diffuse, openended, decentralized, and serendipitous knowledge processes based on open-innovation and technology. These peer-to-peer distributed knowledge systems rival the scope and quality of traditional proprietary products through the diffusion speed and global access of open-source projects, especially in both software and open-source biology.

OSE encourages innovation-smart processes based on the radical non-propertarian sharing of content, cloud data computing, and the leveraging of cross-border international exchanges and collaborations. Furthermore, it encourages a culture of distributed, collaborative, decentralized model research that is genuinely participatory, involving the wider public and amateur scientists along with experts in the social mode of open knowledge production. OSE provides an alternative to the intellectual property approach to dealing with difficult problems in the allocation of resources for the production and distribution of knowledge and information. Increasingly, portal-based knowledge environments and global science gateways support collaborative science. Open-source informatics enables knowledge grids that interconnect science communities, databases, and new computational tools. Open science is seen as a means for revitalizing public institutions and for developing scientific creativity and innovation at a global level through international collaboration.

Open science and open economy provide a good fit for epistemology and practice of 'the creative university as digital public university'. It is only by embracing this model, that the contemporary university can support creation and dissemination of new (types of) knowledge, while simultaneously fostering equality, social justice, and democracy. The creative university as digital public university is critical, but it does not have to have the Foucauldian permanent disposition to critique—sometimes, it can be creatively esthetic, instrumental, entrepreneurial, and so on, without any critique.

At this moment, the majority of public institutions and private companies in higher education are fairly remote from the model of 'the creative university as digital public university'. However, some of their practices do develop in a positive direction, and higher education slowly but surely begins to respond to complex contemporary challenges of peer production, collective intelligence, the logic of openness, and its wider public role. While it is expected that our insights might slightly change in line with further developments, 'the creative university as digital public university' represents an important philosophical goal that might lead present and future transformations of the contemporary university.

NOTE

[1] This chapter is based on a keynote talk given by Michael Adrian Peters at The Creative University Conference, University of Aalborg, Denmark, 18–19 August 2016. The last section of the chapter, *Towards the creative public digital university*, is based on the keynote talk given by Michael Adrian Peters at The Creative University Conference, University of Waikato, New Zealand, 15–26 August 2012. The chapter was first published as Peters, M. A., & Jandrić, P. (2018). Peer Production and Collective Intelligence as the Basis for the Public Digital University. *Educational Philosophy and Theory,* copyright © Philosophy of Education Society of Australasia, reprinted by permission of Taylor & Francis Ltd, http://www.tandfonline.com on behalf of Philosophy of Education Society of Australasia.

REFERENCES

Banaji, S., Burn, A., & Buckingham, D. (2006). *Rhetorics of creativity: Literature review*. London: Centre for the Study of Children, Youth and Media Institute of Education, University of London. Retrieved March 28, 2017, from http://www.creativitycultureeducation.org/wp-content/uploads/rhetorics-of-creativity-2nd-edition-87.pdf

Bangladesh Awami League. (2017). *Cabinet okays proposal for digital university, NSP expansion*. Retrieved March 28, 2017, from https://www.albd.org/index.php/en/updates/news/2105-cabinet-okays-proposal-for-digital-university-nsp-expansion

Barbrook, R., & Cameron, A. (1996). The Californian ideology. *Science as Culture, 6*(1), 44–72.

Benkler, Y., Shaw, A., & Hill, B. M. (2015). Peer production: A form of collective intelligence. In T. Malone & M. Bernstein (Eds.), *Handbook of collective intelligence*. Cambridge, MA: MIT Press.

Bloomberg. (2017). *Company overview of digital university, inc*. Retrieved March 28, 2017, from http://www.bloomberg.com/research/stocks/private/snapshot.asp?privcapId=224284354

Burch, R. (2014). Charles Sanders Peirce. In E. N. Zalta (Ed.), *The Stanford encyclopedia of philosophy*. Stanford, CA: Stanford University. Retrieved April 1, 2016, from https://plato.stanford.edu/cgi-bin/encyclopedia/archinfo.cgi?entry=peirce

Calhoun, C. (2006). The university and the public good. *Thesis Eleven, 84*(7), 7–43.

Coursera. (2017). *About*. Retrieved March 28, 2017, from https://about.coursera.org/

Degn, L., & Sørensen, M. P. (2015). From collegial governance to conduct of conduct: Danish universities set free in the service of the state. *High Education, 69*(6), 931–946.

Fichte, J. G. (1794). *Foundations of the science of knowledge*. Retrieved March 28, 2017, from https://archive.org/details/thescienceofknow00fichuoft

Foucault, M. (1996). What is enlightenment? In M. Foucault (Ed.), *Ethics, the essential works* (p. 312). London: Allen Lane & Penguin.

Fuller, S. (2006). *The philosophy of science and technology studies*. New York, NY: Routledge.

Gardner, H. (2011). *The unschooled mind: How children think and how schools should teach*. New York, NY: Basic Books.

Hayes, S., & Jandrić, P. (2017). Learning, technologies, and time in the age of global neoliberal capitalism. *Knowledge Cultures, 5*(2), 11–17.

Jandrić, P. (2013). Academic community in transition: Critical liberatory praxis in the network society. In T. Issa, P. Isaías, & P. Kommers (Eds.), *Information systems and technology for organizations in a networked society* (pp. 88–106). Hershey, PA: Idea Group.

Jandrić, P. (2017). *Learning in the age of digital reason*. Rotterdam, The Netherlands: Sense Publishers.

173

Jandrić, P., Devine, N., Jackson, E., Peters, M., Lăzăroiu, G., Mihaila, R., Locke, K., Heraud, R., Gibbons, A., Grierson, E., Forster, D., White, J., Stewart, G., Tesar, M., Arndt, S., & Brighouse, S. (2017). Collective writing: An inquiry into praxis. *Knowledge Cultures, 5*(1), 85–109.
Khan Academy. (2017). *About*. Retrieved 20 December, 2017, from https://www.khanacademy.org/about
Kreiss, K., Finn, M., & Turner, F. (2011). The limits of peer production: Some reminders from Max Weber for the network society. *New Media & Society, 13*(2), 243–259.
Olsen, J. P. (2005). *The institutional dynamics of the European university*. Oslo: ARENA—Centre for European Studies, University of Oslo.
Olssen, J. P., & Peters, M. A. (2005). Neoliberalism, higher education and the knowledge economy: From the free market to knowledge capitalism. *Journal of Education Policy, 20*(3), 313–345.
Parker, G. G., van Alstyne, M. W., & Choudary, S. P. (2016). *Platform revolution: How networked markets are transforming the economy and how to make them work for you*. New York, NY: W. W. Norton & Company.
Peters, M. A. (2009). Education, creativity and the economy of passions: New forms of educational capitalism. *Thesis Eleven, 96*(1), 40–63.
Peters, M. A. (2013). Managerialism and the neoliberal university: Prospects for new forms of "open management" in higher education. *Contemporary Readings in Law and Social Justice, 5*(1), 11–26.
Peters, M. A. (2015a). The university in the epoch of digital reason: Fast knowledge in the circuits of cybernetic capitalism. In P. Gibbs, O.-H. Ylijoki, C. Guzmán-Valenzuela, & R. Barnett (Eds.), *Universities in the flux of time: An exploration of time and temporality in university life* (pp. 9–31). London: Routledge.
Peters, M. A. (2015b). Interview with Pierre A. Lévy, French philosopher of collective intelligence. *Open Review of Educational Research, 2*(1), 259–266.
Peters, M. A., & Heraud, R. (2015). Toward a political theory of social innovation: Collective intelligence and the co-creation of social goods. *Journal of Self-Governance and Management Economics, 3*(3), 7–23.
Peters, M. A., & Jandrić, P. (2015). Learning, creative col(labor)ation, and knowledge cultures. *Review of Contemporary Philosophy, 14*, 182–198.
Peters, M. A., & Jandrić, P. (2016). Digital reading. *Review of Contemporary Philosophy, 15*, 153–170.
Peters, M. A., & Jandrić, P. (2017). Dewey's democracy and education in the age of digital reason: The global, ecological and digital turns. *Open Review of Educational Research, 4*(1), 205–218.
Peters, M. A., & Jandrić, P. (2018a). *The digital university: A dialogue and manifesto*. New York, NY: Peter Lang.
Peters, M. A., & Jandrić, P. (2018b). Peer production and collective intelligence as the basis for the public digital university. *Educational Philosophy and Theory* (Online), 1–14. doi:10.1080/00131857.2017.1421940
Peters, M. A., Jandrić, P., Irwin, R., Locke, K., Devine, N., Heraud, R., Gibbons, A., Besley, T., White, J., Forster, D., Jackson, L., Grierson, E., Mika, C., Stewart, G., Tesar, M., Brighouse, S., Arndt, S., Lazariou, G., Mihalia, R., Bernade, L., Legg, C., Ozolins, J., & Roberts, P. (2016). Toward a philosophy of academic publishing. *Educational Philosophy and Theory, 48*(14), 1401–1425.
Platform Cooperativism. (2015). *Main*. Retrieved April 29, 2016, from http://platformcoop.net/
Plato. (360 BC). *The republic* (B. Jowett, Trans.). Retrieved March 28, 2017, from http://classics.mit.edu/Plato/republic.html
Readings, B. (1996). *The university in ruins*. Cambridge, MA: Harvard University Press.
Rowlands, M. (2010). *The new science of the mind: From extended mind to embodied phenomenology*. Cambridge, MA: MIT Press.
Siemens, G., Gašević, D., & Dawson, S. (2015). *Preparing for the digital university: A review of the history and current state of distance, blended, and online learning*. Athabasca: Athabasca University. Retrieved March 28, 2017, from http://linkresearchlab.org/PreparingDigitalUniversity.pdf
Singularity University. (2017). *About us*. Retrieved March 28, 2017, from https://su.org/about/
Sternberg, R. J. (1999). *Handbook of creativity*. Cambridge: Cambridge University Press.
Sumpter, D. (2006). The principles of collective animal behaviour. *Philosophical Transactions of the Royal Society B: Biological Sciences, 361*(1465), 5–22.

Sundararajan, A. (2016). *The sharing economy: The end of employment and the rise of crowd-based capitalism.* Cambridge, MA: MIT Press.
Tapscott, D. (1997). Strategy in the new economy. *Strategy & Leadership, 25*(6), 8–14. Retrieved March 28, 2017, from http://www.cbpp.uaa.alaska.edu/afef/ba635-strategy_in_the_new_economy.htm
Taylor, A., & Jandrić, P. (2016). Unschoolers of the world, unwork! Grassroots lessons and strategies against 21st century capitalism. *Journal of Critical Education Policy Studies, 14*(3), 131–153.
The Digital University of America. (2016). *Get an education absolutely free and a college degree.* Retrieved March 28, 2017, from http://digitaluniversityofamerica.com/
The University of the Commons. (2017). *Mission statement.* Retrieved March 28, 2017, from http://www.uotc.org/wordpress/
UCSD. (2009). *Blueprint for the digital university.* Retrieved March 28, 2017, from http://sites.uci.edu/fasrc/files/2015/05/UCSD-Blueprint-for-the-Digital-University.pdf
University College Cork. (2016). *Ireland's digital university.* Retrieved March 28, 2017, from https://www.youtube.com/watch?v=BqKfrHFwrdY
UNPIdF. (2017). *Digital user guide.* Retrieved 28 March, 2017, from http://cours.mido.dauphine.fr/GUN/gun5EtudGB.pdf
Voltaire, F. (1759). *An essay on universal history, the manners, and spirit of nations: From the reign of Charlemaign to the age of Lewis XIV.* Retrieved March 28, 2017, from https://play.google.com/store/books/details?id=npE-AAAAYAAJ&rdid=book-npE-AAAAYAAJ&rdot=1
Western's Computational Brain Science. (2017). *Computational brain science: The networked language of the mind.* Retrieved March 28, 2017, from https://www.uwo.ca/sci/media/stories/articles/2016/computational_brain_science_the_networked_language_of_the_mind.html

Michael A. Peters
Beijing Normal University
Beijing, P. R. China

Petar Jandrić
Zagreb University of Applied Sciences
Croatia

FARSHAD BADIE

11. LOGICAL FOUNDATION OF INDUCTIVE MEANING CONSTRUCTING IN CONSTRUCTIVIST INTERACTIONS

INTRODUCTION

My point of departure is a special focus on an activity-based approach to communication analysis that argues that 'any communication is a sharing of information, cognitive content and understanding with varying degrees of consciousness and intentionality' (Allwood, 2007, 2013). Correspondingly, an interaction between a learner and a mentor can be interpreted through their co-activations (consisting of their shared actions and transactions). More specifically, within an interaction between a learner and a mentor, they both become concerned with their co-activations (i.e., their collaborations, co-operations, and co-ordinations). In this framework, mentor and learner exchange questions, answers, actions, and transactions concerning their multiple descriptions, specifications, explanations, and justifications.

The central focus of this chapter is on a constructivist theory as well as constructivist model of learning in the context of mentor-learner interactions. Constructivism is an epistemology and is strongly supported by the study of the origins (genesis) of knowledge. Correspondingly, the genetic epistemology is closely related to the developmental theory of knowledge (Geber, 1977; Vuyk, 1981; Driscoll, 2005). It is possible to conclude that the constructivist model of learning could work as an explanatory, heuristic, and developmental framework (Pask, 1975, 1980; Glasersfeld, 1983; Simpson, 1989; Scott, 2001; McIntyre Boyd, 2004).

In my opinion, relying on this model of knowing and learning, the learner-mentor interactions are describable as a constructivist account of their understanding of the world. I shall claim that 'understanding' (or the ability to comprehend) is producible and activable based on one's (a) personal knowings, (b) constructions of knowledge (ultimately, over the constructed extended abstracts in his/her mind), (c) interpretations of the world, (d) constructed meanings of the world, and (e) senses made of world. The abilities of self-awareness as well as interpreting the reality of the world could be recognised as the most valuable products of the phenomenon of 'understanding' (Badie, 2016a, 2016c, 2017a, 2018). In addition, constructivist interactions can be described and specified based on agents' varying degrees of consciousness and intentionality. The constructivist model of learning can, in the context of learner-mentor interactions, explain how the phenomenon of 'interaction' supports the generation of one's meaningful understanding based on his/her produced conception of the world.

This research will focus on a logical analysis of meaning construction within constructivist interactions. The logical analysis will be supported by my designed semantic framework (Badie, 2015a, 2015b, 2016b). I will employ a Concept Language (Description Logics) in order to conceptualise my main logical ideas behind that framework. This chapter will offer a logical and semantic characterisation of 'concept', 'definition', and 'meaning'. Subsequently, a conceptual and logical background for 'semantic interpretation' and 'meaning construction' will be provided. Finally, the outcomes will theoretically be checked within creative universities.

The main contribution of this research is in providing a logical/epistemic backbone for formal semantic analysis of meaning construction (that supports meaningful understanding production) within constructivist interactions.

CONSTRUCTIVISM AND CONSTRUCTIVIST INTERACTIONS

It can be assumed that Giambattista Vico was the first philosopher who proposed an explicit formulation of a constructivist theory of knowledge in his little-known Latin treatise. Vico coined the phrase 'verum est ipsum factum' and explained that 'to know something means to know what parts it is made of and how they have been put together' (Vico, 1710; Glasersfeld, 1995). However, the theory of constructivism was introduced in the modern era by Jean Piaget as a way and style of thinking about the phenomena of 'cognition' and 'knowledge' (Piaget & Cook, 1952; Glasersfeld, 1989, 2001). It's worth mentioning that Piaget's developmental theory of learning argues that the constructivist model of learning is concerned with how the individual learner goes about the construction of knowledge in his/her own cognitive apparatus (Phillips, 1995).

Vygotsky's (1978a, 1978b) theories about human-human interactions and minds in society (and, respectively, the concept of 'social constructivism'), need to be taken into account when considering the phenomenon of 'social interaction'. Vygotsky believed that 'social interaction' plays a fundamental role in the process of human cognitive development. According to Vygotsky's theory, an individual who has stronger understanding (of the world) and higher abilities in particular domains could be a 'mentor'. The concept of a 'mentor' has been labelled with the abbreviation MKO (More Knowledgeable Other). Mentors are advanced learners who construct and develop their personal knowledge through their constructivist interactions with learners. Additionally, Vygotsky introduced the Zone of Proximal Development (ZPD) in order to express the concept of 'learning' by an individual learner (i) under MKO's supervisions and/or (ii) with his/her collaborations with other individuals. It can be concluded that learners can learn (can do 'learning' as their main task and role) in this zone. I shall summarise that mentors (who are aware, intentional, and advanced learners) are required to act as facilitators whose main functions are to help learners become active participants and constructors. In fact, they open the world to the learners and open the learners to the world. According to Badie (2017b), the learners can then:

- relate their new conceptions (of the world) to their preconceptions and experiences,
- integrate their constructed knowledge into interrelated conceptual structures,
- design personal creational patterns for themselves, and
- reflect on their own understandings of the world.

In the context of constructivist interactions, the local meaningful understanding of any concept (at any single moment) gives opportunities to the agents to produce their deeper personal understanding within their collaborative process of knowledge construction. For example, the learner would be given an opportunity to produce his/her more proper understanding of the applications of a mathematical formula, or the mentor would be given an opportunity to produce his/her better understanding of the current problems of the learner concerning that mathematical formula's applications.

At this point I offer my definition of the concepts of 'constructivism' and 'social constructivism'. Constructivism is 'a transformation from the phenomenon of learning into individualistic knowledge structures and, subsequently, into individualistic understanding of the world'. Based on this definition, the concept of 'social constructivism' can be interpreted 'transformation from the phenomenon of 'learning' into united understanding of the world'. There is no doubt that social constructivism is corresponded to the epistemological junctions between the phenomena of 'knowledge' and 'cognition'.

CONCEPT: EXISTENCE AND REPRESENTATION IN MIND

It is difficult to think of a foundational scientific concept about which there is more controversy among experts (in philosophy, linguistics, psychology, cognitive science, computer science, and information science) than the concept of a 'concept' (see Kant, 1781/1924; Bartlett, 1932; Peacocke, 1992; Hampton & Moss, 2003; Margolis & Laurence, 2007, 2010, 2015). Over the years, the term 'concept' has not been used consistently and it is not always clear whether (i) what is meant by this expression is some mental representation of phenomena in the world, or (ii) whether a concept always has to be bound up with some linguistic expression, or (iii) whether concepts refer to assessable phenomena; for instance, sets and classes (Götzsche, 2013). However, some sociologists, anthropologists, educationalists, and educational psychologists believe that a concept can be identified and recognised by the critical characteristics and properties shared by its examples (Encyclopaedia Britannica, 2007; Parker, 2008, 2011). In fact, the examples come under the concepts' labels and indexes.

In this research, I need to focus on my conception of the phenomenon of 'meaning' in order to be clearer on the expression 'concept'. The section below, titled 'Meaning', will be more specific on the logical analysis of meanings. In the framework of constructivism, meanings—to a large extent—influence any person's knowledge constructions based on his/her background knowledge. In fact, meanings could be interpreted as conceptual structures that are constructed based on conceptual entities. Thus, any conceptual entity can be regarded as a building block and basic material of a conceptual structure. My theoretical model names these conceptual entities 'concepts' (see Badie, 2017c, 2017d). Accordingly, a conceptual entity would, as a representation of a piece of reality/fiction in one's mind, be interpreted a basic material of [to-be-constructed] meanings within learning and knowledge building processes.

I believe that my conception of 'concepts' has strong correlation with the assumption that concepts can be identified by the critical characteristics and properties shared by their examples. More specifically, human beings can, with regard to their constructed concepts, reason and discover whether their differently experienced phenomena fall under the label of their own constructed concepts. It should be emphasised that (only) a conceptual entity can be an instance of a concept, and thus a learner/mentor transforms his/her experienced phenomena into conceptual entities[1] (and activates them in his/her mind) in order to consider them as the instances of concepts (that are also conceptual entities). Subsequently, the learners'/mentors' understanding as well as their following actions and reactions materialise in virtue of their personal grasp of their constructed concepts. Regarding my theoretical model, people can express their constructed concepts in the form of their conceptions. In other words, one's conceptions are regarded as expressed and outputs of his/her constructed concepts.

In the framework of constructivism, the agents' conception of the world could be expressed in the form of predicates. Predicates can assign the characteristics of phenomena to statements or even into truth-values (Clapham, 2014; Blackburn, 2016). Predicates are non-logical symbols in First-Order Predicate Logic. They express something about the variable symbols and, respectively, about the constant symbols. Consequently, in my opinion, 'in the framework of constructivism, predicates are assignment functions from characteristics, features, and properties of one's conceptions and respectively, of his/her constructed concepts into subjects'. Relying on this assumption, conceptions and their interrelationships are hierarchically describable. Let me offer an example:

Mentor: What is Linux?
Sarah: Linux is a type of software.

According to the statement 'Linux is a type of software', Sarah has identified Linux as a 'Software'. Assessed by Predicate Logic, the unary predicate 'Linux' has been described as a kind of the unary predicate 'Software'. In Sarah's opinion, Linux has all the characteristics and properties of Software. In fact, she believes that Linux (as a concept) is a sub-concept of the concept 'Software'. Translated into Description Logics (DL), her statement can be translated into 'Linux $\sqsubseteq$ Software'. Let me conclude that the logical term 'Linux $\sqsubseteq$ Software' has provided a concept construction that supports Sarah's specification of her conceptualisation of the concept 'Linux'. This specification of a conceptualisation provides a background for her understanding production based on her conception of 'Linux'.

DESCRIPTION LOGICS

My main reference to Description Logics is Baader (2010). Description Logics (DLs) represent knowledge in terms of concepts, individuals (as instances of concepts), and roles (that relate two or more individuals to each other). Based on DLs, the basic step of any logical construction becomes supported by atomic concepts and atomic roles. In this research, we will see that the general (super) conceptions of human beings can be represented by atomic concepts (that are equivalent to atomic literals in Predicate Logic). The fundamental set of the main connectors in DLs is: {Conjunction ($\sqcap$: and), Disjunction ($\sqcup$: or), Negation ($\neg$: not), Existential Restriction ($\exists$: there exists ...), Universal Restriction ($\forall$: for all ...)}. Atomic Concepts, Atomic Roles, Top concept ($\top$: truth/tautology) and Bottom concept ($\bot$: falsity/contradiction) are the other constructors of a basic DL.

Knowledge in DLs is interpreted to be constructed based upon terminological axioms and assertional axioms (that are fundamental world descriptions). Terminological axioms are introduced to express statements about how concepts and roles are (or can be) related to each other. Correspondingly, assertional axioms propose fundamental descriptions of the world based on concepts, roles, and individuals. A terminological interpretation (like *I*) is a function that is extendable based on concept/role descriptions by inductive rules. Interpretations are applied to define formal semantics. In fact, an interpretation can be regarded as a function that covers a syntax in order to express its meaning. Accordingly, a terminological interpretation is called a 'model' of an axiom if it can satisfy the statement in the conclusions of the fundamental axioms and world descriptions, as shown in Table 1.

Table 1. Terminological axioms and fundamental world descriptions in description logics

Axiom	Syntax	Semantics
Concept Inclusion Axim	$C \sqsubseteq D$	$C^I \subseteq D^I$
Role Inclusion Axiom	$R \sqsubseteq S$	$R^I \subseteq S^I$
Concept Equality Axiom	$C \equiv D$	$C^I = D^I$
Role Equality Axiom	$R \equiv S$	$R^I = S^I$
Concept Assertion	$C(a)$	$a^I \in C^I$
Role Assertion	$R(a, b)$	$(a^I, b^I) \in R^I$

In order to analyse and specify formal semantics, we need to apply terminological interpretations over triples like (Concept, Role, Individual). More particularly, any terminological interpretation consists of:

- a non-empty set 'Δ' (that is the interpretation domain and consists of all variables that occur in any of the concept descriptions), and
- an interpretation function '$\cdot^I$' (or an 'interpreter').

The interpreter assigns to every individual symbol (like a) a '$a^I \in \Delta^I$'. Also, it assigns to every atomic concept (like A) a set $A^I \subseteq \Delta^I$ and to every atomic role (like P) a binary relation $P^I \subseteq \Delta^I \times \Delta^I$.

At this point I feel the need to be more specific on the term 'interpretation'.[2] The phenomenon of 'interpretation' expresses the act of elucidation, explication, and explanation. It's possible to have different conceptions of the interpretations (Badie, 2017b). I would like to assert the following conceptions:

- As analysed earlier, through the lenses of logics, an interpretation can be perceived as a mapping from a meaning into a non-logical symbol/word. In fact, based on our own conceptualisations, we give meanings to symbols, words, and terms.
- The interpretations construct bridges between (i) one's 'expressions and explanations' and (ii) the phenomena of 'meaning' and 'semantics'. For example, a learner, based on his/her conceptualisation of the world, focuses on expressing and explaining himself/herself in order to make meanings for his/her mentor.
- An interpretation could be understood as a continually adjusted relationship between (i) one's intentions behind his/her conceptions and (ii) his/her actual mental universe of his/her conceptions (that are based on his/her accumulated experiences). Subsequently, as I have analysed in Badie (2016c, 2017a, 2018), all understandings are caused by interpretations. In fact, the concept of 'understanding' is the sub-concept of 'interpretation' (i.e., *Understanding $\sqsubseteq$ Interpretation*). On the other hand, not all interpretations will necessarily produce understanding.

The section 'Semantic Interpretation' will specify further regarding the concept of 'interpretations' in the framework of constructivism and in the context of mentor-learner interactions.

CONCEPT CONSTRUCTION

Learning in the framework of constructivism and in the context of learner-mentor interactions is heuristically supported by:

- factual, structural, and existential questions (that are concerned with WhatNesses as well as essences of phenomena in the world),
- inferential questions (that are concerned with WhyNesses of phenomena in the world), and
- methodological and technical questions (that are concerned with HowNesses of phenomena in the world).

Note these heuristic questions invite the responder (the interlocutor) to search through a hierarchy of multiple related concepts in order to produce an appropriate answer. Any appropriate answer shapes a part of a construction that is—mutually and collaboratively—constructed by the learner and mentor. Any agent, by asking a heuristic question, manages to guide his/her interlocutor to producing either heuristic answers or updated heuristic questions.

Forming concepts (by the agents) over their mental structures is an initial step. Educationalists see concept formation as a process by which a person learns to sort specific experiences into general conceptions. More specifically, some educationalists and social scientists, such as Taba et al. (1971) and Du and Ling (2011), define concept formation 'an inductive teaching and learning strategy that supports learners in learning something through studying a set of examples of that thing' (see also some approaches in McCracken, 1999; Sell et al., 2014). The process of concept formation is a sub-process of a greater process which I have called *Concept Construction*, see Figure 1, section II.

According to Badie (2015a, 2015b, 2016b, 2016c), concept construction processes are structured over the union of three sub-processes consisting of:

- *Concept Formation*. Concept formation is an intra-psychological process.
- *Concept Transformation*. According to concept transformations, concepts could be transformed (either from one's mind into another's mind or from environment into one's mind) by, e.g., speaking, listening, hearing, touching, smelling, or tasting. Concept transformation is an inter-psychological process).
- *Concept Reformation*. Concept reformation is an intra-psychological process.

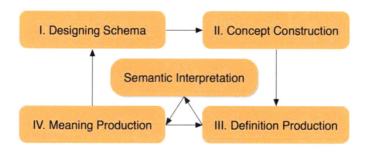

Figure 1. Meaning construction within constructivist interactions

Concept reformation happens either after transforming concepts or at the more specific levels of one's conceptualisations of his/her formed concepts. According to the process of concept construction and its inductive nature, my theoretical model has assumed that learner and mentor generate logical cases for their case-based reasoning and, logical rules for their rule-based reasoning. In this framework, they will be able to use as well as reuse their achievements for case-based and rule-based learning and mentoring. Additionally, they can interpret and reason whether their experienced phenomena could come under the label of their own constructed concepts.

CONCEPT LEARNING

I draw your attention to the following conversation between John (the learner) and Diana (the mentor):

John: Bats fly.
Diana: Do you know that bats are mammals?
John: Really?
Diana: Yes!
John: So, some mammals can fly.

In this conversational exchange, John has, initially, declared that 'bats fly'. This statement is expressed based on the concepts 'Bat' and 'Fly'. Later on, hearing the word 'mammal', that is the most central concept of Diana's question (Do you know that bats are mammals?), conduces John to inducing that 'Fly' and 'Mammal' are the most significant concepts relevant to 'Bat'. Obviously, the concepts 'Bat', 'Fly' and 'Mammal' have been transformed between John and Diana. Subsequently, John attempts to reform the concepts 'Bat' and 'Mammal' in his mind and, thus, to produce the updated conceptions of his personal preconstructed concepts 'Bat' and 'Mammal'. The most significant product of this constructivist conversation is that John has learned something based on an induction-based conclusion. As the main consequence of learning, he has generated the rule 'there exists a mammal that can fly' (formally: $\exists\, isFlying.Mammal$).

The processes of 'concept formation', 'concept transformation', 'concept reformation', and 'reasoning based on the constructed concepts' are collectively known as 'Concept Learning'. John's concept learning is supported by his inductive reasoning[3] processes (Badie, 2017b, 2017c, 2017d, 2018). His concept learning is logically designed based on a system of evidential support that is constructed over his less-than-certain inferences. John's concept learning is generated based on:

- his preformed concepts 'Bat' and 'Mammal',
- his preconceptions of 'Bat' and 'Mammal',
- his constructed concepts 'Bat' and 'Mammal', and
- his updated conceptions of 'Bat' and 'Mammal'.

Note that John's conceptualisations of the characteristics and properties of the constructed concepts 'Bat' and 'Mammal' have prepared a supportive basis for his concept learning. There is no doubt that John's concept learning is highly supported by his experiences (e.g., observations, hearings, and studies) of various groups of examples of bats, flying, and mammals. It should be emphasised that John has become concerned with the specification of his conceptualisation of his constructed concepts 'Bat', 'Fly', and 'Mammal' within his concept learning process in the context of his interactions with Diana.

Let me focus on another example: James has a conception of 'Spring' (based on his constructed concept 'Spring'). Accordingly, he, with regard to his conception of 'Spring', may say something to his mentor (Anna), ask a question, or answer a question. Accordingly, hearing different words from Anna is conducive to developing his conception of 'Spring'. See the following conversational exchange:

> *Anna*: James, what could you tell me about spring?
> *James*: Spring is the season of the moderate weather; when all the trees are green.

Based on DLs, James' statement can be translated into: 'Spring $\doteq$ Season $\sqcap$ ($\exists$hasWeather.Moderate) $\sqcap$ ($\forall$hasTree.Green)'. This description is structured over the elements of the set C = {Season, $\exists$hasWeather.Moderate, $\forall$hasTree.Green}. The concept descriptions '$\exists$hasWeather.Moderate' and '$\forall$hasTree.Green' (that are the elements of C) can be divided into atomic concepts. Thus, C is structured over the set C' = {Season, Moderate, Weather, Green, Tree}. These five concepts (in C') have supported James' conception of the concept 'Spring'. In fact, Anna could focus on these concepts in order to conceptualise James' conception of Spring. For example, the dialogue can be continued by Anna's statement as following:

> *Anna*: In my opinion, spring is the season of the moderate weather; when some of the trees are green.

In fact, Anna has focused on the elements of C' (that are James' expressed conceptions) and has then focused on the elements of C. Subsequently, she has—by declaring 'in my opinion, spring is the season of the moderate weather; when some of the trees are green'—attempted to modify an element of C. More specifically, Anna has tried to construct C_2 instead of C, where C_2 stands for {Season, $\exists$hasWeather.Moderate, $\exists$hasTree.Green}. More particularly, she has focused on James' concept description '$\forall$hasTree.Green' (i.e., all the trees are green) and has transformed it into '$\exists$hasTree.Green' (i.e., some of the trees are green). In this example, C and C' are the sub-concepts of the concept 'Spring'. Formally, 'C $\sqsubseteq$ Spring' and 'C' $\sqsubseteq$ Spring'. In fact, based on James' conception of the world, C is the sub-concept of Spring. Also, based on Anna's conceptualisation of James' conception, C' is the sub-concept of Spring.

It shall be concluded that if the mentor and the learner look forward to achieving a satisfactory negotiation of a concept description, they will need to focus on the atomic concepts within that concept description. Accordingly, the mentor:

- conceptualises the learner's constructed atomic concepts,
- conceptualises the learner's conceptions of those atomic concepts,
- observes other related concepts from the perspective of that conception,

- compares the results with his/her own conceptions, and
- guides the learner to improve as well as to reform his/her conceptions.

DEFINITION

A definition is an equivalence (and, formal-semantically, an equation) between a concept and a description. Definitions assign concept descriptions to concepts. Inductive rules are employed in order to describe more specified concepts based on more general ones. A set of an agent's definitions must be explicit in order to be meaningful. Any agent may revise and reorganise his/her definitions during his/her interactions with another agent. This process could be named *Definition Updating* or reorganising and reforming the proposed concept description. Consequently, the more organised concept descriptions support the agents in constructing their more understandable meanings on higher levels of their interaction. Note that the levels of an interaction are as follows:

- Level 1: learner says/does something.
- Level 2: mentor says/does something.
- Level 3: learner says/does something.
- ...
- Level n: learner/mentor says/does something.

or:

- Level 1: mentor says/does something.
- Level 2: learner says/does something.
- Level 3: mentor says/does something.
- ...
- Level n: learner/mentor says/does something.

Terminology Generation

In my theoretical model, a finite set of an agent's definitions generates a *Terminology* if, and only if, no atomic concept has been defined more than once by him/her at the same level of his/her interaction with another agent. The subscripts L and M stand for the terms 'corresponded to learner' and 'corresponded to mentor', respectively. Subsequently, T_L and T_M represent the finite set of the learner's and the mentor's definitions. Consequently, for every atomic concept A_L (and A_M), there will be (at most) one axiom in T_L (and T_M). Therefore, we can conclude that there will be (at most) one A_L (and A_M) to the left-hand side of any individual definition that constructs an axiom. The agents can, by interacting and conversing, interchange any member (as well as any subset) of their own terminologies (T_L and T_M). Formally:

- Considering C_L as the product of the learner's conceptualisation of the concept C, the learner creates a terminological set like $D_{C_L} = \{D_1, D_2, ..., D_n\}$ for his/

her multiple definitions of C. Accordingly, for $i \in [1,n]$, D_i denotes the learner's definition of C on the ith level of interaction.
- Considering C_M as the product of the mentor's conceptualisation of the concept C, the mentor creates a terminological set like $D'_{C_M} = \{D'_1, D'_2, ..., D'_n\}$ for his/her multiple definitions of C. Accordingly, for $i \in [1,n]$, D'_i denotes the mentor's definition of C on the ith level of interaction.

Therefore, the definitions D_i and D'_i will be located on the same level of the mentor-learner interaction based on the learner's and the mentor's conceptualisation, respectively. Subsequently, both agents can move to one upper level. Consequently, the learner's definition becomes modified (from D_i to D_{i+1}) and the mentor's definition becomes modified (from D'_i to D'_{i+1}). Therefore, learner and mentor approach their more satisfactory agreements on their developed definitions.

At any level of the interaction, the learner (as well as mentor) selects an element or a subset of D_{C_L} (as well as of D'_{C_M}) in order to exchange it with the interlocutor. Therefore:

- *For learner*: $\forall i, j \in [1,n]$, $\exists D_{C_L}^* = \{D_i, ..., D_j\} \subseteq \{D_1, D_2, ..., D_n\}$. Thus, he/she interacts with his/her mentor. So, there will be a *Definition Transformation* (like t_L) from the set of his/her selected definitions (that is dependent on his/her terminology) into the mentor's set of definitions and, subsequently, into the mentor's terminology. Formally, $t_L: \{D_i, ..., D_j\} \to D'_{C_M}$.
- *For mentor*: $\forall p, q \in [1,n]$, $\exists D'_{C_M}^* = \{D_p, ..., D_q\} \subseteq \{D'_1, D'_2, ..., D'_n\}$. Thus, he/she interacts with his/her learner. Then, there will be a Definition Transformation (like t'_M) from the set of his/her selected definitions (that is dependent on his/her terminology) into the learner's set of definitions and, subsequently, into the learner's terminology. Formally, $t'_M: \{D'_p, ..., D'_q\} \to D_{C_L}$.

It shall be concluded that the collection of definition transformations leads both agents to their most-negotiable (i) conceptions of the atomic concepts and, subsequently, (ii) conceptions of the concept descriptions over the atomic concepts.

Allow me to focus on an example in order to offer another definition. Suppose that Martin has said something about 'Information Systems'. Regarding my theoretical model, he initially has produced a definition transformation function like $t_1(InformationSystem)$. The function t_1 expresses the operation of Martin's first definition (that is, a subset of his terminology) on the concept *InformationSystem*. Subsequently, Lara (who is Martin's mentor) has transacted and produced a transformation function like $t'_1(InformationSystem)$. The function t'_1 expresses the operation of Lara's first description (that is, a subset of her terminology) on the concept *InformationSystem*. Obviously, t'_1 has been generated and applied (by Lara) with regard to the output of t_1 in her mind. This procedure will sequentially be continued. Any statement/question will cause a transaction/answer. Ultimately, the concatenation of the multiple functions

187

conduces Martin and Lara into their most-negotiable understandings based on the concept 'Information System'. This understanding is the product of the *Composite Definition Transformation Function* (of the concept 'Information System'), or *CDTF(InformationSystem)*.

The Composite Definition Transformation Function of the concept C is equal to:

$$CDTF(C) =$$
$$[t'_i \circ t_i(C)] \circ [t'_{i-1} \circ t_{i-1}(C)] \circ ... \circ [t'_1 \circ t_1(C)] =$$
$$[t'_i \circ t_i \circ t'_{i-1} \circ t_{i-1} \circ ... \circ t'_1 \circ t_1](C) =$$
$$t'_i(t_i(t'_{i-1}(t_{i-1}(...(t'_1(t_1(C)))...)))).$$

The logical term $t'_i(t_i(t'_{i-1}(t_{i-1}(...(t'_1(t_1(C)))...))))$ expresses a definition development (and, in fact, a conception development) within mentor-learner interactions. *CDTF(C)* prepares the agents for approaching their most satisfactory understandings of each other's conception of the concept description C.

MEANING

In my theoretical model, meanings are conceptual structures that are constructed based on concepts. More specifically, a meaning is a *Concept-Update Function* (*CUF*). This function utilises a concept (as an input), updates it, and returns its updated one. It is worth mentioning that some approaches (in dynamic semantics) have considered meanings as context-update functions (Chierchia, 2009; Gabbay, 2010).

Suppose that C stands for a concept and M represents a meaning (in the form of a function). Considering meaning as a concept-update function, we have:

$$M(C) = C'.$$

Let me offer an example. Suppose that Maria has initially produced a meaning for C in her mind. Maria would—after more interactions with Bob (who is her mentor) and on higher and more specified conceptual levels—be able to produce the mental function $M_1(C) = C'$ and, then, the mental function $M_2(C') = C''$. Obviously:

$$M_2(M_1(C)) = M_2(C') = C''.$$

It shall be concluded that C'' is the most-updated meaning of C. Such a procedure could be continued. In fact, the function $M(C)$ can develop itself during Maria-Bob interactions and conversational exchanges. $M(C)$ is inherently a *Composite Concept-Update Function* (*CCUF*).

Suppose that $M_i(C)$ is a *CCUF* that represents the 'meaning of C on level i' of the mentor-learner interactions. More specifically, $M_i(C)$ is the composition of i

concept-update functions on i levels of mentor-learner interactions, where i belongs to $[1,n]$. Formally:

$$M(C) =\\ (M_i \circ M_{i-1} \circ \ldots \circ M_1)(C) =\\ M_i(\, M_{i-1}(\,\ldots(\,M_1(C)\,)\,\ldots\,)\,) =\\ M_i(\,\ldots\,(C)\,\ldots\,).$$

Subsequently, the agents on the ith level of their interactions have achieved their most-satisfactory agreement on the meaning of C. Obviously, $M_i(C)$ is more satisfactory than $M_{i-1}(C)$.

SEMANTIC INTERPRETATION

In order to analyse the formal semantics, I focus on an interpretation (like I) that consists of:

- a non-empty set D (as the domain of the interpretation), and
- an interpretation function (like $.^I$).

Therefore, considering the individual symbol a as an instance of the concept C, an interpretation assigns the world description $C^I(a^I)$ to the concept assertion $C(a)$. It also assigns to the role assertion $R(p, q)$—where p and q are the instances of two concepts—the world description $R^I(p^I, q^I)$ that is a subset of $D^I \times D^I$.

Suppose that Mary had proposed the definition 'spring is the season of the moderate weather; when all the trees are green'. Translated into DLs, she has stated that:

$$Spring \doteq\\ Season \sqcap \exists hasWeather.Moderate \sqcap \forall hasTree.Green.$$

This definition is the product of her own interpretation of the concept 'Spring'. More specifically, (i) the concept 'Season', (ii) the description '∃hasWeather.Moderate', and (iii) the description '∀hasTree.Green' have logically been connected to each other in order to construct her personal definition of the concept 'Spring'. It should be drawn into consideration that Mary has interpreted the concept 'Spring' over the elements of the set:

$$D = \{Season, Moderate, Weather, Green, Tree\},$$

and, in fact, she has semantically focused on the interpretations of all members of D. In fact, she has mentally produced the set:

$$D^I = \{Season^I, Moderate^I, Weather^I, Green^I, Tree^I\}.$$

189

Informally, Mary has interpreted that the conjunction of the concepts 'Season', 'Moderate', 'Weather', 'Green', and 'Tree'—semantically—satisfies the concept 'Spring'.

Note that if an interpretation could satisfy a definition, then it will be identified as a 'model' of that definition (Prior, 1955; Simpson, 1989). It can also satisfy the semantics of terminological and assertional axioms, as shown in Table 1. In fact, Mary attempts to construct a mental model in order to validate and authenticate her definition of 'Spring'. Hence, the interpretability of her definition by her mentor's mental models determines the acceptability of that definition over the mentor's conceptions and, in fact, over the mentor's terminology.

Formal Analysis of Semantic Interpretations in the Context of Learner-Mentor Interactions

Regarding the mechanism of the Composite Definition Transformation Function of the concept C or $CDTF(C)$ (see 'Definition' section), the co-constructed terminologies can balance any agent's personal terminology. Thus, it shall be claimed that the most optimistic (as well as valuable) outcome for the agents is co-constructing a unified terminology based on which they can reorganise and update their own definitions of the world. A more specific on formal analysis of meaning co-construction in the context of interactions follows below:

An interpretation (like I) can be utilised in order to interpret the concept-update functions and to produce meanings. The agents at any level of their interactions find a proper mental model in order to:

- update their own constructed concepts,
- satisfy their own produced concept-update functions, and
- satisfy the interlocutor's terminology.

The meaning M is a concept-update function. Therefore:

$$M(C) = C'.$$

This function is representable in the form of a functional role as follows:

$$M(C, C').$$

Then, according to role inclusion axioms:

$$(C^I, C'^I) \in M^I.$$

This conclusion encodes the fact that an agent's interpretation has certified his/her constructed meaning as a functional role. Utilising the Composite Concept-Update

LOGICAL FOUNDATION OF INDUCTIVE MEANING CONSTRUCTING

Function (*CCUF*) and the role inclusion axiom, we have the following logical descriptions at different levels of the interaction.

- Level 1 of interaction: $M_1(C, C') \Rightarrow (C^I, C'^I) \in M_1^{I1}$
- Level 2 of interaction: $M_2(C', C'') \Rightarrow (C'^I, C''^I) \in M_2^{I2}$
- …
- Level n of interaction: $M_n(C^{(n-1)}, C^{(n)}) \Rightarrow (C^{(n-1)I}, C^{(n)I}) \in M_n^{In}$

where:

- C is a concept. It is also the co-domain of the functions $M_1, M_2, …, M_n$,
- $C^{(n)}$ represents C after n times of being updated,
- $C^{(n)I}$ represents the interpretation of C after n times of being updated, and
- 'In' represents the desired model of an agent on the nth level of his/her interaction with the interlocutor.

How the collection of n interpretations (on n levels of interaction) works now needs to be checked. Suppose that a learner and his/her mentor have participated in an interaction. In order to define 'Composite Interpretation Transformations', an inductive focus on the conclusion of the following processes is required.

First Process: The learner utters his/her description of his/her conception. Subsequently the mentor interprets the learner's conception. This semantic process involves determining whether the mentor's interpretation (or $M^I_{(1)}$) of that concept description could produce a concept inclusion with the learner's interpretation (or $L^I_{(1)}$). Semantically: $M^I_{(1)} \subseteq L^I_{(1)}$. In fact, the first domain of the mentor's interpretation must be the subset of the domain of the learner's interpretation.

Second Process: The mentor transacts and utters his/her own description (based on his/her interpretation) with regard to the learner's conception. The learner has to interpret the mentor's uttered description. The first semantic process is inversely becoming organised on the second level. This higher, as well as more specified, semantic process involves determining whether the learner's interpretation of the mentor's interpretation (or $L^I_{(2)}$) could produce a concept inclusion with the mentor's real interpretation (or $M^I_{(2)}$). Semantically: $L^I_{(2)} \subseteq M^I_{(2)}$. It means that the second domain of the learner's interpretation must be the subset of the second domain of the mentor's interpretation.

The ith Process: According to the logical characteristics of the first and second processes and their interrelationships, we can inductively analyse the *Composite Interpretation Transformation* (*CIT*) as follows:

If i represents the learner's utterance, then: $M^I_{(i)} \subseteq L^I_{(i)}$ & $L^I_{(i+1)} \subseteq M^I_{(i+1)}$.
If i represents the mentor's utterance, then: $L^I_{(i)} \subseteq M^I_{(i)}$ & $M^I_{(i+1)} \subseteq L^I_{(i+1)}$.

Collectively, we can induce that:

$$(M^I_{(1)} \subseteq L^I_{(1)}) \cap (L^I_{(2)} \subseteq M^I_{(2)}) \cap$$
$$… \cap$$
$$(M^I_{(n)} \subseteq L^I_{(n)}) \cap (L^I_{(n+1)} \subseteq M^I_{(n+1)}). \quad (*)$$

Note that an agent's interpretations at any lower level of his/her interactions with another agent is the subset of his/her own interpretations at the upper levels. Formally:

$$L^I_{(1)} \subseteq L^I_{(2)} \subseteq \ldots \subseteq L^I_{(n)}$$
$$\&$$
$$M^I_{(1)} \subseteq M^I_{(2)} \subseteq \ldots \subseteq M^I_{(n)}. \quad (**)$$

According to (*) and (**), we have:

$$(M^I_{(1)} \subseteq M^I_{(n)}) \cap (M^I_{(n)} \subseteq L^I_{(n)})$$
$$\&$$
$$(L^I_{(1)} \subseteq L^I_{(n)}) \cap (L^I_{(n+1)} \subseteq M^I_{(n+1)}).$$

Therefore:

$$M^I_{(1)} \subseteq M^I_{(n)} \subseteq L^I_{(n)}$$
$$\&$$
$$(L^I_{(1)} \subseteq L^I_{(n)}) \cap (L^I_{(n+1)} \subseteq M^I_{(n+1)}).$$

In fact, they both have optimised and restricted their individual interpretations by activating inclusions over their interpretations.

Suppose that $n \to \infty$. Thus, we will have:

$$M^I_{(1)} \subseteq M^I_{(n)} \subseteq L^I_{(n)}$$
$$\&$$
$$L^I_{(1)} \subseteq L^I_{(n)} \subseteq M^I_{(n)}.$$

Therefore:

$$M^I_{(n)} = L^I_{(n)}.$$

This logical term encodes the assumption that there could be an equivalence and stability between the mentor's and the learner's interpretations (after the infinite levels of interaction). In other words, it expresses that the learner/mentor has satisfied the mentor's/learner's interpretation by his/her own interpretation at level ∞. Furthermore, as I have mentioned in section 'Description Logics' and analysed in Badie (2016c, 2017a, 2018), the concept of 'understanding' is the sub-concept of 'interpretation' (i.e., *Understanding* $\sqsubseteq$ *Interpretation*). Consequently, considering *UND* as 'the semantic model of understanding', we will have:

$$M^{UND}_{(n)} = L^{UND}_{(n)}.$$

This conclusion is the most valuable product of the frequent interpretation transformations in the context of mentor-learner interactions. According to $M^{UND}_{(n)} = L^{UND}_{(n)}$, the agents have produced the same understanding of the world.

THE OUTCOMES WITHIN CREATIVE UNIVERSITIES

According to this research, a creative university can be regarded as a *Constructivist Learning/Mentoring Community* that is corresponded with (i) constructivist learning/mentoring processes, (ii) constructivist interactions between mentors and learners (as well as learners and learners), and (iii) collaborative meaning constructing that could support collaborative knowledge building. In Badie (2016b) I focused on constructivist knowledge building in the context of mentor-learner interactions in. In addition, I have worked on logical modelling/analysis of understanding production in Badie (2017a, 2018). Note that knowledge building in the context of mentor-learner constructivist interactions deals with the concepts of pervasive knowledge building and knowledge of community.

It should be stated that this research has mainly dealt with meaning construction based on mentor-learner constructivist interactions in creative universities. Subsequently, we need to recognise the creative knowledge as one of the most significant outcomes of constructed meanings in the context of constructivist interactions. Therefore, the state of knowledge of a community in a creative university is correlated with collaborative constructed meanings by learners and mentors. There are some significant assumptions:

i. In creative universities, meanings are interpreted to be related to the importance, value, worthiness, authentication, authenticity, and precision of what learners and mentors express. Accordingly, it is assumed that the phenomenon of 'meaning construction' is highly related to the phenomena of 'interpretation', 'explanation', 'sense making', 'comprehension', and 'construing'.
ii. Creative universities must consider meanings as the active and dynamic processes of knowledge construction. Thus learners/mentors, by constructing meanings, become connected to their own constructed models of knowing and subsequently to their own constructed models of knowledge.
iii. Regarding the fact that constructivism is a style of thinking about knowing as well as knowledge, creative universities must take into consideration that there is a strong bi-directional relationship between meaning construction and constructivism. Consequently, meaning construction must be regarded as the most significant task of constructivist learning as well as constructivist mentoring. This means that creative universities need to put 'meaning construction' at the centre of constructivist learning/mentoring processes.
iv. In creative universities, learners and mentors construct their own meanings with regard to their own conceptions of the world. More specifically, as this research has analysed, the semantic phenomenon of 'meaning' can be interpreted a

function from any individual's conceptions into his/her own updated and developed conceptions.
v. In creative universities, the constructed meanings by any individual become reflected in his/her personal meaningful understanding of the world.

Regarding the aforementioned points and taking into consideration my research in Badie (2017e), the state of knowledge of an individual learner (as well as mentor) could—relying on his/her constructed meanings—be highly reflected on the meaningful knowledge of the creative university (that is, a constructivist learning/ mentoring community). Based on the fact that learners/mentors reorganise and update their constructed meanings, it is reasonable to expect that any individual's achievements are connected to the developments and advancements of meaningful knowledge of the creative university. It is emphasised that the main belief of any learning community in a creative university is that the phenomena of 'meaning' and 'development' are tied to any individual's communicative and social interactions with other individuals. In the context of learning communities in creative universities, any individual learner must be permitted to express, explain, defend, prove, and justify his/her conceptions (and, subsequently, definitions) of the world. Accordingly, all learners must be allowed to communicate their conceptions to each other as well as to their community in order to move toward the most appropriate meanings and, subsequently, toward the most proper meaningful understandings of the world.

CONCLUSION

This research has focused on conceptual and logical analysis of constructivist interactions between mentors and learners within an explanatory and developmental framework of meaning construction. The chapter has presented a conceptual and logical description of how constructivist interactions support the agents through constructing their own meaningful understandings based on their constructed as well as co-constructed meanings. The main contribution has been to provide a logical support for the formal semantic analysis of meaning construction within constructivist interaction.

More specifically, I have logically analysed the agents' conceptualisations, constructed concepts, produced conceptions, expressed concept descriptions, described definitions, generated terminologies, produced semantic interpretations (and semantic models), constructed meanings, and produced meaningful understandings. I have concluded that the following items are the most significant products of the agents within their constructivist interactions:

- Constructing concepts and, subsequently, producing the updated conceptions of the world (based on the own preconceptions of the world).
- Defining the world based on the produced conceptions of the world.
- Interpreting the world based on the individualistic definitions of the world.

- Constructing meanings based on the own interpretations of the world.
- Making negotiations on constructed meanings (based on personal and the interlocutor's produced meanings).
- Reflecting the produced meanings on the own background knowledge.
- Reflecting the personal developed knowledge on the phenomenon of 'universal knowledge' and, accordingly, developing the universal knowledge.
- Producing the own understanding of the world over the built-up universal knowledge.
- Moving towards a mutual and united understanding of the world.

The last section of the chapter has focused on the outcomes of this research within creative universities. I have regarded the creative university as a constructivist learning/mentoring community that is strongly corresponded with constructivist learning/mentoring processes and constructivist interactions between mentors and learners (as well as learners and learners). I have stated that creative universities must consider meanings the active and dynamic processes of knowledge construction. In fact, as per the analysis in Badie (2017b), learners/mentors become connected to their own constructed models of knowing and, subsequently, to their own constructed models of knowledge by constructing meanings. It is important to take into account that the constructed meanings by any individual (in creative universities) become reflected in his/her personal meaningful understanding of the world. Therefore, the learners must be allowed to express their own conceptions of the world. Their existing conceptions must be taken seriously. If not, they will revert back to their own conceptions of the world outside of the university.

NOTES

[1] In my opinion, human beings' mental images of concepts (that are conceptual entities) are displayed based on their mental structures in their minds. In addition, the mental structures are constructed based on mental entities (or schemata), see Badie (2017b). In Kantian philosophy, a transcendental schema is the procedural rule by which a category or pure, non-empirical concept is associated with a sense impression, see Kant (1781/1924). For Piaget, schemata first emerge as concrete actions and then gradually develop into more abstract mental entities (Husén & Postlethwaite, 1989; Spiro et al., 1992; McGaw & Peterson, 2007; Sawyer, 2014).
[2] See https://en.oxforddictionaries.com/definition/interpretation and http://dictionary.cambridge.org/dictionary/english/interpretation
[3] See https://plato.stanford.edu/entries/logic-inductive

REFERENCES

Allwood, J. (2007). *Activity based studies of linguistic interaction (Gothenburg Papers in Theoretical Linguistics 93)*. Sweden: Goteborg University, Department of Linguistics.
Allwood, J. (2013). A multidimensional activity based approach to communication. In I. Wachsmuth, J. de Ruiter, P. Jaecks, & S. Kopp (Eds.), *Alignment in communication* (pp. 33–55). Amsterdam: John Benjamins.
Baader, F., Calvanese, D., McGuinness, D., Nardi, D., & Patel-Schneider, P. (2010). *The description logic handbook: Theory, implementation and applications*. Cambridge: Cambridge University Press.

Badie, F. (2015a). *A semantic basis for meaning construction in constructivist interactions* (pp. 369–376). Proceedings of the 12th International Conference on Cognition and Exploratory Learning in Digital Age: International Association for Development of the Information Society (IADIS), Maynooth, Greater Dublin, Ireland.

Badie, F. (2015b). *Towards a semantics-based framework for meaning construction in constructivist interactions* (pp. 7995–8002). Proceedings of the 8th International Conference of Education, Research and Innovation. International Association of Technology, Education and Development (IATED), Seville, Spain.

Badie, F. (2016a). *A semantic representation of adult learners' developing conceptions of self realisation through learning process* (pp. 5348–5353). Proceedings of the 10th Annual International Technology, Education and Development Conference. International Association of Technology, Education and Development (IATED), Valencia, Spain.

Badie, F. (2016b). A conceptual framework for knowledge creation based on constructed meanings within mentor-learner conversations. In V. Uskov, R. Howlett, & L. Jain (Eds.), *Smart education and e-learning* (Vol. 59, pp. 167–177). Cham: Springer.

Badie, F. (2016c). *Towards concept understanding relying on conceptualisation in constructivist learning* (pp. 292–296). Proceedings of the 13th International Conference on Cognition and Exploratory Learning in Digital Age. International Association for Development of the Information Society (IADIS), Mannheim, Germany.

Badie, F. (2017a). *A formal semantics for concept understanding relying on description logics* (Vol. 2, pp. 42–52). Proceedings of the 9th International Conference on Agents and Artificial Intelligence (ICAART), Porto, Portugal.

Badie, F. (2017b). *A theoretical model for meaning construction through constructivist concept learning—A conceptual, terminological, logical and semantic study within human-human-machine interactions* (PhD thesis). Aalborg University Press, Aalborg. doi:10.5278/vbn.phd.hum.00073

Badie, F. (2017c). On logical characterisation of human concept learning based on terminological systems. *Journal of Logic and Logical Philosophy*. Retrieved from http://dx.doi.org/10.12775/LLP.2017.020

Badie, F. (2017d). From concepts to predicates within constructivist epistemology. In A. Baltag, J. Seligman, & T. Yamada (Eds.), *Logic, rationality, and interaction* (Lecture Notes in Computer Science, Vol. 10455). Berlin: Springer.

Badie, F. (2017e). Knowledge building conceptualisation within smart constructivist learning systems. In V. Uskov, J. Bakken, R. Howlett, & L. Jain (Eds.), *Smart universities, smart innovation, systems and technologies* (Vol. 70). Cham: Springer.

Badie, F. (2018). *A description logic based knowledge representation model for concept understanding.* Agents and Artificial Intelligence, In Selected Papers of 9th International Conference on Agents and Artificial Intelligence, Springer International Publishing (ICAART), Porto, Portugal.

Bartlett, F. C. (1932). *A study in experimental and social psychology*. Cambridge: Cambridge University Press.

Blackburn, S. (2016). *The Oxford dictionary of philosophy*. Oxford: Oxford University Press.

Chierchia, G. (2009). *Dynamics of meaning: Anaphora, presupposition, and the theory of grammar*. Chicago, IL: The University of Chicago Press.

Clapham, C., & James N. R. (2014). *Concise Oxford dictionary of mathematics*. Oxford: Oxford University Press.

Driscoll, M. P. (2005). *Psychology of learning for instruction* (3rd ed.). Boston, MA: Pearson.

Du, J., & Ling, C. X. (2011). *Active teaching for inductive learners* (pp. 851–861). In SDM—Proceedings of the 2011 SIAM International Conference on Data Mining. SIAM/Omnipress.

Earl, D. (2017). *Internet encyclopaedia of philosophy*. Retrieved from http://www.iep.utm.edu

Encyclopaedia Britannica Online. (2017). *Academic edition*. Retrieved from https://www.britannica.com

Gabbay, D. M., & Guenthner, F. (2010). *Handbook of philosophical logic* (Vol. 15). Heidelberg: Springer Science & Business Media.

Geber, B. A. (Ed.). (1977). *Piaget and knowing studies in genetic epistemology* (3rd ed., pp. 13–16). London: Routledge and Kegan Paul Ltd.

Götzsche, H. (2013). *Deviational syntactic structures*. London: Bloomsbury Academic.

Hampton, J. A., & Moss, H. E. (2003). Concepts and meaning: Introduction to the special issue on conceptual representation. *Language and Cognitive Processes, 18*(5–6), 505–512.
Husén, T., & Postlethwaite, T. N. (1989). *The international encyclopaedia of education* (Vol. 1, pp. 162–163). Oxford & New York, NY: Pergamon Press.
Kant, I. (1781). *Kritik der Reinen Vernunft*. Wiesbaden: VMA-Verlag.
Margolis, E., & Laurence, S. (2007). The ontology of concepts: Abstract objects or mental representations? *Noûs, 41*(4), 561–593.
Margolis, E., & Laurence, S. (2010). Concepts and theoretical unification. *Behavioral and Brain Sciences, 33*, 219–220.
Margolis, E., & Laurence, S. (2015). *The conceptual mind: New directions in the study of concepts.* Cambridge, MA: MIT Press.
McCracken, D. D. (1999). An inductive approach to teaching object-oriented design. In J. Prey & R. E. Noonan (Eds.), *SIGCSE* (pp. 184–188). doi:10.1145/299649.299748
McGaw, B., & Peterson, P. (2007). *International encyclopaedia of education* (3rd ed.). Oxford: Elsevier.
McIntyre, B. G. (2004). Conversation theory. In D. H. Jonassen (Eds.), *Handbook of research on educational communications and technology: A Project of the Association for Educational Communications and Technology (AECT Series)*. Florence, KY: Taylor & Francis.
Parker, W. C. (2008). Pluto's demotion and deep conceptual learning in social studies. *Social Studies Review, 47*(2), 10–13.
Parker, W. C. (2011). *Social studies in elementary education* (14th ed.). Boston, MA: Allyn & Bacon.
Pask, G. (1975). *Conversation, cognition and learning: A cybernetic theory and methodology*. New York, NY: Elsevier.
Pask, G. (1980). Developments in conversation theory, part 1. *International Journal of Man-Machine Studies, 13*, 357–411.
Peacocke, C. (1992). *A study of concepts*. Cambridge, MA: MIT Press.
Phillips, D. (1995). The good, the bad, and the ugly: The many faces of constructivism. *Educational Researcher, 24*(7), 5–12. Retrieved from http://www.jstor.org/stable/1177059
Piaget, J., & Cook, M. T. (1952). *The origins of intelligence in children*. New York, NY: International University Press.
Prior, A. N. (1955). *Formal logic*. Oxford: The Clarendon Press.
Raivo, S., Rüütmann, T., & Seiler, S. (2014). Inductive teaching and learning in engineering pedagogy on the example of remote labs. *International Journal of Engineering Pedagogy, 4*(4), 12–15.
Sawyer, R. K. (2014). *The Cambridge handbook of the learning sciences* (2nd ed.). Cambridge: Cambridge University Press.
Scott, B. (2001). Conversation theory: A constructivist, dialogical approach to educational technology. *Cybernetics and Human Knowing, 8*(4), 25–46.
Simpson, J. A., & Weiner, E. S. C. (1989). *The Oxford English dictionary*. Oxford: Oxford University Press.
Spiro, R. J., Feltovich, P. J., Jacobson, M. J., & Coulson, R. L. (1992). Cognitive flexibility, constructivism, and hypertext: Random access instruction for advanced knowledge acquisition in ill-structured domains. In T. M. Duffy & D. H. Jonassen (Eds.), *Constructivism and the technology of instruction: A conversation* (pp. 57–75). Hillsdale, NJ: Lawrence Erlbaum Associates.
Taba, H., Durkin, M. C., Fraenkel, J. R., & McNaughton, A. H. (1971). *A teacher's handbook to elementary social studies: An inductive approach*. Reading, MA: Addison-Wesley.
Vico, G. (1710). *De antiquissima Italorum sapientia*. Naples: Stamperia de' Classici Latini. (1858, Chapter I, 1, pp. 5–6)
von Glasersfeld, E. (1983). Learning as a constructive activity. In C. Janvier (Ed.), *Problems of representation in the teaching and learning of mathematics* (pp. 3–17). Hillsdale, NJ: Lawrence Erlbaum Associates.
von Glasersfeld, E. (1989). Cognition, construction of knowledge and teaching. *Synthese, 80*(1), 121–140.
von Glasersfeld, E. (1995). *Radical constructivism: A way of knowing and learning*. London: Falmer Press.
von Glasersfeld, E. (2001). The radical constructivist view of science. *Foundations of Science, Special Issue on: The Impact of Radical Constructivism on Science, 6*(1–3), 31–43.

Vuyk, R. (1981). *Overview and critique of Piaget's genetic epistemology, 1965–1980* (Vol. 2). New York, NY: Academic Press.
Vygotsky, L. S. (1978a). Interaction between learning and development. In M. Gauvain & M. Cole (Eds.), *Readings on the development of children* (pp. 34–41). New York, NY: Scientific American Books.
Vygotsky, L. S. (1978b). *Mind in society: Development of higher psychological processes.* Cambridge, MA: Harvard University Press.

Farshad Badie
Department of Communication and Psychology
Center for Computer-mediated Epistemology
Aalborg University
Aalborg, Denmark

Printed in the United States
By Bookmasters